For thou hast made him a little lower than the angels.

PSALM 8:5

Your sons and your daughters shall prophesy,
and your young men shall see visions,
and your old men shall dream dreams.

ACTS 2:17

WAY BELOW THE ANGELS

the pretty clearly troubled but
not even close to tragic confessions
of a real live Mormon missionary

CRAIG HARLINE

WILLIAM B. EERDMANS PUBLISHING COMPANY
Grand Rapids, Michigan / Cambridge, U.K.

Published 2014 by
WM. B. EERDMANS PUBLISHING CO.
2140 Oak Industrial Drive N.E., Grand Rapids, Michigan 49505 /
P.O. Box 163, Cambridge CB3 9PU U.K.
www.eerdmans.com

Printed in the United States of America

20 19 18 17 16 15 14   7 6 5 4 3 2 1

Library of Congress Cataloging-in-Publication Data

Harline, Craig.
Way below the angels : the pretty clearly troubled but not even close to
tragic confessions of a real live Mormon missionary / Craig Harline.
          pages   cm
ISBN 978-0-8028-7150-3 (cloth : alk. paper)
1. Harline, Craig. 2. Mormon missionaries — United States — Biography.
3. Mormon missionaries — Belgium — Biography. 4. Church of Jesus Christ
of Latter-Day Saints — Biography.   I. Title.
BX8695.H36A3   2014
266′.93092 — dc23
[B]
2014023376

Rendering of the angel on the Nauvoo Temple weathervane by William Weeks, from
"William Weeks Nauvoo architectural drawings, circa 1841–1846" (MS 11500), used by permission of the Church History Library of the Church of Jesus Christ of Latter-Day Saints.

For

Paula and Kate
missionaires extraordinaires

Andrew
非常好的传教士

Jonny
misionero extraordinario

Names of most living persons, and some dead, have been changed.

Bible quotations are from the King James Version,
which we Mormons still not-altogether-defensibly prefer.

Contents

De Brouckère Square

Pretty Recently. Like May 23, 2011, 1:00 pm Central European Time.

That's at least the third feeble *Pardon monsieur* I've had to mumble this afternoon for bumping into somebody out here on the roller-derby-rules sidewalk of the Boulevard Jules Anspach, right in the middle of Brussels.

I'm doing all this bumping not so much because of all the jamming going on (because when is that not going on?), but almost entirely because walking along on this particular patch of reinforced concrete has as usual got me seriously distracted.

Oh, it's not what you're thinking. It's not the dazzle of a classic-European-boulevard-lined-by-six-story-buildings that's doing the distracting, though that'd be a good guess. It's not even the gauntlet of fake-smiling waiters standing outside the endless stretch of touristy cafés, waving me in and calling me by name *(Sucker!)*. And believe it or not it's not even all the fun historical facts, plaques, and monuments crying out to me at every corner, which you'd assume would be the most serious cause of distraction for a fun-loving historian guy like me.

Nope, the real reason I'm bobbing and weaving at near-acute angles down Monsieur Anspach's eardrum-pounding boulevard today, and going right on past one irresistible plaque after another, is that I'm thinking about missionary history, not Brussels history.

See, a long long time ago (like way before I was a fun-loving historian), in a place really close close by (like right where I'm walking), I was a missionary, stopping every single guy I saw to tell him about my religion. The relief that comes from not having to stop anyone anymore, the relief that-knows-no-words at being able to just walk along period, is enough all by itself to put me in an ozone-level daze. Oh, I was glad to be a missionary, mind you, glad to tell people about my religion. But there wasn't a single g, l, a, or d in even the distant neighborhood of stopping someone on the street. And so even though the five-star Grand Place and the EZ-flowing Manneke Pis are just a block or two away from where I'm walking along period, and even though a tired but interesting-in-a-kitschy-sort-of-way casino is coming up on my right and a movie theater stuffed behind radically repurposed nineteenth-century facades is flashing away on my left, I'm not paying any more attention to any of them than most of my students usually pay to me.

But then making the daze even more ozone-ish than usual today is that I'm also thinking about *why* I'm walking down this particular boulevard on this particular day, which is not to just walk along period, as is my wont, but to commemorate on purpose a miserable little event that happened just up ahead, on big non-square De Brouckère Square, exactly 35 years ago today. And that thought's got me feeling just a little weepy.

A lot of thoughts in Belgium get me feeling weepy, even though I mostly don't actually weep, so as not to embarrass myself again. Things like the huge Arc of Triumph in Jubilee Park in Brussels, because my first look at that told me just how unwelcome my foreign little missionary message would be; or the old castle ruin near Zichem in winter and the yellow fields outside Brussels in summer, because my missionary eyes had never seen beauty like that before; or the dismal upstairs bedroom in Hasselt, because my missionary self was saved there; or just about any Gothic church, because those first scared the heaven out of missionary me but now they're where I seem to find God all the time. But I especially get feeling weepy when I catch full sight of big non-square De Brouckère Square and now at last step onto it, because 35 years ago today on this very same May 23 I stood on this very same Square in the shadow of this very same French-styled trapezoidal building with the very same Coca-Cola sign on top and started, well, weeping. Really weeping. Not just feeling like it, like a wimp. But actually weeping, like a baby. In public. Weeping because I'd been out on my two-year-mission almost a whole year by that point, and to put it mildly things weren't exactly going as planned.

That long-ago May 23 wasn't just a bad day, which even 19-year-old I was starting to understand was something you might have to expect once in a while from Life. It wasn't even just the hands-down worst day of my mission, which is saying something, given the line of contenders for that crown. No, it was a catastrophic, ocean-liner-flipped-upside-down, universe-turned-inside-out sort of day, the sort you think you'll never get over, the sort that not only singlehandedly pops your good dream of a mission but then goes and leaves a new one in its place — and this one's not good at all.

Instead it's the dream that doesn't show up until a few years after you're back from your mission, but then has the nerve to hang on for about 30 years more.

It's the dream so skin-touchingly real that even while you're in the middle of it you actually tell yourself *this is not a dream but the real genuine-article thing, so don't think you're going to get out of it by waking up or something.*

It's the dream so Madame-Tussaud's lifelike that when you wake up anyway in the usual heart-racing panic you have to pinch yourself to make sure it didn't really happen.

It's the dream so epidemic among former Mormon missionaries that it makes you a big believer in Jung's collective unconscious.

It's the dream that says you have to go on another mission.

Even though you're lying down whenever the dream hits, your knees manage to buckle anyway. But you still agree to go again, every time, thanks to the mighty sense of duty you learned on your first mission and because you actually do finally want to have a legendarily good mission. But then you wake up in the heart-racing junior-Post-Traumatic-Stress-Disorder panic anyway, because it turns out you can't handle after all the possibility of something like the miserable little event on De Brouckère Square ever happening ever again. Ever.

Now, I've gone happily back to Belgium many times since my mission, to do my fun-loving historian thing, and of course just to walk around period. But I've also always gone way out of my way to avoid the Square itself — scampering across, shivering past, tiptoeing around, coming into the hair-raising vicinity only when absolutely necessary — and never ever marching there on purpose the way I have today. Which can mean only one happy thing: the Square doesn't scare me anymore. And neither does the bad old dream it started. It's Gone. Vanquished. Declawed. Neutered. Even Funny. I'm not here to wallow, or feel sorry for myself (again), but to march a fetchin'* Victory march, an *I Will Survive* march. Because the bad dream is dead. Of De Brouckère Square, and of every other rough missionary place in Belgium.

Standing here I'm a little embarrassed about the fuss I'm making over such a miserable little event, so even though I'm swelling like a North Sea storm on the inside, I stay calm on the outside: I don't want bypassing people looking at me funny again. Or worse yet, recognizing me.

I'm also face-in-hands embarrassed to admit that it took me so long to get over that event, and the bad dream, because my fun-loving historian self knows full well that my petty little mission suffering was in the world-historical and even mission-historical scheme of things pretty small Belgian potatoes.

But being embarrassed to admit embarrassing things like how hard a mission sometimes/often was for me or how short I fell or how guilty I felt for falling short was exactly how the bad dream kept on keeping on for so embarrassingly long. You shouldn't have been so weak, I told myself. You shouldn't have been so bothered by the rough stuff, because everyone had rough stuff, so just forget about it, and just remember the good stuff, like how going on that mission actually gave you something approaching genuine faith, and helped you feel so connected and grateful to your church that you couldn't imagine not always being part of it, and yes turned you

---

* Along with *flippin'*, a long-popular substitute cuss-word among especially male Mormon missionaries.

into the fun-loving-historian self you so love being and which you never without that mission would've ever had a prayer of becoming, much less of going *back* to Belgium all these happy times since. And that's not to mention all the other things on your mile-long list of good stuff that still make you bottom-of-your-heart-glad you went on a mission. And that good stuff should just cancel out the rough stuff, I told myself — should just swallow it up in victory, so to speak. But it didn't.

In fact the only thing that believe it or not started making the bad dream go away was when I finally if almost accidentally started admitting some of the rough stuff, instead of pretending that it didn't matter or that it'd been more or less obliterated by good stuff. And then the only thing that made the dream go completely poof was when I finally admitted *all* the rough stuff. So I'm not not admitting rough stuff anymore. Even if it is embarrassing. Even if it did take roughly 35 years to sort out. Even if I won't be as nauseatingly enthusiastic about the whole humiliating process as that champion admitter Augustine was.* Even if my Autobiographical Memory is only Pretty and not Highly Sensitive† and thus probably not 110-percent trustworthy.

And I'm not not visiting De Brouckère Square anymore either, or any other rough missionary place. I'm not afraid to remember now, or to admit. Or even to tell.

---

* I have in mind here his famous *Confessions,* from around 400 AD, which invented the genre of the really long written confession. If you want to know how to confess at length, on paper, you have to start with Augustine's fat book and its impressive range of sins.

† Pretty Sensitive Autobiographical Memory is not a clinical term, but Highly Sensitive Autobiographical Memory, or Hyperthymesia, is. Something like only six people in the world have been diagnosed with HSAM, and I'm not one of them.

one

VISIONS

A Long Long Time Ago. Especially July 7, 1975.

When you were a Mormon boy there was only a good mission dream, with no unreachable stars in sight.

It started with dreamy songs I yelled out at church about going on a mission and converting people who *really* wanted to know the truth. It got stronger with all the dreamy talk I heard at church too — *the best thing you'll ever do, you'll never be so happy, wish I was out there again.* And it took on some real Plato-style form when I finally stopped goofing around in the pews during services and started listening to the legions of missionaries who came marching home after two long years away, telling their dreamy tales.

Before my star-filled eyes the dream became flesh, as one returning missionary hero after the next grabbed for dear life onto the remote-controlled height-adjusting pulpit and white-knuckledly told another epic tale of adventure and conversion. Lots of conversion. By the time the hero neared the end of his story, which he signaled by saying a few spine-shivering sentences in the exotic new language he'd learned, the pulpit was on fire, and so were my insides, because I so badly wanted to be just the sort of guy I was sure these guys actually were.

A guy like these wasn't just a regular guy, or even one of the regular missionaries you saw working around town, but a haloed revelation. Oh, the missionaries working around town glowed pretty nicely too, sure they did, but they were still works in progress, illuminatively speaking: you didn't know what they were like before their mission, and you probably wouldn't see them again after they went home. But for the guys who left on faraway missions from your hometown and then came back you saw the before and the after picture, and the difference was like firefly and sun, night and day, oil and water, bond and free, Dodger and Giant. Seeing the after version was like seeing Koufax pitch, or Tammy Carr walking into sixth grade, or Saint John himself striding onto Patmos.

Can you believe how mature he is now?(!) head-shaking people would ask. *Can you believe that language he learned, whatever the heck it was?(!) Did you hear him stumble around in English?(!) What a missionary he must have been if he can hardly remember English!(!) And what about those miracle stories?(!)* I wanted to do miracles too, and make converts, and get the gift of tongues, and be mature, and become a spiritual giant, like these guys, and have people say things about me with implied and even explicit exclamation points.

The vision big-bangingly ended with me coming triumphantly home to tell my own miracle and conversion stories from my most assured record-setting mission, and wowing everyone with my own exotic new language, and most of all saying near the end of my homecoming talk what every returning missionary seemed to say, was practically required to say because everyone in the audience was waiting to hear it, waiting to hear again what they already knew about missions even though most of them hadn't actually been on one themselves. Here it was: *Those were the best two years of my life.* The magic words. The cue to smile and nod. Ah. Yes. Reassured. Once again. *We knew it. Goes to show. Knew that's what you'd say once you got back. That's what a mission is all about.* In fact, if the missionary didn't say the words, then people wouldn't know what to think about his mission, because there really was no other way to think about it, at least in public.

Oh, there'd be a *little* drama in it: the returning missionary might drop his head a bit after saying *the best two years,* and start to choke up. Then he'd recover and lean on the pulpit and say, *They were also the hardest two*

2

years, which'd make him choke up and go all quiet again, and make people maybe wonder for a second whether he was maybe reconsidering the best-two-years part, or whether there was something more to the best-two-years part that he wasn't bothering to say. But then he'd lift his head back up and say that those two years were the best *because* they were hard. *Well, that's okay then,* everybody breathed out; *a little hard work never hurt anyone.*

The hard part might have scared some guys off, but not me. I'd been mowing lawns in 100-degree heat forever, and driving to the dump once a week to pitchfork out foul-smelling layers of (in descending order) green yellow brown black white grass clippings from a rickety trailer onto sweltering piles of disgusting muck straight out of Dante's *Inferno.* Maybe converting people would be hard too, but once they converted I wouldn't care one bit how hard it'd been.

There were things besides my vision pushing me to go on a mission too, of course. People at church talked about my going like it was a sure thing, and reminded me every week or so that unlike the lilies of the field I'd better spin and toil to get enough money for all the raiment I'd surely need for the mission I was most definitely going on. In 1974, the prophet of the church, God's mouthpiece, had even come right out and said that every Mormon boy ought to go on a mission. Girls went on missions too, sometimes, but from what I heard only if something wasn't quite right with them. Boys were the opposite: if something wasn't quite right with them, they stayed home. My future wife and daughter, both future missionaries too, would have set me on the non-proverbial concretely molecular porch with Fred Flintstone's saber-toothed cat for thinking that way, but that was how I soaked things up, without a second thought, or come to think of it (finally) even a first.*

In fact maybe pushing me as much as anything to go on a mission was the unthought thought of all those girls *not* on missions. Because the first thing any Mormon girl worth her modest clothing would want to know

* In my time and most others, maybe 15 percent of the missionary force was female, so that missionary culture was still overwhelmingly male. That changed dramatically in 2012, and now around 50 percent of all new missionaries are female.

about any sub-19 Mormon boy was whether he was going on a mission, and you knew what the answer had better be. Sub-19 girls were supposed to encourage you to go, and they'd promise to write, and really would write for a while, but by the time you got back they'd usually already be taken by some R(eturned) M(issionary). The girl I'd liked for the past three years, for instance (I couldn't say she was my girlfriend, since she never let me call her that), would actually be taken by an RM before I even left, which had to be a world land-speed record. But it was okay if a girl didn't wait or if she got engaged in record-setting fashion, I told myself, because another thing I knew without thinking was that by going on a mission I'd at least be investing in the next crop of Mormon girls who *would* be around when I got back.

With all that non-thinking going on I couldn't say down to the nearest decimal exactly what was pushing me with exactly what force to get out on a mission. I could've been laid out in some sort of spiritual anatomical theatre, like in one of those old Dutch paintings, and been sliced up in front of a bunch of curious people jostling to see which of my motives for going were pure and which came from all the social conditioning around me, and the results would've been as muddled for me as for most people. Oh, I felt like I had the *testimony* or witness that Mormons are always talking about, the feeling from God telling you that what you were doing was right and that the church was true, but maybe even some of that came from all the pats on the back I was getting because I was doing something everyone/everygirl at church wanted me to do, or from the pats I was sure not to get if I didn't.

I wouldn't have cared about sorting it out like that though, or even have known it was possible. I just knew I wanted to go.

On that hot July 7 when hope was still running up and down and across, I hustled my skinny little self out to the middle of the L-shaped street that confluenced so suburbanly right in front of my kitty-corner house, because I wanted to see the mailman as soon as he came swaying around the corner.

It was so hot out today you could actually *see* the heat, rolling across the street in crazy, hazy waves, like the asphalt was melting or something and the two mingy arms of the L were actually and not just metaphorically confluencing. But I hardly even noticed, for one because it was this hot and wavy every day, and for two because I was busy calculating that if church leaders met in Salt Lake on Thursdays to decide on missionary calls, and put them in the mail on Fridays, then my own call would probably arrive at my house here in the center of central California on a Monday. Today.

No way was I going to stand politely on the curb for something that big. I wanted to be clear out over the manhole cover so I could look all the way down the block, even if it meant Mrs. Dinkel sticking her head out the door real fast as usual and yelling from somewhere beneath her armor-plated curlers *You kids get out of the street!*

And suddenly there he was, stopping and starting at every house until finally he stopped, against every regulation of the postal driving code, right next to me in the middle of the street, because a veteran mailman like that knew that a young guy like me didn't stand out waving his arms in a street rolling with heat waves unless he was waiting for something big.

A few of my many brothers and sisters were standing out in the street now too, their soles also going into meltdown. *Just a bunch of junk mail,* I thought, bummed, as I flipped through the pile, but I kept flipping and whadda ya know in between the ads from Kmart and Sears and Woolworths was a big white official-looking envelope from Salt Lake City with my name on it. *Here it is!* I yelled, and the people standing around made some noises while my parents ran outside too.

Years later it would practically be against Mormon rules to just rip open the call right there on the street to see where you were going. Instead you'd have to wait until that night so 300 of your closest friends could squeeze in for the big occasion and the crowd could really go wild. But I didn't know about any fancy ritual like that, so I ripped away and moved my eyes straight to where my teachers said a good thesis sentence should be, right at the end of the first paragraph: *Belgium Antwerp Mission!* I yelled again. Everything started going in slow motion with those words, because even though I'd hardly ever heard them before, even though one of the words had *twerp* in it, and even though they were listed backwards in that odd way Mormons had of writing mission names by country (or state) first and then city, I was sure they would change everything.

Everyone cheered, but they would've cheered even if I'd said *Montana Bozeman!* Still, these cheers had some genuine *Wow!* or even *Wow?* to them, because no one had the faintest clue in the world where in the world Belgium was. *Where's Belgium?* they all asked in hot-footed puzzlement. So did everyone else I told over the next few weeks. No one even bothered asking *Where's Antwerp?*

I wasn't exactly sure myself where Belgium was, much less Antwerp: both were in Europe, I knew that, and Europe was good. And I was as surprised as anyone, because just the week before in order not to be surprised I'd studied a list of all 150 or so Mormon missions around the world and Belgium Antwerp had not been on it. Wait a minute, I thought: that meant it was a brand-new mission. And that meant — shiver — I would be one of the first missionaries there! Oh, missionaries had probably set foot in the place before, because they'd set foot everywhere, but not in the sort of concentrated biblical-proportion numbers a brand-new mission would mean.

I ran into the house ahead of everyone to get at the *World Book Encyclopedia* first, and read everything I could about Belgium, at least two whole pages, including that it was right above France, that it was about the size of Maryland, that it had about 10 million people, and that — can you believe this — they were almost all Catholic.

Catholic! That got me shivering again, the way a guy might shiver before playing a big game or fighting an epic battle. Almost *all* Catholic! Now that was the sort of challenge I'd hoped for. My teachers at church said that every church had a *portion* of the truth in it, but that portion couldn't be very big, I thought, not in those plain-looking Protestant churches I'd visited once or twice, and especially not in the evil Catholic Church I wouldn't on my life set foot in. Even though the Catholic Newman Center around the corner actually looked a lot like my own church, and even though I had a couple of Catholic friends at school who looked a lot like I did, I knew that beneath all that if you kept digging you'd eventually uncover that the Catholic Church was wicked. And weird. The Church of the Devil. The Whore of All the Earth. The Great and Abominable. What great news!

Wouldn't all those Belgian people in Catholic darkness be glad to see me? And Catholics there were bound to be a lot more wicked than the pretty ordinary-looking sort I saw walking out of the Newman Center every Sunday morning in the same polyester dresses and rumpled suits I saw at my own church. How fantastic!

See, the harder farther and newer a mission, then the more heroic it was, not to mention *the greater the share of honor* it'd bring, as Shakespeare's Henry V might've put it if he'd been stirring up fellows for Mormon missions instead of for the Battle of Agincourt.* Privately, I also calculated, like a medieval knight calculating the payoff of a really big joust, that this greater share of honor just had to mean a big boost in my standing among girls — because I was sure that the second thing a Mormon girl worth her modest clothing would want to know about me was *where* I was going on a mission.

I was sure that being able to say Australia, Japan, or Belgium would make me bigger and more spiritual and more heroic in especially female minds than saying Nevada, Kansas, or Ohio would. I'd tried telling myself and others that I'd be content with a mission to some ordinary place, but I'd said that only because wishing for somewhere special might bring bad luck, or make God teach me a lesson in humility by sending me to Montana.

Why just the year before, no less an authority than a Returned Missionary who'd gone to Japan had casually asked me while we were casually walking along casually talking about missions whether I'd like to *go foreign. Yes,* I admitted, *I would.* Big mistake: I'd walked right into his casual-looking trap. Because when he heard my answer, RM got serious, looked down at the ground, and said like he was uttering some law laid down at Creation and understood by every going-foreign missionary ever since: *Then you*

* English troops were outnumbered by French troops something like six to one at this famous battle in northern France in 1415, but as Shakespeare tells it, Henry's motivational speech saved the day more than English arrows or French mud did.

won't. That was it. Decided. Over. Finished. Like John Calvin and a whole bunch of saints, this guy believed that God's will for you just about always came in the form of what you *least* wanted to do. So if you wanted to *go foreign* then you could bet your hoped-for passport you wouldn't. In fact the best thing you could do to help yourself go foreign was to wish to go to Montana, but you had to *really* wish it.

Thank God that this guy and Calvin and all those saints were wrong, at least this time, because even though I yanked and tugged mightily I just could not root out my hope to go foreign — but then I went foreign anyway. What luck! How would I have survived *not* going foreign, or *not* speaking English, I wondered? Speaking English would have felt too close to ordinary life, too close to my regular self: I needed something bigger than that. A going-foreign mission was just the thing to bring out my *true* self, instead of the pretty ordinary self that'd been pretty convincingly on display so far. In fact a going-foreign mission, it hit me now, was what God had been saving me for all these years.

That must've been why God had snatched me from certain death in that near fiery-crash in the desert when I was 13, when the other three Scouts in the car headed to the big Mormon Scout Jamboree in Utah dozed off, and the mom who was driving caught a bad case of road-daze in the hot sun and so didn't notice when the long straight four-lane freeway turned into a modest two-lane road with two-way traffic and so she just stayed in the left lane, and pretty soon a big shiny car started coming at us really fast and she didn't notice that either but I did, and when the big shiny car which never once slowed down was almost in our laps and I was sure I was going to die I simultaneously (a) wondered if I would make it to the Celestial Kingdom (the highest level of Mormon heaven) and (b) yelled *Look out!,* shocking the road-dazed mom into action and saving us all, just so I could go on my going-foreign mission.

That must also have been why God had given me enough talent to be on the high school basketball team but not enough to be a star: God knew that basketball stardom might sidetrack me from a mission, like it was doing to the other Mormon kid on the team who *was* a star, and who no doubt because of that was also a partier and not going on any sort of mission, and the purpose of whose existence was apparently to be a warning lesson to me about the perils of basketball-stardom, and as a sort of reassurance that God really did care about me more than He did most kids. Sure, the other kid got earthly stardom, but God gave me the eternal sort of the going-foreign missionary.

That also must've been why God had made sure my non-girlfriend didn't like me *too* much, because even though there was no way I would've stayed home from a mission even for her, if she'd really liked me then I'd have been distracted too much while on my mission, so God had caused her to like me only enough to keep me hanging on pathetically until it was almost time for me to go, at which point it was too late for me to find an actual girlfriend, but at least I'd have no distractions now.

And that must've also been why I, though lazy at school, had been such a demon scripture-chaser at church, blessed with the memory and athleticism needed to look up verses faster than anyone. I was bad at school but good at scripture-chase because guess which one would help me most on a mission?

Now it all made sense.

All that while I'd been being groomed for a going-foreign mission. That's where my true self, my still-dormant special self, would come out. Oh sure, my leaders were always telling all the kids they were special, but it couldn't really be true or no one would be special. There had to be ordinary for special even to exist. Or okay, say everyone was special, well then there had to be extra-special, and that was where I and a few others apparently came in.*

Right on cue, the telephone rang: it was a friend across town who'd just

---

* I wasn't so much hopelessly egotistic as hopelessly egocentric, which all the psychology books said 19-year-olds were supposed to be, especially by (enough said) 1975: in other words, even though I had some serious inventory-shortages in the confidence department, I had absolutely no doubt that the universe revolved around me. One famous study showed that around 1900 only 7 percent of American teenagers thought they were something special; by the late 1980s that figure had climbed to 80 percent. I was just doing my part to raise that figure.

opened his mission call too. The friend said with a bit of disappointment and a lot of *You won't believe this* in his voice, *Guess where I'm going?*

Me, blurting out the first horrifying mission that came to mind: *Utah!*

The friend, gasping: *How did you know?*

Me, more out of sheer relief and mile-deep repressed fears than out of any actual prognosticatory gifts or deliberate meanness: *Because that's where I did not want to go, and I knew one of us would. Ha ha!*

The friend, wounded: *Where you going?*

Me, cup running over and on my fiftieth actual exclamation point of the day plus an implied one: *Belgium! Can you believe it?!(!)*

The friend, flatly: *Wow.*

Oh, I felt the smallest sliver of guilt over talking like that, but joy at my unaccustomed bit of good fortune overwhelmed any sting. *That could have been me going to Utah,* I thought, after hanging up. What if the church leaders in Salt Lake had mixed things up? What if the two applications had been lying right next to each other on the massive brown table and the leaders reading them had said, *Let's see, one of these kids from Fresno has got to go to Utah and one to somewhere special,* and they'd switched things around? But they hadn't! They (and thus God) had chosen me for the special mission that no doubt required a lot more still-dormant talent than Utah did.

I couldn't wait to start spreading the news, one lucky listener at a time. I ran to tell my bishop* in person, which was easy because my dad and I were helping to put a new roof on the bishop's house. I shot up the ladder to that roof and excitedly announced I was *going to Belgium to fight Catholics!* The bishop surprised me by looking up from his nailing and saying calmly, *You just need to love them.*

Now that made no sense at all. A mission to an all-out Catholic place just had to be about fighting. Ironically I was actually thinking a lot like a sixteenth-century Jesuit missionary here,† except a Jesuit wasn't going out to fight Catholics (well, not usually). A Jesuit getting ready to go off on

---

* The non-mitred leader of a Mormon ward, or congregation.

† Members of the famously effective and sometimes controversial religious order called the Society of Jesus, founded 1540.

some faraway mission was definitely expecting to fight enemy religions and to vanquish them through conversion, which must've sounded a lot more exciting to them than teaching catechism classes on perfectly good Sunday afternoons in some boring little parish in rural France did. The lucky few Jesuits chosen for going-foreign missions to Brazil or China went into ecstasy over the news, thrilled at the thought of being boiled to death or crucified upside down in some strange new world, rather than just dying at home in bed of gout. Up there on the roof pounding in shingles, I had visions of myself suffering heroically too, being kicked around or shot at in Belgium, for the sake of the truth.

I loved it! I had no idea yet what a Jesuit was, but I'd heard something about the old Christian martyrs of olden times, and had even read a little about Reformation martyrs in John Foxe's famous sixteenth-century *Book of Martyrs*. An odd guy in my ward, who spoke with a trembly voice that probably came from reading too much Foxe, somehow thought I'd be interested in the grisly thing and loaned me a copy. The guy was right: I ate it up. Of course those martyrs hadn't died for real truth, but you had to admire them anyway.

Reading Foxe made me realize that I'd had a little practice being a martyr myself — just beginner's stuff, mind you, to help me get ready for the real thing. Like the time in seventh grade that Big (Catholic) Ricky O'Connor and Even Bigger (also Catholic) John Burke chased me and stuffed a cigarette butt down my mouth and laughed, because they knew I didn't want anything to do with cigarettes; I spit out that wet old bad-tasting thing as fast as I could so I wouldn't go to the lowest kingdom of heaven (Telestial), which was actually the Mormon version of hell. Or there was the time in eighth grade that Big Ricky O'Connor chased me again, this time around the block while holding a bottle of whiskey that he said he was going to make me drink: *Damn Mormon!* he yelled when he couldn't catch me, which he followed up with a terrifying *We'll get you yet!* Luckily I was fast, and finally smart enough to find some new friends.

Up there pounding in shingles on the bishop's roof, I started having visions of mission victory too, even more than of persecution. I saw myself converting whole crowds of grateful people who would — I could hear it — utter my name in reverential tones to their equally grateful descendants for bringing them the truth. The vision got so strong I had to stop nailing, because a number suddenly came into my head from up in the blue sky: 84. That's how many grateful Belgian converts would be reverently uttering my name.

What a great number! In fact it was even better than I knew. Just reading around in the Bible, you could see pretty fast that two of God's favorite numbers were 7 and 12, both of which were individually too small to be my conversion goal, but *multiply* those two divine favorites by each other and guess what you got? 84! 84 was 7 and 12 in Ecstasy. And it wasn't even really that big if you thought about it. It wasn't even a convert a week — and since I'd heard that you usually converted whole families, then you could go a few weeks without converts and still make 84. Why wouldn't God want me to reach a goal like that, or want 84 Belgians to find the truth?

I'd heard about missionaries in Latin America converting 200 people all the time, and what about the famous Mormon missionary Wilford Woodruff in the olden days making thousands of converts in England, which was close to Belgium, and how about Ammon, in the Book of Mormon, converting a whole kingdom of people? Some people tried to tell me that it was probably easier to make converts in Latin America or olden England or the Book of Mormon than it was in present-day Belgium, but how could that be if the Holy Ghost's converting power was the same everywhere and at all times? Why couldn't a missionary right now do the same thing if he had enough faith and talent? Especially me, since even returned missionaries (who knew what it took) were already telling me what a top top missionary I would be?

So 84 was probably decided upon for me like this: maybe in ordinary circumstances I'd be a 200 sort of guy, but even I had to be handicapped for going to Europe. So taking into account my still-dormant talents and the predictions of experts about my likely success, the total, to be a challenge but not too showy, came back up to 84 — which would still be phenomenal. In fact 84 in Europe would be like 840 in Latin America.

God knew how long I'd been getting myself ready for something phenomenal, though. I'd been getting ready temporally for years, earning money not just by pulling weeds and cutting lawns in the relentless sun, but rolling out of bed at 4:00 in the morning to go janitor at Montgomery Ward, until finally landing a real glamour job at Orange Julius. And I'd been getting ready spiritually too, attending three church meetings every Sunday my whole life, going to 45 minutes of *seminary* every weekday morning at 6:15 all four years of high school, reading all four books of Mormon scripture (yes, including the Old Testament) more than once, praying every morning and evening, chasing down my boss at Orange Julius in order to give her ten dollars for food I'd eaten without paying, not usually cussing or smoking or drinking or doing drugs or being immoral, and confessing to my bishop about the times when I had slipped up — including when I'd touched those three girls where you weren't supposed to (it might have been only two, but I wasn't sure about the third so I'd included her just in case). Confessing that had been the absolute worst, because here I was one of the Mormon youth leaders and destined, said everyone, to be a great missionary, and there I was doing stuff like any ordinary youth non-leader, including the ones who kept saying that yes you were supposed to touch girls there. I was sure that my confession disappointed the bishop because it disappointed me too: I didn't want anything to do with ordinary. But I knew I had to confess to be pure, and become great.

The trouble was, even though it'd been a year or two since I'd told the bishop about that, I still didn't feel pure, or great, even after getting my mission call. So a week later, I went to talk to my bishop again, in his office this time, not on the roof where someone might hear. He listened kindly and said that if I was feeling so badly then maybe I should apologize directly to the three (maybe two) girls themselves, instead of just to him. And Good Lord I did it, even though it was ten times more embarrassing than telling the bishop had been, and even though it took me forever to pick up the phone, because how in the world were you supposed to start a conversation like that with someone you hadn't seen in years and explain that you were going on a mission so you had to be pure, so *I'm just calling to say I'm sorry*

13

for anything improper I might have done a few years ago? What if they didn't think there'd ever been anything improper, or, even worse, what if they didn't know what I was talking about? But I bumbled through, and they were all (three) very nice, and wished me good luck, and I felt a little better.

But still not as pure as I'd hoped.

I just wanted to get myself worthy, so I could be the missionary I'd dreamed of being.

two

Super Model

What we want is for you to look like the local businessmen, said the booming voice as a few prospective local businessmen staggered back into the main meeting room, still disbelieving that their hair could even go as short as it had just gone.

More than a hundred such creatures, plus a few well-dressed young women, had arrived that Saturday morning at the Mission Home in Salt Lake City to begin their new lives. The President of the three-story institutional-looking institution and the owner of the booming voice, a firm-handshaking retired FBI agent named Obadiah Hunt, had just a couple of hours before briefly gathered all the newcomers and boomed out a short welcome, but then he'd fittingly gotten right down to business, the first order of which was to do something about everyone's hair.

The mildly shocking results coming back from the barbershop next door were at least helping the prospective local businessmen get their minds off the scenes of emotional carnage that'd filled the main hallway even earlier that morning, when they'd been dropped off at the Mission Home by family and friends and maybe girlfriend, and when the once harmlessly abstract and even heroic-sounding idea of not seeing said family and friends and maybe girlfriend for two whole years had suddenly become disturbingly concrete, causing the prospective local businessmen and their assorted entourages to break down into long sobbing goodbyes that ended only when a 70-something lady with souffléed hair and cat glasses and really sharp jaw-line waded into the mess and started strong-arming family and friends and maybe girlfriend out the door.

Well, not quite all of them. Had broken down, that is. I hadn't. I'd just smiled amusedly, maybe even superiorly, at the whole thing. And wondered why everyone else wasn't smiling too.

Oh, I wasn't above breaking down, as I'd prove soon enough. But I'd had plenty of chances to break down the last few days and still hadn't.

I could've broken down at my farewell talk the Sunday before, when multitudes came to hear me, including my non-girlfriend, who wore her reward for helping get me on a mission: an engagement ring from her Returned Missionary. That by itself could've broken me down. I also could've broken down when the 12 speakers I'd arranged to have talk at my farewell (way more than the usual three or four) stood up and said a lot of nice and probably exaggerated things about me. And I could've broken down during my own talk, when I wrapped the meeting up by saying a lot of nice and probably exaggerated things about myself too, so many that the usual hour-and-a-half meeting had run 15 minutes over. But even hearing (and saying) all those nice things hadn't broken me down.

I hadn't broken down either at my setting-apart a couple days later, when the Stake President (even higher than a Bishop) had laid his hands on my head and officially made me a missionary, getting me so emotional that I swore right on the industrial-grade-carpeted spot never to sin again, but I still hadn't broken down. I hadn't even broken down at the airport the day before in California saying goodbye to my family. I'd flown up into the heavens as cheerful as Elijah on his chariot of fire, whistling probably the same tune Elijah had too.

No, the reason I hadn't broken down during any of that or much less today was because it all marked the official beginning of making my mission dream come true, of the gun going off ceremoniously at the starting line as it were. Why would anyone want to cry about that?

Of course crying didn't mean you were automatically sad. I knew that. Years of churchgoing had taught me that anyone in the hallway that morning who was crying and smiling at the same time was probably more glad than sad, because crying and smiling at the same time was despite its physiological challenges the preferred Mormon way to let everyone know you were in happiness heaven, and that you were really feeling the Holy Ghost. In fact, if like me you were just smiling and not crying then fellow Mormons might wonder whether you were really truly happy or even really feeling the Holy Ghost at all, an unthought thought that caused me to feel that maybe I should cry a little too instead of just smile, to send the right message. But I didn't cry, because I was sure I was so really truly happy to be at the Mission Home.

I'd kept on being happy until we were all briefly gathered in the main meeting room and President Hunt had boomed his *Welcome to the Mission Home* and then just like that had started walking behind each row of missionaries and tapping the shoulders of anyone who needed an immediate haircut, including the astonished me. I'd sinned already, already breaking my promise of just a couple days before.

I was *sure* that my hair was short enough: I'd studied the picture that'd come with my call and had told the barber back home to cut it just like that, and then *wham* (tap). But maybe I shouldn't have felt so astonished because every last fellow there (except the very last, whose hair even President Hunt had to admit just couldn't go any shorter) had ended up being tapped too. Maybe my hair had grown past acceptable limits in a week. Maybe I'd seen the accompanying picture wrong, even if not as wrong as my friend who'd shown up at the Mission Home wearing an absolutely forbidden mustache. Maybe President Hunt was just getting us used to taking orders, just hitting hard at the start the way Machiavelli said a leader should, to establish his authority. Or most likely of all maybe short to me and these other sons of the 1970s just wasn't short to President Hunt, an FBI guy.

Even the hair of the *Sisters* seemed too long for him. He didn't go into specifics with them about how to wear it, just saying (something like) *you Sisters won't have time to fuss around with curlers anymore so you might think about cutting it short.* With the *Elders,* though, he was as specific as Leviticus: even though our hair was already off collars and ears, which for the 1970s was practically a flippin' crew cut, it wasn't *miles* off, the way he liked it, with all hair in the danger zones cut to the nub.

To get that sort of cut, (almost) every last Elder had been ordered to march immediately to the barbershop that just happened to be next door and that just happened to be reserved for us and that just happened to have more barbers assembled in one place than had ever been assembled before, or at least since last week. A Guinness-World-Record's worth of barbers. A group that got together every Saturday and knew exactly what to do with missionary hair: whatever Obadiah Hunt told them to do. Which meant *really short and as unattractive as possible without being totally offensive.* If he'd told the assembled barbers to rub a little Brylcreem in, or even half a bottle of Vitalis the way he did himself, they'd have done that too.

Like most others, I'd exited the barber superstore with the shortest haircut I'd have my entire mission. I wasn't sure what the Sisters had been up to during that hour or two, as no haircutting provisions had been made for them and they wouldn't have wanted to come within a mile of the assembled barbers anyway. Maybe they'd spent the time in their dorm room, flinging curlers out the window or lopping off big chunks of hair, I imagined. While the last of the reduced Elders wandered disorientedly back into the main meeting room, President Hunt was taking the trouble to explain to the regathering crowd the metaphysical foundations of the famous (male) missionary *toilette:* (really) short hair, suit, white shirt, and tie.

Now I know some people like to say, explained the President (who'd heard it all before from smart-alecky missionaries), *that Peter and Paul and even the Lord Himself didn't wear short hair or a suit or white shirt or tie.* But that was just the most pathetic argument he'd ever heard, because *of course not, they dressed differently in those days and didn't have the conveniences of modern shaving. But what you can be sure they did do,* he assured everyone, *was to blend in with the local businessmen — because that's what they were.*

They were *not,* he assured even more emphatically, *hippies,* as some people nowadays liked to say, a thought that seemed to really rile him up.

If I had already been even just a little historically minded then I might have raised my still-thickening eyebrows at the more than slightly questionable claims that Paul the tentmaker and Jesus the possible carpenter had somehow dressed more like the Chamber of Commerce of first-century Palestine than like the local union, and that ancient Romans somehow didn't know much about shaving. And I would have wrinkled my nose at the whole idea that the local businessman was the guy we (especially the Sisters) should necessarily want to look like. Weren't missionaries more like local teachers than local businessmen? Or even like local machinists? Was a local businessman the first guy who came to mind when you were way down deep in the spiritual quicksand, so to speak?

But my historical-mindedness was still lying as dormant as most other things inside, so I accepted the local businessman as our rightful sartorial model, and also the implication that our particular American version of that model wasn't just a particular American version but a look so universal and reassuring that it transcended all cultures.

Even more foundational than (really) short hair to that look, and thus requiring even less explanation, was the (preferably) dark suit. Nobody had to be sent next door for one of those, because every Elder sitting there listening to President Hunt was already wearing one, with another in reserve upstairs. What luck for present company to live in the age of the new revolutionary top-of-the-line wrinkle-proof spot-proof two-pant special-weave-polyester just-for-missionaries suit that looked and felt like stainless steel and that would last through the Millennium even if you didn't want it to, and also in the age of the equally revolutionary and indestructible missionary shoe that came with a 60,000-mile warranty and that you wouldn't be caught dead wearing in real life.

Only a lucky few in the audience were wearing these still recent and thus costly innovations though, I noticed. Most guys were, like me, wearing whatever happened to be on sale at JC Penney the day they'd gone missionary-clothes shopping with their parents. I'd selected a thin wool blend (mostly blend) gray suit that would wear out cataclysmically in the seat after only four months on a Belgian bicycle, plus a bottom-of-the-line traditional-weave brown polyester that would soon sprout tiny balls of polyester everywhere. My shoes, a pair of good-old wingtips, were the worst choice ever in the history of missionary work, worse even than Paul's dusty sandals, because good-old wingtips pinched while walking and slipped while biking.

There was only one tiny innovation evident on my person, and that was my special sort of white shirt. For some reason, my usually compliant self just hadn't been able to accept the idea of plain old white. Oh, I knew going into the missionary business that my shirts would have to be white: that wasn't negotiable. But I rightly imagined here in exuberant 1975 that I'd be able to find something a little less pasty than the usual model, something a little livelier, something that maybe didn't go translucent after only three washes — something that maybe had a little pattern in it.

I'd tried explaining the pattern thing to my dad while we were still at JC Penney, the explaining necessitated by my dad's price-is-right radar having located deep in the ninth circle of hell a *Sale!* table full of the usual sort of plain white shirt, sending me into a panic. Upon hearing my sheepish explanation of the shirt I actually wanted, my dad looked as bewildered as Mary at the tomb. *How can an all-white shirt have a pattern?* he wondered.

Wonder was right. The shirt I had in mind, probably possible only in the 1970s as a shirt, truly was a miracle, because it (a) was rare and (b) went against nature. Ironically, however, it tried to incorporate nature, as strings of white vines or scallops were sewn or stamped onto the sleeves, trunk, collar, and everything. There might have even been a white grape on the buttons. You looked like a tablecloth at high tea wearing a thing like that, but better a tablecloth than a cadaver, or a clone, I thought (or more accurately unthinkingly felt).

All that worry over the shirts had surprised me, not to mention my dad. But maybe deep deep down, maybe even in the vast untouched subconscious of the 19-year-old American male, maybe I feared I'd lose my personality if I put on that plain old pasty shirt from the *Sale!* table, maybe feared that a shirt like that would fly up with some little demon, snatch my soul and turn me into a clone. That pasty shirt was the last thing standing between me and clonehood, I thought/felt. If I could find something that was just a little different from the rest but that would still pass inspection, then I'd be saved.

Luckily for me, but to the chagrin of my dad or anyone else later unfortunate enough to catch a glimpse of my missionary pictures, we found a whole pile of white-on-white shirts at a hipper store. But the fancy variation didn't make as much difference as I'd hoped: I still looked pretty much like the other missionaries, and maybe even less like a local businessman than they did. In fact sitting there listening to President Hunt discourse on the virtues of our new outfit, I started having serious doubts about the local-business-viability of my shirts. I pulled my coat a little tighter so the President couldn't see the leaves and vines running all over me. If I got in trouble for those too, I'd be two sins down already, after barely walking in the door.

We never did hear many details about who the Sisters were supposed to look like.

Make no mistake though: even with the king of bad haircuts on my head, even though slumping over to hide my viticulturally-themed shirt, I was still really truly happy.

You had to expect in the 1970s that a teenaged guy and an FBI guy were going to clash a little on a few points of fashion, but even then it was only in the teeny details: I agreed completely on the essentials. Plus once President Hunt started talking about other subjects I went into total ecstasy. The man just sounded so certain about everything, just the way I wanted to sound too.

In fact when it came time for the big testimony meeting later in the week, meaning that anyone was free to stand up and *bear testimony* to the truthfulness of the church and its missionary program, I found myself actually talking like President Hunt, right down to the booming voice. I must have been good at it, because the President himself complimented me on what I'd said, which was mostly a summary of what the President had been saying all week long.

In other words, I was with the exception of the pasty white shirts mostly and truly eager to conform. Beaver eager. I would dam as high, build as sturdily, and gnaw as vigorously as told. You just had to tell me.

I got my wish in a big way, because during those five days of initiation in the Mission Home the President and top top leaders of the church walked across the street from church headquarters and told us more things to do than I'd ever been told before, even by my big sister. We all got a sort of *working model,* as a sociologist might've put it, of what a missionary was supposed to be. Now, guys like me had been developing a working model our whole lives, of course, even if we didn't know that's what it was called, just by watching missionaries around us, and by pestering every Returned Missionary in sight with annoying questions, and of course by reading a few how-to books. But here at the Mission Home we were getting the fine print, the inside scoop, the technical know-how, right from the top.

From what I'd learned growing up and from what I heard here, my model said that good missionaries knew the scriptures inside and out. That except for little humorous glitches they always basically got along with each other. That they knew just how to respond to the questions of people they were teaching *(investigators).* That they were usually busy teaching but if not then they knew exactly what to do with the precious time they never had enough of and that just flew by. That the best missionaries converted people at least every month. That any troubles they faced they got over pretty fast because they were full of faith and the Holy Ghost, which you could tell from how they were always laughing and smiling and hand-shaking and testifying and go-getting and healing and devil-out-casting. The real miracle was that investigators could somehow *not* convert after hearing missionaries.

Sure I'd heard a few exceptions to the model even before getting to the Mission Home, but that's all they were. They weren't enough to make me throw out the model altogether, or make me think I couldn't become it.

Like maybe when I was 13 driving with my mom, and we saw two missionaries on bicycles riding 50 yards apart from each other, and I said, *Hey the guy in front must not see how far ahead he is!* But my mom said, *Well maybe they're not getting along, they don't always, you know.* I couldn't believe that.

Then there was that missionary I met when I was 18 who was from the South and who started boasting about how he and his friends had made the four black kids at his high school stand up and sing Dixie and how funny that was. I wasn't sure about that, but I wasn't a missionary so maybe I was missing something. Or maybe this guy was one of those rare slacker missionaries I'd heard about but had never actually seen.

There was also the brother of my friend, who said during his homecoming talk that a mission wasn't one big spiritual experience and then just sat down without telling one funny story or miracle story or even mentioning the best two years. Maybe he was one of the slackers too. When I found out that he'd also been in a fight on his mission, then I was sure he was a slacker.

And there were the troublemaking missionaries I'd heard about from my brother-in-law, like the guy who souped up his mission car and raced it at the drag track one Saturday (and won and got his name in the paper, which was how he got caught), or the two guys who spent their days supervising a gym and chaperoning dances, or the guy who got so mad that he cut one of his companion's suits into tiny pieces. But these guys couldn't have been real missionaries.

No, hearing what I heard here at the Mission Home made me sure that my model still held, especially because President Hunt and the other church leaders said so, all five days long, and they knew better than any slackers. I wrote down everything they said, like John writing his Revelation. They said you had to have faith to convert people. That you had to have a testimony that the church was true. That you had to be worthy to be led to converts. And that you could be sure that if you had faith and a testimony and were worthy then people would convert. In fact people actually wanted to convert, even if they didn't know it, but it was up to you to be ready to help them see it. You could do it though, in fact you could do whatever you wanted on your mission, even move a mountain like Moses or convert multitudes like Ammon or Wilford Woodruff or present-day Latin American missionaries, if you had multitude-level faith and worthiness.

That *could do whatever you wanted* scared me for just a second, as in existentially scared me, like when my dad and my teachers used to tell me I could be *whatever* I wanted to be in life. It would've been a whole lot easier if they'd drawn up a short-list, instead of leaving things so wide-open. But then I remembered that at least for my mission I already had a short-list and didn't have to be scared about the *whatever:* I had 84. That was my *whatever.* My only worry now was whether 84 was maybe shooting too low, since thinking about *whatever you wanted* sort of did that to you.

I wrote down the specific techniques the leaders told us about too, like that studies showed missionaries would convert people pretty regularly if they spent about half of their 60 proselyting* hours a week actually *teaching* people lessons instead of spending most hours just *looking* for people to teach. I wrote that magic number down too, right next to 84: 30 teaching hours a week to get to 84.

When not listening to President Hunt and other church leaders over those five days, we were being divided up into small groups to hear even more specific details from a few specially hand-picked Returned Missionaries just home from the trenches, which was exciting because in some ways these guys seemed to know even more than the old authorities just exactly what missionaries needed at this particular moment in missionary history. Some of the details they gave us were pretty basic. Like that we all had to call each other *Elder* now (not because we were old but like in the New Testament), or *Sister* (not clear where that came from). That we all had to get out of the habit of going anywhere alone because we always had to be near our companion, except maybe in the bathroom — in fact absolutely not in

---

* As some observers have pointed out, Mormons might be the only people who say *proselyting* rather than the proper *proselytizing* — either because (1) the correct word is too hard for us, (2) someone in authority once used it and we all dutifully repeated it from that day on, or (3) we just wanted to give it our peculiar twist.

the bathroom (and in fact if your companion ever made any sort of move on you, then you were, said the teachers, perfectly justified in punching him out). That we needed to strictly obey the rules, especially the official white handbook we were supposed to carry in our shirt pocket next to our heart. That we needed to pray and read scriptures like never before.

But all that stuff (except for the bathroom part) I'd already heard. What I mostly wanted to hear was their stories about miracles. And fighting devils. And they didn't let me down. At the end of every class, these guys broke out their most incredible stories — about converts they'd found at the last house on the last street in the most impossible ways, about people they'd healed, about being protected by God's own hand, and — it got really quiet — about the times they'd had to cast out the devil himself.

Now that was more like it! The devil so hard at work was a good sign you were doing something the devil hated. And the devil, as any Jesuit knew as well, hated missionaries most of all, because they were doing the most divine thing on earth. If the devil could take out a missionary, then it was like he was taking out hundreds of other people too. That's how special you were.

I was so happy to be at the Mission Home that on the very first night, when we all went to bed in our huge dormitory with 50 or so bunk-beds and the lights went out and it got quiet and only a little moonlight shined through the windows in that upper-story room, I got on my knees right there on my upper-bunk to pray, even though all those other missionaries were in there too. I didn't pray as long or as fervently as one of those saints whose knees got stuck in the ground after a while and got infested with worms or something, but it was impressive anyway for me to do that, in fact so impressive that pretty soon everyone else in the room noticed and got up on their knees too, and then every night afterward it was just taken for granted. But I'd started it, which was one of the first signs that I probably really was meant for big things, just like people had predicted.

Praiséd be God and not my name for it, I would have quoted Shakespeare's Henry V again, after he'd sent the French whimpering from Agincourt, if I'd known about Henry.

Maybe it was my piety, or all the talks about purity, but whatever it was on the third day at the Mission Home some guys began forming a line in the hallway again — not for the barbershop this time but for the door to the President's office. There were whispers that they'd already had enough and wanted to go home, or that they'd decided they'd better confess some sin they'd been holding back and oh man they might have to go home because of it. I was really glad now that I'd called those (three) girls, but even with that I was still never sure whether I'd confessed enough sins myself, because I could always think of something else I'd done that was probably wrong too. But I was sure that I wouldn't just leave the Mission Home unless I was forced to. That night some of the beds in the huge dormitory room were empty. All those guys headed home were probably crying again, I guessed, just like when they first got here, but they must have been totally sad tears now. And they must have been slackers. Or never had the good dream.

But I did. In fact I could see it better than ever now — one big landscape filled with grateful people standing like a marching band on a football field in the shape of the number 84, gratefully uttering my name in even more reverential tones than before.

three

The Really Big Hand of Jesus

Right where a shadow fell over the top of a giant dune, a young local businessman with the supremely un-Mormon name of Sebastian St. Croix was sculpting something in the sand, way down deep in the slightly moist layer he'd uncovered by pushing away the shifty stuff on top. A little crowd, including me, was starting to gather, because Sebastian St. Croix was as annoyingly good at this as he was at everything else.

Probably the last place you expected to find yourself if you were preparing to be a local businessman in Belgium was out in the middle of the Idaho desert on a sand dune, but that's exactly where I, Elder St. Croix, and about 80 others like us were today.

We'd come here, or more precisely to nearby Rexburg, Idaho, straight from the Salt Lake Mission Home, to study for two months the respective exotic languages we'd need for our respective exotic missions. Most days we studied our brains out inside a classroom, but Saturday afternoons we got a few hours off for some fun, and on this particular Saturday we'd bussed out to the nearby dunes to run around. Out here we didn't even have to dress like local businessmen or Sisters, just 19-year-old boys and 21-year-old young women in jeans and t-shirts and bare feet, though I noticed that Elder St. Croix's t-shirt was of course tucked business-casually in.

And of course Sebastian St. Croix would be the only guy here not running and jumping around, thought slightly jealous I. If anybody was going to do something different out here on the dunes, then you could've almost guaranteed it'd be future big-shot trial lawyer Sebastian St. Croix.

Everything about him was different. His diction was way too good for a 19-year-old (no wonder: he was actually 23). His skin was way too olive for a Mormon (no wonder: he was a recent convert who'd been Jewish or French or something different like that). His posture, straight as a cypress even when (always) carrying his fully loaded executive briefcase or even when leaning way over to sculpt something on a sand dune, was way too upright for a missionary. And his personality, though fronted by a perpetual smile and cheerful voice and enthusiastic handshake, was way too serious, as he always had to be doing something productive, even out here on the dunes.

The shape starting to emerge beneath his skillful hands was that of yet another hand, a giant hand, about ten feet across, palm up, with lines and bumps and texture that looked as close to skin as sand could get, and that caused the growing crowd to ooh and aah. A few scrunched foreheads wondering why he'd chosen a hand as his subject. And elite insiders eagerly whispered their insider knowledge that this guy was also an expert at (besides much else) stained glass. But he just kept working away, either because he suffered from the same false modesty that afflicted so many of his fellow local businessmen, or because unlike so many of them he was actually tuned in to what he was doing at a given moment.

Then suddenly he leaned over to the middle of the palm and started shaping something else there, something big and square. *What in the heck?* filled the thought-clouds forming over local businessheads. Was that a nail? Good Grief it was. Good Grief this wasn't just any hand, it was Jesus's hand, with a nail in it. Which meant Good Grief that this was Jesus's hand on the Cross. Mormons didn't do Crosses, didn't he know? Not even part of the Cross. Catholics did, and maybe Protestants. But Mormons and especially missionaries Good Grief didn't. We might say *Good Grief,* originally a swear word that was very possibly referring to Jesus's suffering on the Cross, but no missionary knew that so it was okay to say. We just knew that Crosses were bad, and even idolatrous.

Some of the local businessmen started trickling away, while a few others offered faint praise *(the fingers are good)* or broke into quiet debates about whether he should be doing what he was doing. I was eager to hear the views of Elder Downing, leader of the 20 going-Belgian missionaries, but Elder Downing just half-smiled and shrugged his shoulders like *well it's not really right but he's a convert.*

Elder St. Croix didn't hear any of the muffled commotion, and probably didn't have the slightest twinkle of an idea that he might be doing anything even remotely offensive. Word went around fast about the convert thing, which mostly excused him, and besides, how much sand-sculpting would he be doing on his mission anyway?

Soon after he finished, the sun went down behind the biggest dune, Jesus's hand was left intact for whatever surprised person came along next (though I wondered whether some missionary might sneak back and knock off the nail), and all the local businessmen and Sisters packed into the busses that had brought us here. During most of the ride across the desert, I thought about Elder St. Croix's talent, which even though it was obviously as wrong as you could get had still managed to turn the fading light above the sand into some sort of magical super essence.

I hadn't been thrilled about coming to Rexburg (or Idaho), I had to admit.

Five days of spell-binding initiation in Salt Lake listening to top top church leaders was one thing, but two whole months 8,000 miles away from where your actual mission was going to be, in a place so small and old-fashioned that the local businessmen actually looked like missionaries, was another.

But if your going-foreign mission required you to learn a new language, then before actually going foreign you took a detour to one of the church's three Language Training Missions. This particular LTM was located in such an unlikely place as Rexburg not because missionary language-learning was top secret, like the nuclear-acting-and-reacting going on down the road at the INEL* just a short ballistic-missile-ride away, but because the church happened to own a college here, Ricks College, that was full of Returned Missionaries With Relevant Languages who could teach at the LTM for cheap.

Except for maybe that big day on the dunes, life in Rexburg was a lot less exciting than it'd been at the Mission Home, and not just because of location location location. The kind but astonishingly fatigued President of the LTM, Rulon Jorgensen, a retired linguistics professor, had something to do with it too. Despite heroic efforts to stay awake by raising his eyebrows to unheard-of heights above his forehead, he dozed off two minutes into any meeting, the eyebrows ultimately defeated by pendulous eyelids made heavy by years of lost battles with sleep. No alert FBI stuff for him. One **bold-type** missionary had already to everyone's horror stood up and boldly reprimanded the President for nodding off all the time, but the President just opened his eyes briefly to explain, as he probably had to do to many a **bold-type** missionary, that he had a sleep disorder, which made everyone feel bad, including those who nodded off themselves during the President's arcane talks on language. And by the way there was no chance that this President ever noticed anyone's haircut, including his own, which was perpetually loaded with static and stuck out wispily on all sides (nothing on top but eyebrows). It took me a lot of years to realize that this sort of President with his arcane interests and disdain of meetings and haircuts was actually my kind of guy.

But the biggest cause of unexcitement at the LTM was the sort of work you did there, all day long. Conjugating verbs and memorizing huge stacks of vocabulary cards that disfigured your pockets just wasn't as exciting as converting people and casting out devils all the time, or at least talking about such.

My new language, Dutch, wasn't exciting either, at first. My mission call hadn't been clear about what language I'd be learning, had just said I'd be going to Rexburg after the Mission Home. But somehow after reading in the *World Book* that around 60 percent of Belgians spoke Dutch and around 40

---

* Idaho National Engineering Laboratory, near Arco, pop. 1244, where the signs proudly say *The first city* [sic] *in the world lit by atomic power!*

percent spoke French I'd bet against the odds and guessed that I'd be learning French, probably because it sounded so impressive to tell someone that.

Dutch didn't sound impressive at all, in the telling or the speaking. The first Dutch noises ever to stir the hair follicles of my youthful ears were close to alarming, like the maker of the noises was hocking something up every third syllable or so; I had a sore throat my whole first week of making Dutch g's and ch's. The r's were trouble too, because they required some tricky rolling or trilling, depending on what letters they lay next to. As for diphthongs, well, there were a few that were similar to English — Dutch *heet* sounded something like *hate* but with the *ee* drawn out extra-long by coathangering your mouth a few beats. But forget about *ui* as in *huis* (house), because you had to make a sound that you as a foreigner supposedly could not make after age seven, no matter how hard you tried, because by age seven the mouth, cheek, and throat muscles needed for that particular sound had already taken their final English-speaking shape. That was the word on the missionary street anyway. So usually you just gave up and said *house,* American style, which no Belgian was going to understand.

The head-banging memorization of verbs regular and irregular with their assorted conjugations, and of millions of nouns each with their proper form of *the (het* or *de),* couldn't be blamed on Dutch, since you had to memorize things like that for lots of languages. But what was this splitting and joining of so many annoying things called compound conjunctions, which when joined together could make a word a mile long but when split into pieces might spread across a sentence like debris after a hurricane? Or what about never using *do* and *are* unless you really meant them? I.e., you could say *Do that* or *I am happy,* but not *Do you like to read?* or *Are you going to the store?* Instead you weirdly said *Read you gladly?* or *Go you to the store?* Or what about throwing all verbs but the first to the end of a sentence or clause? Why would you want to say *I go dinner ready make* when you could say it the normal way *I'm going to make dinner?* And what about all the idioms, like at dinner never saying *I'm full,* which for some strange reason in Dutch had the more pregnant meaning of *I'm pregnant,* so instead you said (and here went those secondary verbs into action) *I have enough had?*

Add it all up and you basically had another whole way of saying just about everything. Prissy Mrs. Feely, my teacher for first-year German (twice), had been right: learning another language wasn't just about plugging in one word for another and learning a few new noises. It was about learning a whole new way of thinking, and even feeling.

Luckily for me, I ended up, despite other-purposed facial muscles and early disappointment, really liking Dutch, especially the Belgian version called Flemish.* It wasn't what you'd call a beautiful language, not on the level of say French or Italian, but somehow the sounds and words and idioms of Flemish Dutch made you feel like whatever you were saying was more sincere or hilarious than it'd be in any other language.

In fact the better I got at Flemish, the more I not only felt like I was thinking in a new way, but that maybe I was in Flemish an even better version of myself. Flemish-speaking me didn't have all the back-breaking baggage of English-speaking me, and Flemish-speaking me had a lot more available memory too. Talk about a fresh start! This was one big way a going-foreign mission would bring out my true and special self, I thought. If only the girls back home could have known this version of me!

In fact it wasn't long after observing the talents of Sebastian St. Croix out on the sand dunes that I realized what talent I could put on display out here in the wilds of Idaho under a less-than-watchful-eyed President: namely, my full Flemish-speaking self.

Oh sure, everyone at the LTM had some sort of talent, with our olive-skinned maybe-convert maybe having more than his rightful share. And most everyone was eager to let it shine, eager to show what they had to offer the big new missionary world, and also to show to themselves and others that the big hand of Jesus was operating in their particular life too. Not the big spooky hand out on the dunes, of course, but the invisible one that could reach down and touch someone, as a sign of divine favor. If your God-given talent was singing, you let others hear it, especially since that was

* Flemish Dutch (from Belgium) is basically to Dutch Dutch (from the Netherlands) what American English is to English English: the same language but with different usage and idioms and things going on with upper lips and throats.

something actually useful in missionary life. Same with piano: if you played that, you pounded it out every chance you got, especially if you could play like my nemesis Elder Furtwangler, who could rip through a Scott Joplin rag at 100 miles an hour and who thought playing simple old hymns was like talking baby talk. If you could lean your body forward at a Tower-of-Pisa-quality angle, without falling over, like my companion Elder Youngblood could, you even did that, even if it wasn't clear how that might come in handy on your real mission. And if you could sculpt in the sand like Sebastian St. Croix could, then of course you did that too.

Nothing wrong with those other talents, I admitted. In fact I was a little jealous of the ones that got oohs and aahs and laughs. But I was also sure that the best God-given talents anyone could have at this particular stage of missionary life just happened to be the ones I was showing signs of: namely, learning my new language and culture, fast. I'd leave the crowd-pleasing stuff to others and stand out at the things we'd supposedly all come here to master but that turned out to be pretty hard to get excited about or even to be really good at. I'd get the gift of tongues (and cultures) most and first, as humbly and conspicuously as possible.

And so I girded up my polyester-blend-covered loins and worked hard to unravel the mysteries of Flemish, once again praising God and not my own name for it whenever the unraveling seemed to go better for me than it was going for others.

And I mastered my new culture too by dominating a special Belgian water-bottle game we learned during culture class, and played a few afternoons a week in front of the college's old administration building.* Students passing by and looking oddly at us were surely thinking, I thought, *Look at*

---

* It went like this: the missionaries divided into two teams out on the grass, each team standing about ten yards apart from each other. In front of each team stood a narrow-necked cider-like gallon bottle full of water. The teams took turns chucking a volleyball or soccer ball at the other team's bottle. If you hit it then you ran like mad to where it was gushing out, picked it up and dumped out as much water as you could before the person who'd run after the rolling ball came back across an invisible line. Whichever team got all the water out of the bottle first won. I should've doubted its authenticity from the start, because no Belgian would've wasted water like that.

those missionaries mastering their new culture! In fact nothing made me feel like I had my finger more squarely on the cultural pulse of my new country than the Belgian water-bottle game did, even though I was still in a place of mountains and deserts that except for the potatoes couldn't have resembled Belgium less. Oh, and even though it turned out that no Belgians ever actually played the Belgian water-bottle game. Or had ever even heard of it.

I was good at the rest of our cultural training too, which turned out to be about as helpful as the non-Belgian water-bottle game. Usually this training consisted of a teacher getting bored with diagramming sentences and instead telling stories about the various bicycles he'd owned in Belgium or the apartments he'd lived in or the sorts of food he'd liked: chocolate sprinkles on bread was a real favorite, as were fries — invented in Belgium, not France! Who knew? What great stuff!

There was nothing in these cultural training-sessions about such big Belgian things as the Crusader Godfrey of Boullion, or the Warrior Charles the Bold, or the Heavenly Jan van Eyck, or the Medieval Women Called Beguines Who Altered Female Religious Life, or the Emperor Charles V, or the Rebel William of Orange, or the Sublime Pieter Bruegel, or the Independence of Belgium in 1830, or the Flemish Movement, or the Suffering of Belgium in World War I, or its Repeated Suffering in World War II, or the Magical Hills of Brabant, or Belgium's Dominant Religion Catholicism, or even about How Public Restrooms Are Organized in Belgium, or anything else that might have been actually useful. But who needed big things like that when you were getting the essentials, plus lessons in Charity (which transcendeth all cultures), plus the two pages I'd read in the *World Book* back home? All that would surely be enough to understand the local businessmen.

In all that striving and excelling and not-learning of Flemish culture, I was as eager as anyone to see the big hand of Jesus. Out in the real mission field Jesus's big hand would be obvious, I was sure, but here at the LTM, where you weren't really a missionary yet but ate and slept and studied among students and spent your days inside temperature-controlled rooms and weren't making converts, you had to look a little harder, including in the past participles. But look I did, because there was no distant clockmaker God for me, not even any slightly withdrawn Liberal Protestant God, but only a sparrow-seeing hair-numbering God who didn't just put the clock together but was still moving its hands around Personally, even during grammar class.

And so when I learned more Dutch words a day than I thought I could, I was sure it was from God. When I suddenly couldn't learn, I was sure I'd offended God — maybe forgetting to make my bed, or laughing too loud (again), or being rude (again). When my companion Elder Youngblood sprained his ankle, causing him to walk even more slowly than he usually did, I was at first impatient, but then I realized the sprain was probably just God reaching down to teach me a lesson in patience, in preparation for some situation in Belgium that would require patience (a prediction that had a 100 percent chance of coming true). That Elder Youngblood had to suffer a little so that I could learn the lesson, the way the other Mormon kid on the high school basketball team had had to party in order to teach me the value of non-worldly-stardom, didn't seem to me terribly unfair but just one of those ways that God moved mysteriously in.

Another clue that Jesus's hand was right there with me was of course that the devil's hand was too. Or was trying to be. The fellows at the Mission Home had warned about the devil trying to infiltrate, because wherever God went the devil was close behind, trying to ruin things. But who knew he'd show up this fast, right in the LTM, before we were even doing any actual proselyting?(!) It was the devil that made us forget a conjugation, or made us think about girls, or even made us swear, like Elder Youngblood one day so frustrated trying to say something in Dutch that he just blurted out the forbidden English adjective *goddamn*.* This caused Elder Furtwangler, a guy never to be outdone, to use the word even more creatively. That had to be from the devil.

---

* Forbidden *in toto,* not just as an adjective or an English word.

35

And what about the missionary in another language group who'd recently said that he'd felt the devil right in the hallway of the dorm — not in New York or Chicago or supposedly big targets like that, but a little old dorm right here in Rexburg, Idaho? Then just a couple of nights after that I'd had a dream that the devil was trying to stop me from going to convert one of my old coaches by throwing me into a huge pit with all sorts of horrible noises that just had to be Hell. I couldn't wait to tell about that at my group's weekly testimony meeting, not only to edify others but to not-so-subtly let them know that I was getting that level of personal attention from the devil, not just run-of-the-mill stuff like forgetting a noun and its accompanying article, which obviously meant that I was an extra-special target.

Maybe my favorite clue of divine favor at the LTM though, actually there was no maybe about it, was the magical appearance of Rachelle. Achingly staggeringly beautiful Rachelle. After the record-setting defection of my non-girlfriend back home, I'd thought I was done with girls for two years. Now I'd really be able to concentrate on my mission, just like the official white book in my vine-stamped shirt pocket said: *Lose yourself in the work. Put out of your mind all thoughts and discussions of home, school, and girlfriends.* But that didn't last long. Within weeks I'd started looking for someone to write seriously, not only because I wanted to but because everyone else seemed to be. Even Elder Furtwangler claimed to be writing someone seriously, which I didn't believe for a second, but I wasn't going to be left behind.

It wasn't all that hard to get someone to write you, because being a missionary suddenly made you a hundred times more attractive to Mormon girls than you'd been in civilian life — partly because like most people you were better in theory than in person, and partly because as a missionary you were now only one step away from being a Returned Missionary, and that's what Mormon girls seemed to care about most. In fact it didn't take long to see that girls you hardly even knew might suddenly start sending nice-smelling letters to you. But finding someone who wanted to write you seriously and vice versa was another matter — and a big one, because even though girls were off-limits in person for two years, writing seriously to one somehow made you more legitimate as a missionary.

I in my search didn't put up a notice on the bulletin board in the college cafeteria the way some missionaries did (sometimes successfully), but used the more tried and proven technique of finally noticing the younger sister of a friend. Someone I ran into at the college mentioned a mutual friend who had a sister (Rachelle) just the right age (almost finished with high school), which meant young enough to be impressed by a missionary, probably too young to get married while you were gone, and old enough not to make you feel creepy for writing her. On the next free Saturday afternoon, I wrote to Rachelle on some pretext, taking care to mention some of my exploits in a culturally complex self-effacing way that ultimately didn't actually self-efface. And she wrote back. Several times. A few letters did not serious writing make, but Rachelle soon bothered to send a picture, and the unwritten laws of missionary correspondence said you did that only if you were at least *thinking* about writing someone seriously. And what a picture it was, beyond my most aching staggering beautiful dreams. Not a vague, distant, strategically lighted, and over-flattering picture, like the one I'd sent her of me, but up-close in clear and living color. She was way too beautiful for me, at least for English-speaking me. But I had two years to make a good impression on paper, enough time to maybe make her think when she finally met me for real that, just like in one of those psychology experiments, I was what she'd been conditioned to think I was.

I knew that catching Rachelle after my mission wasn't a sure thing, but this unexpected potential elevation to a higher league of beauty than my English-speaking self was accustomed to just had to be yet another sign of God's favor smiling already upon special Flemish-speaking me. Only God could have nudged someone that beautiful to write me, was the thing, as a sort of reward for my hard work and worthiness so far, a sort of tantalizer for what was in store if I kept it up on my actual mission, as in maybe a more permanent reward in the form of, say, marriage. Because I was sure that ending up with Rachelle would depend almost entirely on my worthiness, and the continued if gradual coming-out of my special Flemish-speaking self. That was one reason I immediately put her achingly staggering, beautiful picture in a place that would remind me to always be worthy and special:

right in my scriptures. The other reason was of course so that other missionaries would see the picture too whenever I casually opened my scriptures, which like most missionaries I did all the time.

There was one last clue of Jesus's hand reaching down and touching me: I was soon big pals with the leader of all 20 going-Belgian missionaries, Elder Downing. I'd been star-struck by him since the first day at the LTM, when he burst into our classroom and babbled away in Dutch with the teacher as if he'd been speaking the language forever instead of for only a month, then babbled some more to us as we left class that afternoon. It turned out that Elder Downing was actually saying *Grow up,* as we filed past and shook his hand, which was something he liked to say a lot, but as far as I could tell he was the ideal missionary who seemed to know just how to handle himself and who as far as I could tell already spoke fluent Dutch. No wonder he'd been chosen as our group leader.

I wanted to be just like that, including the leader part. That's why I was happy when it was clear Elder Downing liked talking and joking with me. It was no accident that out at the sand dunes I'd been able to seek out his views on the Jesus hand just by turning my head, because as usual I was standing right next to him. Maybe leaders attracted leaders, I thought. Elder Downing was the group leader for now obviously, of the 10 older and 10 younger going-Belgian missionaries (the Olders were simply a month ahead, and the group leader always came from their ranks). But when the Olders left, the Youngers would become the new Olders for their second month, a new group of Youngers would come in, and a new group leader would have to be chosen. That was where I came in. Possibly. Probably.

My big sister had said that I'd be a leader, lots of people had said I would, and I'd shown leaderly skills so far, like in learning my language, or my skill at the non-Belgian water-bottle game. So it didn't take me long to include being a leader in my working model of my missionary self — a big leader, not just Senior Companion like almost everyone would be someday, but more like District Leader (24 of them in Belgium), or even Zone Leader (only 12 of those), or even, can you imagine, Assistant to the President (only two!).

Being Group Leader at the LTM was the first step, I thought. I tried not to think about it too much or look forward too much to the day when Elder Downing would leave for Belgium, because I didn't want to be proud or jinx myself. But surely hanging out with him couldn't hurt. I thought.

four

STONED

The trouble started the day Elder Youngblood and I were trying to figure out during afternoon grammar class what the heck the conditional pluperfect even was, and in the process of that figuring out I started talking in English.

I didn't usually talk that way, preferring as I did my new Flemish-speaking self, and mindful as I was of the inviolable rule that from the third day on at the LTM you were supposed to speak your new language all the time, *Or Else*. There were a few exceptions to the rule, like out on the dunes during recreation-time. And also, I assumed, during afternoon grammar class. Because trying to explain to your companion some major or even obscure point of Dutch grammar in Dutch was useless when you could hardly say anything more yourself than hello and goodbye (which happened to be the same word).

But I assumed wrong, because only two or three words into my all-English explanation I suddenly saw looming out of the corner of my eye my nemesis Elder Furtwangler, wearing a big grin on his face and lugging a huge stone in his hands.

This was the *Or Else*.

Elder Furtwangler dropped The Stone on my desk with a big thud and said in his never-once-modulated voice, *Thanks Yink!*

I was mortified.

If you spoke English illegally, then you had to lug around The Stone as punishment, an utterly horrible barbaric and fatuous tradition invented by a prison guard, or maybe a PE major, I thought. And you had to lug it everywhere — to the cafeteria, to class, yes even to the bathroom — a prospect that was meant to scare you straight, straight back to talking really bad Dutch. And you had to keep lugging The Stone everywhere until you heard someone else evil enough to speak English too, which allowed you to unload it on him.

Like a lot of rituals, The Stone was part initiation for newcomers and part payback for oldtimers who'd suffered the ritual themselves as newcomers. See, The Stone was meant only for Youngers, supposedly because Youngers needed more reminding than Olders did about speaking Dutch all the time, but really because this little ritual gave Olders a good superior laugh at the sight of a Younger lugging the thing around. Now *that* was funny!

Only later did I learn that the whole business of The Stone was yet another thing in Mormon missionary life that'd come straight from Jesuits. The Jesuits wanted boys at their famous sixteenth-century schools to speak their new language (Latin) all the time, instead of the local vernacular, and they motivated those boys both positively and negatively to do so — say, positively handing out lists of everyday Latin phrases sure to come in handy *(Throw me the ball,* or *I'm late because the maid forgot to wake me up),* and negatively hanging around the neck of anyone sinful enough to speak the vernacular a big *signum* (sign), like a badge of sin. The only way to get rid of the signum was, you guessed it, to hear some other kid speaking the local tongue, allowing you to run over and strap the thing on him. Which of course made the *signum*-wearing boy care a lot more about spying than about his lessons.

If the local businessmen at the LTM had known that little tidbit about the provenance of their utterly horrible barbaric and fatuous tradition, then maybe The Stone would've never gotten off the literal ground, because everyone would've been sure there was no way in heaven that anything from Jesuits could've been inspired. The Jesuits were right about speaking a new language all the time if you wanted to learn it fast, I would've admitted.

But I would've also insisted they were out to lunch and dinner too about punishment.

I hadn't paid much attention to The Stone at first, because there was no way in the lithic world that Flemish-speaking I was ever going to get it. Until that fateful afternoon when Elder Furtwangler loomed.

My first thought was to heave The Stone right back at Elder Furtwangler for saying *Thanks* in English (*Yink,* as a proper noun, didn't count). But EF was protected by the sacrosanct rule about no givebacks. So my second thought was just desperately to blurt, *It doesn't count during grammar class!* and other patheticisms I imagined were inscribed in the Official Stone Rulebook. But blurting in English just sealed my fate, and EF walked away still grinning, and now also looking around to make sure everyone else was looking too.

Elder Furtwangler was having fun because he didn't really care if he got The Stone. If he was dying to say something in English that just had to be said, then he said it, and with his mouth still yapping away he'd stick out his hand to take The Stone from whoever came running to hand it to him. Everyone knew that he was still the best at Dutch anyway, even better than I was. Giving Elder Furtwangler The Stone was like dropping a dunce cap on the smartest kid in class: the picture was so wrong it just reinforced how smart he was. He even carried The Stone around up high, like a shot-put, to show off his strength. *It's not that heavy,* he'd say. It was a joke all the way around for him.

But not for me: The Stone was the Scarlet Letter R (Rule-breaker) or E (English-speaker). English-speaking me, just who I didn't want to be. How could I be the next Group Leader if I did something as ordinary as getting The Stone? Just as Elder Furtwangler hoped, people started chuckling as he returned to his seat. Oh, they usually chuckled anyway whenever The Stone changed hands, but this chuckling had some real vinegar to it, maybe because with that big old thing from the pre-paleolithic age sitting on my desk, I the fanatical speaker of Dutch looked just like anyone else. And that made me fume.

After another half-hour of fuming, and grumbling, and of perking my ears for the slightest English sound, I finally heard it, from somewhere in the corner. I ran right over and dropped The Plague-covered Stone on the offender's desk, without any of the usual apologetic smiling or joking. I felt the tiniest bit like a jerk, because the offender hadn't done anything more than I'd done to earn it, and because I'd declared my own treatment unfair but had still gone ahead and inflicted it eagerly on someone else. Which the offender bothered briefly to point out, sort of putting a damper on The Stone business that afternoon. But Stoneless I at least felt almost pure again, and that's what mattered most.

Unfortunately for me, that wasn't the end of the story. Or the humiliation. News of my little fit spread to the Olders next door. Maybe one of Group-Leading Elder Downing's aides-de-camp whispered the troubling news to him between repetitions of the past perfect. But however he heard, Elder Downing decided something had to be done about that level of irreverence, and fast. A little complaining was fine when you got The Stone, because it added to the hilarity, but serious complaining along the lines of mine could threaten the whole sacred institution, not to mention the Olders' sense of fun. Elder Downing would therefore mixed-metaphorically nip it in the bud, kick it in the shins, and stop it in its tracks, that very night.

Every night 17 devil-fighting going-Belgian local businessmen crowded into the two-bed two-desk dorm room of Elder Downing and his companion for a short devotional to ceremoniously end the day (only 17 instead of 20 because three of the going-Belgian missionaries were Sisters, and they weren't allowed in the Elders' dorm, and vice versa). Devotional was a sort of daily recreation-time, because during these 10 minutes of announcements, scripture verse, and prayer there wasn't a local businessman in sight: everyone just wore pajamas. And best of all for these 10 minutes you didn't even have to speak Dutch, allowing you to finally get out in English what you'd been pulling out your hair to say all day.

On that fateful night, as everyone noisily pushed inside, standing skinny in a corner or perching on a few inches of bed or packing like sardines across the linoleum floor, something besides stale socks smelled fishy. Elder Downing wasn't joking around as usual as he sat in his usual spot on top of his veneered desk, but just stared at the floor. Even when the last person finally squeezed in and the door was muscled shut across assorted limbs, Elder Downing didn't crack wise or make an announcement or ask someone to read a scripture verse, but just opened his own Bible and started to read. He was going to do the verse himself tonight, without any laughs or warm-up.

This felt serious. Oh it was. Elder Downing read a verse that even this pajama'ed assembly of scriptural novices knew, a famous verse from 1 Corinthians 13: *When I was a child, I spake as a child, I understood as a child, I thought as a child: but when I became a man, I put away childish things.*

Ah yes, thought I, totally missing the meta-message. We were indeed grown up now. And doing a man's work. What a manly message. And serious message. Enough to sober anybody up. No wonder Elder Downing wasn't laughing.

But that wasn't the exegesis Elder Downing had in mind. Instead he shut his Bible, ignored 16 centuries of theological commentary on the verse, and declared its true meaning in one simple sentence: *You Youngers need to grow up about The Stone.* Then he shut his Bible.

That was it.

Silence.

All the Youngers in the crowded crowd knew exactly what Elder Downing was talking about, so there was no need to look over at me — and good thing, because swinging your chin around in there could've hurt somebody. But even if you were an Older who hadn't heard what'd happened, even if you were an alien who just happened to be looking in through the third-story window from outside, you could have guessed I was the guilty one just by the second-time-that-day horrified look on my face.

Even the alien would've noticed that even though I was sitting down on the hard linoleum, I looked a little dizzy. And not from the circulation-cut-

45

off caused by pulling knees up to chest and wrapping arms around them and being crowded in, but from the mortification and shock. I, by my own estimation the leading light of the Youngers, was being busted in public by my own chosen role model for something that was based on the flimsiest and most controversial pretext ever. I, heroically Flemish-speaking, was being held up as an example of what not to be by the person whose place I'd surely soon be taking.

It couldn't be. I tried calming down and taking a deep breath, but there wasn't room for it. So I just thought, don't speak out against your leader. Don't even think out against your leader. A leader was put there by inspiration, so he must be right and you wrong. What torture going on inside that body, an alien would've noticed.

All this in a moment. A moment later, Elder Downing soberly asked someone to say a short prayer, which was done in our baby Dutch, thus with no verbs rightly conjugated and no secondary verbs thrown to the end of sentences and not a conditional or pluperfect in sight. Then everyone stood up and did the usual handshaking all around as they filed slowly and quietly (for once) out the door, back to their own two-bed two-desk rooms. I was so upset I could hardly look Elder Downing in the eye when it came time for us to shake hands, but even that brief look should've let him know how sorry I was.

I hadn't cried when I'd left on a mission, or at the Mission Home, or at any time since then, including now, but I at least felt like crying — and not because I was happy, or wanted to clean out my eyes or kill bacteria or expel toxins like some health-conscious crier might.

Back in my room lying on my bed, my guilt was running ocean-deep. I *had* acted like a baby. And I was sure I was *fully* guilty, never thinking to divide things up a little, the way later books about guilt would say to do — like assigning maybe 40 percent to the Jesuit who'd inspired The Stone, maybe 15 percent to the missionaries who'd hauled it from the river, maybe another 15 to the ringleaders who'd never made the rules clear, maybe another 15 or more to me for not hearing the rules right and then acting like a baby and making it a big deal, and maybe another 15 or less to Elder Downing for making it an even bigger deal by humiliating me in front of everyone when actually only the Youngers had witnessed the original ugly act.

But I couldn't divide it up like that. I was 100 percent guilty. Maybe even 110 percent. I knew from Mormon scripture that God couldn't *look upon sin with the least degree of allowance.* And what if Elder Downing didn't recommend me as his successor now? A real Group Leader would never do anything that childish, which Elder Downing had only confirmed by his tone and his I-did-it-for-your-own-good handshake at the end of the devotional.

I never liked that verse in Corinthians again.

I had to find a way to make up for my wretched foe pa* if I wanted to be a standout missionary (in the good sense) again. And I thought I knew just the way.

Not just through patching things up with Elder Downing, although that happened, partly by never giving him cause to chew me out again and mostly by taking some goofy pictures together just before he and the other Olders left for Belgium, because there was nothing like taking goofy pictures to help you feel like you'd patched things up with someone. And not by never getting The Stone again either, although that happened too, mostly because the new going-Belgian group leader, Elder Larson, decided to get rid of The Stone as soon as the Olders left, disappointing those who'd been looking forward to inflicting it on the new Youngers. Getting rid of an old and venerable tradition like that surprised most people, because it was like saying that the old and venerable tradition hadn't been a very good one after all, and also because Elder Larson had served in the Army and according to everyone's vocational calculus he should've loved something like The Stone — but instead he tossed it personally into some nearby body of water.

---

* I wasn't sure how a phrase that I could only imagine had been used to refer to an *enemy father* somehow came to have the idiomatic meaning of *mistake.* I just used it as I heard it.

But the way I made up most for my big mistake with The Stone was by bringing Flemish-speaking me to my final logical LTM form: I would become King of the Discussions, the most important sort of Flemish we'd ever speak here or in Belgium.

That's right, I wasn't named the new Group Leader. But I almost didn't mind: Elder Larson was not only 25 and a veteran, but had been a Lieutenant-something, for gosh sakes. But the main reason that I almost-but-not-quite didn't mind being named Group Leader was that in my estimation the King of the Discussions was the real leader of the group anyway — the guy most likely to make lots of converts, the guy most likely to rise to serious leadership positions in Belgium itself.

The Discussions were the seven one-hour lessons we used to teach investigators about the church and try to persuade them to convert. If missionaries had the Holy Ghost and investigators had soft hearts, then these lessons were irresistible, I knew. You started working on them at the LTM full-time after you had a month of grammar behind you, and though my talent for memorizing had certainly come in handy for learning grammar, well it was at the top of the toolbox for conquering 200 large-spaced pages of Discussions. These had to be word-perfectly and not vaguely memorized, our teachers explained, so that (1) missionaries were teaching the same official things all over the world, (2) even missionaries who could barely say a word outside of the Discussions were at least saying something partly coherent about their religion, and especially (3) the Holy Ghost could really go to work on investigators.*

It didn't take long for me to pull ahead of everyone in Discussion-learning, which I knew because everyone's progress was up on the chalkboard for all to see, another little motivational tactic the Jesuits would've

---

* Not many years later missionaries were given a new set of Discussions and told *not* to be word-perfect any more, but to use their own imperfect words, which the Holy Ghost was now said to like better. But in my time the Holy Ghost liked word-perfect. In fact some missionaries a little older than I was would one day start a big software company by that very name, and any former missionary of a certain age who heard that name could've guessed where it came from.

loved. I liked this chalkboard method though, unlike The Stone, because this one made me look good. When morning class started, everybody walked to the board and wrote down which concept of which Discussion they were working on, such as D-2, because each Discussion was assigned a letter and then subdivided into concepts.* When you passed a concept off, meaning that you said it word-perfectly to your companion with just a few flub-ups and hints, then you walked back up to the board, erased what you'd written, and wrote down your next concept.

I loved walking to and from the board, because the farther ahead I got with my memorizing, the louder the sounds of disbelief grew. Everyone always took a look when someone walked up to the board, to see where other people were, but they especially took a look when I walked up — and the sounds they let out were my siren song. *No! It Can't Be! What?! Psssh! Impossible! Are you kidding?* Unlike Ulysses, I couldn't resist them, nor the sights and sounds of palms striking desks, hands going to heads, sighs being expelled, and heads dropping in disbelief. It was like pro baseball players watching Koufax pitch: in theory they were all pros, but Koufax was so great that even his peers were in awe.

Even my nemesis Elder Furtwangler, usually unimpressed by anyone, would look up to watch me, though he wouldn't make any noises. He'd just stare at what I'd written, then at me, and do that slow blink of his. Elder Furtwangler probably couldn't believe anyone was ahead of him, I guessed, because there he was, Math *(Mathematics)* genius and possible race-car driver and maybe concert pianist and *supposedly* the best Dutch-speaker of us all. But there I was, farther along in the Discussions than he was, and the Discussions, I kept telling myself, were the Dutch that mattered most. Who cared if you knew a fat vocabulary notebook full of bizarre and sometimes risqué words, the way Elder Furtwangler did?

I tried not to look proud. When walking up to write my goal, I was all business, even though I was often wearing my favorite unbusinesslike tie

* The first Discussion was improbably lettered C, then came D, E, F, H, I, and J. G was a partial Discussion, for reasons explained in the next chapter. A and B remain mysteries.

that my grandma had given me, the one that said *Hello Handsome* on it over and over again, backwards. And when going up to erase something or when sitting back down, I looked as pious as a nun going to prayers, never returning anyone's stare or responding to the clamor but just looking straight ahead with my head hanging down and a face as sober as Jeremiah's.

But inside I was as proud as King Herod. Or as King Herod's wife Herodias. Or as Solomon when he went bad.

Or as Elder Furtwangler.

Wait. What?(!) Elder Furtwangler was loud and brash and arrogant and boastful and I couldn't fathom how in the world some of the other missionaries liked him, including some of the new Youngers. That couldn't be me. But it was: I was just as proud as he was. In fact I was probably even prouder, because at least he didn't pretend not to be proud. He boasted straight out, which was committing only one sin, while I was committing two: being proud, plus acting like I wasn't. When I walked back and forth so humbly between my desk and the board, I was actually using my uncannily strong peripheral vision to take reactions greedily in. When Elder Furtwangler walked to the board to write down his own progress, I pretended not to notice, but I was as alert as a guard dog and knew exactly where he was in the Discussions. When he was passing off a concept to his companion, I pretended to be deaf but my ears were perked, all the way across the room, listening for how well he had really learned it. *Ah ha! Just as I suspected. He doesn't really know it: he had to be prompted too many times. And he's counting it anyway* (head shake)!

Still, I didn't let up, because Elder Furtwangler was really smart and things might kick in for him all of a sudden, the way they can when learning a new language. And so after walking back from the board, I'd go right back to my desk, turn it to the corner again so no one could bother me, put my elbows on the desk and my hands across my forehead in the shape of one of those old green visors journalists used to wear, and start memorizing again. Spiritual Giant Busy. Superstar Missionary in Training. Do Not Disturb.

Most missionaries left the LTM with maybe three or four shaky Discussions not quite under their belt and were patted on the back for it. Some tried so hard to memorize that they put the Discussion book under their pillow at night, hoping to learn by osmosis, or they left headphones in their ears when they fell asleep. I just memorized straight-up, with no gimmicks, and had a real chance to finish all seven Discussions, which I'd heard no one had ever done in Dutch, and which made me sure that God was helping me be extra-special again. Someone in Belgium must be waiting for me to come teach one of those later Discussions, like an H or an I, right after I arrive, I thought, so I have to be ready, and God was helping me.

Discussion-King I never really stopped to think that all my passing-off kept interrupting the memorizing of my own companion, Elder Young-blood, who was way behind me in part because of me, or to think that maybe someone else in Belgium was waiting for him to come give them a later Discussion too. Discussion-King I never really stopped to think that maybe the reason even Elder Furtwangler was behind me was that he actually took a lot of time to listen to his companion pass things off, whereas Discussion-King I saw pass-off time as something mostly for my high-achieving self.

No, Discussion-King I just knew that my gift was memorizing, that thanks to it I'd almost certainly made up for the little incident with The Stone, and that I was ready to go to Belgium and start doing some multitude-level converting.

five

IN THE CLOUDS

None of the local businessmen cared that they'd had to catch the bus at four in the morning for the four-hour ride from Rexburg to the airport in Salt Lake City, because it meant they were finally going Belgian at last.

Plus a lot of family and friends would be at the airport to say goodbye again. And girlfriends.

In fact the hands-down biggest topic of conversation during the days leading up to departure was not how to conjugate *travel* or how to get your bags under 44 pounds or whether you should bother bringing anything electrical what with all the weird sockets in Europe, but instead just one supremely important thing: whether it was okay to kiss your girlfriend goodbye at the airport.

Not everyone sitting on the bus had a girlfriend, much less a girlfriend within driving distance of the airport, but it was a topic of such universal interest and still-vague decrees that everyone had an opinion anyway.

Those in the anti-kiss camp stood shakily on some vague authoritative statements they'd supposedly heard supposedly forbidding any sort of inter-gender contact beyond a non-lingering handshake. That would be good enough for my future wife, who before flying away to her mission wouldn't get any closer to me than to offer the most fleeting of handshakes, arm fully and bulwarkly extended.

Her strong-arm tactics might've had more to do with me than with any rules, of course, but if it was rules she had in mind then her view was decid-edly of the minority sort, because even more missionaries stood even more shakily in the pro-kiss camp, insisting that a kiss goodbye was not only a fine thing to do but practically a categorical imperative. The unstated foun-dation for such a view was that two years were such a long time that even the most supposedly loyal girlfriend might be gone by then, and so maybe you were kissing her goodbye for good. But the stated foundation was a lot of even vaguer authoritative statements than the anti-kiss camp could mus-ter. Elder Downing, for instance, had it on good third-hand authority that some unnamed church authority had authoritatively declared that *If I were going to be away from my girlfriend for two years, then you'd better believe I would kiss her goodbye, especially if she was good-looking.* No one rushed out to fact-check this claim, but it was canonized in a flash and memorized faster than any Discussion ever was. Elder Downing had a serious conflict-of-interest going on here, because his girlfriend lived only ten minutes from the airport, but as a zealously obedient fellow he was determined to follow even the most perilously shaky authoritative declarations.

The greatest champion of the pro-kiss camp, however, was my own companion, Elder Youngblood, who'd been collecting vague authoritative statements all week, and who once inside the airport terminal started obey-ing them right away, promptly getting lost in a *series* of kisses and hugs with his girlfriend. He wasn't the only one getting lost, but he was the only one who caused Sister Acey, watching off to the side with all other curious non-participants, to laugh and turn away and red-facedly declare *Mercy!*

Exponentially less engaged than Elder Youngblood was Poor Elder Hart, whose girlfriend was more accurately a near-girlfriend. He'd met her just weeks before in the college cafeteria, but their relationship so far was based on a few glances across several tables, a couple of semi-flirtatious conversations across the dirty-dish conveyer belt, and some enthusiastic letters full of colored-in exclamation points. A relationship with a founda-tion like that not only made things awkward at the airport but raised all sorts of thorny theological problems, even for some in the pro-kiss camp. Were a few glances and a couple of conversations across a conveyer belt and some artful punctuation enough to qualify her as a girlfriend and thus for a kiss goodbye? Should a farewell kiss be your first kiss? A couple of even mediocre medieval scholastics would've seen the essential problem right away: if you were allowed to kiss a girl who couldn't reasonably be called a girlfriend, well, then you could justify kissing anyone who walked by.

There wasn't much danger of missionaries jumping out to kiss strange girls, even though movies like *Kidnapped by the Mormons** had long suggested exactly that scenario and worse. Some of the anti-kiss missionaries feared that scenario too, and would've preferred some rule saying that anyone wanting to kiss a girl goodbye should have to prove that she'd been his girlfriend for at least several months in advance, maybe by passing around a few dated letters or a framed certificate or something.

Even though he was one of the lucky pro-kiss participants, Poor Elder Hart would've been completely onboard with a rule like that, because after only two awkward minutes he was already realizing how difficult it was to attain with a mere near-girlfriend the expected levels of affection that certain pro-kiss observers had been expecting and hoping for from him. While they watched eagerly from the same perimeter where anti-kiss observers watched suspiciously, and as the flimsiness of his near-relationship suddenly hit him floppily on the head, Poor Elder Hart froze. He tried touching his near-girlfriend's arm, but he mostly just kept sighing and trying to look as sad as it was possible to look when you were leaving behind someone you hardly knew, and when you weren't really sure you wanted to show any affection at all but felt a certain obligation to the pro-kiss observers who'd encouraged you, not to mention to the near-girlfriend who'd followed your bus all the way from Rexburg and was hoping for more than to be almost touched on the arm.

I didn't have any girl to worry about at the airport, since Rachelle lived too far away, and thank goodness for that, I thought while watching Poor Elder Hart. I was happy just to talk to her for the first time the day before,

---

* The 1911 Danish film was silent but its message didn't really need any words beyond the title.

when we'd been allowed to telephone family and friends for a final long-distance goodbye. I'd said to her in so many words that *missionary work in Belgium is really taking off and will take off even more once I show up,* but what I was really saying in a displaced sort of way was *I can't believe how beautiful you are and I'm hoping that my exploits will make you like me.* Maybe Rachelle was displacing too, because in her next letter she said that her phone-answering mother had favorable things to say about my voice, but Rachelle couldn't dare say such things herself, of course.

After everyone was finally herded aboard their respective planes, my biggest concern was not girls but how I was supposed to behave now. Because for the first time we were real missionaries now, turned loose in public among real potential converts: if one or more sat next to you on the plane, you were supposed to talk about the church with them and get their name and address if possible. Most missionaries ended up sitting next to other missionaries, though, which sort of threw a wrench into any neighborly proselyting, but rumor had it that such **bold-type** missionaries as Elder St. Croix weren't going to be stopped by mere seating arrangements and somewhere over the Atlantic were going to stand boldly up in front of the whole Economy section (and First Class if possible) and boldly make a bold presentation, or even two.

That level of boldness made me shudder. Why couldn't I ever think up something like that? Or do something like that? Or at least *want* to do something like that? Wasn't I a leaderly guy too? Leaderly guys like Elder St. Croix were always thinking up and doing stuff like that instead. I was sort of glad I wouldn't be on his plane, to tell the truth, so as not to be shown up. I decided to leave all the potential converts alone on the plane, and just study my Discussions, but once in Belgium I would boldly talk to everyone! Yes sir, once in Belgium I'd just like Sebastian St. Croix put my right hand out for a firm shake and lean the top half of an otherwise Washington-

Memorial-straight body forward just a little, to punctuate my smiling face and cheerful voice.

The best part of the long and silent trip was at the end when our second plane, a big Sabena 747 from New York, dropped softly through the rainy clouds outside Brussels and offered sleepy but wide-eyed missionaries their first glimpse of Belgium, a land filled with clusters of orange roofs set off by magical shades of green — more shades and more green than I'd ever seen before. Whenever I flew into Belgium in later years, the same fairy-tale quality would always hit me, more than it would when I flew into view of say the Vikingesque forests and lakes of Sweden, or the medieval-illumination fields of France, or even the Renaissance fields of northern Italy, because the orange rooftops and green fields of Belgium seemed to me to come from another dimension and not just another time. But that fairy-tale quality hit me hardest the first time through the clouds, because it fit so neatly my vision of a mission.

During my entry-interview in Antwerp with my real Mission President, I was hoping to work into the conversation all the Discussions I'd been blessed to memorize already, thinking this might help him see that he needed to send me to a really special place. But somehow it never came up.

He assigned me instead to the eastern town of Hasselt, a to-put-it-kindly drab provincial town, whose official motto according to one local travel writer should've been *Always a Disappointment.* Unfortunately the motto fit the local Mormon missionary scene too.

Even on my first day I could see that the four of us local businessmen in town didn't look like real local businessmen after all. No real local businessman wore a stainless-steel suit or indestructible shoes, or even the good-old wingtips and special white shirts I favored. Some of the worst-off real local businessmen came close to my JC-Penney-plus-bad-haircut look, but most wore fancy big-lapelled suits over colored and severely-tapered shirts (that some really shouldn't have been wearing), with hair spilling out over ears and collar. The only sort of local businessman we looked like, I realized, was from the American 1950s — somebody like Ward Cleaver, whose TV job never was exactly clear but you knew it had something to do with local business. And the only sort of local businessman who still looked like that anywhere wasn't properly speaking a businessman at all, or come to think of it even local: an FBI guy. Like President Hunt back at the Mission Home.

Now since we were foreign-gone and not domestic, that look had to be translated to its overseas equivalent: a CIA guy. I knew this because the locals told us so, all the time. I'd been understandably expecting a cheery greeting from real local businessmen on the street — *Hail brother merchant! Well met!* — but all I got instead were real local businessmen walking past with heads deliberately down, who left the actual task of greeting to the inevitable packs of local teenaged boys who shrieked at us what every other local was too polite to say aloud: *CIA!* Then the boys would laugh and run like crazy in the other direction, to avoid the special kicks and punches they were sure to get to sensitive pressure-points if caught by CIA guys. I wanted to yell back, *Don't you know the difference between a local businessman and a CIA guy?* But I gave up, or moved my oversized raincoat just enough to reveal the big double-holster pack I wore underneath to carry books and pamphlets in, because the boys were sure to think it was a gun and shriek again.

At least my first companion, Elder Shepherd, who seemingly like all first companions was from Idaho, wasn't a disappointment, but even that was uncertain for a while. Because during our very first morning of role-play, when we practiced Discussions, I seemed to know the F we were rehearsing better than he did. The teenaged Tristan Jaspers, a local Mormon who often rode his bike over to help us practice, noticed too, and, in that hypnotizing way he had of moving the top of his head back and forth while talking, complimented me on it. I hadn't quite finished all seven Discussions before leaving the LTM (I'd gotten through six-and-a-half, which I was sure was still a record), but what I knew I knew cold. I would be even more disappointed when I found out the reason why Elder Shepherd was rusty on F — and H,

I, and J too: you almost never got that far with any investigator, and so you didn't recite them much.

But Elder Shepherd proved otherwise to be a good and mostly helpful companion (*mostly* because after that initial Discussion-practice he took a liking to putting me in my place). In fact he arranged on only my second night in town for us to give a Discussion, my very first live one. It was just a C, which was sort of disappointing, sure as I'd been that something advanced was waiting for me, but I said my lines so well that once again everyone complimented me and was in disbelief that I'd just arrived in the land. Maybe it was sort of disappointing too that I couldn't understand a word of those compliments or anything else, but at least we got a return appointment for a D in a couple of days, plus the family was big and friendly and obviously had honest hearts, so with a Discussion every other day or so they'd be up to H, I, and J soon enough, and then probably convert. But what another disappointment when Elder Shepherd and I showed up for the next Discussion and the family turned us away at the door and handed back the pamphlets we'd left behind.

Maybe most disappointing of all, though (because I was sure some other family would appear soon), was my first Sunday of what could loosely be called *church*. It consisted of six or so brave local Mormons, plus four kind-of-brave foreign local-businessmen, and was held above a pretty seedy bar that stood right across the street from (just to finish the cliché) a pretty seedy train station.

It would've soothed me a little to know that there was in fact a long tradition of start-up religions meeting in pretty seedy places for church, and that real churches weren't invented in Christianity until almost 200 years after it began. The earliest Christians just met in a cave or in someone's living room, the latter not necessarily seedy but enough to make you feel like an oddball, because if everyone interested in your brand of religion could fit into a single living room, well that wasn't exactly a big reassurance about your brand of religion, even if you did try to put a positive spin on it by insisting you were part of some blessed elite. A lot of centuries later the pretty seedy locale of choice for new religions in the western world would be the abandoned storefront in a nearly abandoned street, or, to get really depressing now, in a nearly abandoned strip mall. Even Mormons didn't put up any real churches their first 30 years or so, but met together in the open air or under a big tent. Had I known all that, I might've thought that maybe our little bar-top church wasn't so bad and was maybe even a little ahead of schedule: missionaries had been in Hasselt for only a couple of years now and here we were already meeting *above* a bar instead of just inside it.

But I didn't know about the really slow road to a real church and so sitting there only kind-of-bravely on that Sunday I felt disturbingly out of whack. Sure, I'd assumed that church in Belgium probably wouldn't be exactly like church at home, in a big familiar comfort-giving brick building with a fully-occupied cushioned-pewed chapel separated from a full-court gym by a gigantic metal curtain. I'd even sort of liked the theory that church wouldn't be the same in Belgium, in keeping with the innate heroism of the going-foreign mission. But the reality was proving harder to take.

Deep deep down I had to admit that I'd been expecting a Mormon church in Belgium to be just a smaller comfort-giving version of a Mormon church in California, with just a smaller cushioned-pewed chapel and smaller metal curtain separating off okay maybe just a half-court gym, and with a smaller but still devout and smiling congregation who mostly did things the way I did — kind of the same way I still expected Belgians, even after all my hard work at Dutch, to actually speak English for their real language.

No one had ever said anything to me about meeting in a Dark Shadows bar-top church with a microscopic and mostly sullen group of believers wondering just exactly how much longer they could put up with feeling like oddballs. What I saw wasn't a smaller comfort-giving version of church at all, but a non-church that except for the songs and white shirts I hardly recognized. And that was terrifying. Without cushioned pews and a gigantic metal curtain and at least 10 rows of smiling people, the church as an institution seemed about as sturdy as a soggy Belgian fry. Who said institutions weren't made of brick and mortar? And gigantic metal curtains?

It turned out that a bar was the cheapest and most available room for rent on a Sunday morning in Belgium (or maybe anywhere). The rent was even cheaper for the second floor than the first, plus up there you didn't have to be out until 11:00 or so. I wasn't so sure that the second floor wasn't actually part of the bar, because we'd had to pick up a lot of damp Stella Artois coasters and move aside a bunch of sticky tables to set up our church, which included four rows of chairs with an aisle down the middle, a small table up front for the Sacrament,* a second smaller table for a pulpit, and a lot of non-liturgical posters and unintentionally-stained-glass windows all around. But even that modest seating plan ended up being ambitious, because when church started at 9:00 only the aforementioned 10 people were scattered across those chairs. If you left a chair between yourself and the next person, and put your arm up on the chair on one side of you, and stretched your legs out in front of the chair on the other side, then the rows didn't look quite so empty.

Elder Shepherd, not only my companion but the local District Leader, led the service, which right away was a bad sign because it meant that there was no genuine local businessman to do the job. Kindly *Broeder* De Smet tried to help, but he was a railroad man, not a businessman. In his orange jumpsuit with fluorescent leg stripes he blended in with locals even worse than missionaries did, but more fundamentally he was overwhelmed at the prospect of conducting a meeting with 10 whole people in it. He had a wife and two teenaged sons, but they hadn't converted along with him, so he was here alone.

Seated in the front row so she wouldn't have to wade through the crowd to lead hymns was Emmalina, 18 or 19, who was genuinely bright and

* What many Protestants call Communion or the Lord's Supper, and Catholics the Eucharist.

friendly and who'd just converted despite the objections of her recently immigrated Austrian mother.

Rounding out the non-crowd were several members of the Jaspers family, which in full bloom numbered five but only a partial set came to church each week. Tristan, the oldest at 16, was always there, and always dressed like a Belgian kid trying to look like an American Mormon missionary, putting him at least two removes from a local businessman. Despite his head movements, he was pleasant enough, though he sometimes got angry fast and liked to boss the missionaries around a little.

There was also Tristan's shifty-eyed younger brother, Willi, black hair slicked unfashionably forward, who looked decidedly like he'd rather be downstairs flinging darts than sitting up here arms folded and feebly mouthing hymns. He wore one of those sweatshirts plastered with semi-sensical English phrases that filled European storefronts in the days before English was widely spoken there: something like *Team Class* ran across his chest today, then underneath that *Royal First,* and on the sleeve a nice *1972* for the final touch. There was usually an even younger brother or sister near Willi too.

Their father wasn't present because he wasn't Mormon and because he was divorced from their mother, *Zuster* Jaspers, who was always sassy toward the missionaries, but that was okay because she was sassy toward everyone and because word was she'd had a really rough life. Maybe she was also sassy because she felt guilty about still smoking: she pretended she didn't smoke, but she smelled like a smoke-filled bar even outside this smoke-filled bar and you could see the nicotine stains on her fingers. Her already hollow cheeks would be even hollower in 18 months when she died from the cancer that would soon ravage her body.

Where were the entire families, I thought? Oh, but there was good news on that front! There were two families in fact, the Lambrechts and the Blommaerts, who lived 30 kilometers from church and right next door to each other. But they weren't here today. Or most Sundays. Not because they'd given up, but because they were so far beyond everyone else in their Mormonism, and also they lived so far away from town that coming to church wasn't exactly easy for them — or for that matter for the others, who seemed to sense they were in a different churchgoing league. It didn't even help that *Broeder* Blommaert was a real live local businessman, because no one here knew him well. Plus he and his family, and the Lambrecht family, traveled around a lot on Sundays to different Mormon branches* in Belgium because they were among the top Mormon leaders in the land. Or maybe they traveled around a lot on Sundays to protect themselves and their kids from the feeling of oddballness and feebleness that just seemed to go beer-mug-in-hand with meeting in a bar-top church.

The congregants made the most of things. Missionaries gave two of the talks and played the piano and prepared and passed around the Sacrament with help from Tristan. *Broeder* De Smet struggled to make an announcement that everybody already knew. Emmalina smiled her way through the music. It was a lot leaner than I was used to, and a lot faster too, mostly because it took only about two minutes to pass the Sacrament around, something that in my California ward could take 20 or 25 minutes. This meant that there was that much more time for talks, which wasn't necessarily a good thing: all talks were given by local members or missionaries, as there was no professional local Mormon clergy anywhere, and from the frown on *Zuster* Jaspers's face and also Willi's you could pretty much tell that they were all tired of hearing the same people every week. Not that Willi really paid attention to who was speaking anyway, but just scooted out as fast as possible when he heard the first syllable of the last Amen. He didn't even bother attending Sunday school or other meetings, which divided people up by age and gender, because when there were hardly any people to begin with then dividing them up even further only made things seem even more oddball and feeble than they already were.

Sitting on the front row feebly singing one of the hymns and wondering how it was possible to feel both depressed and terrified at the same time, I was in an actual and not merely jet-lag-induced fog. But I still had

* A branch was a smaller version of a ward, but a more accurate arboreal label for some was probably *twig.*

plenty of hope inside, and coped by opting for my usual heroic approach to things, making right there on the beer-stained spot the latest of many unfulfillable missionary vows: namely, that we would not be over this bar for long because I was going to fill this sad little room with converts. Then everyone could feel a little less oddball, and we could justify asking the Mission President for something better to meet in.

That'd take care of any disappointment, alright (and oh by the way everybody would of course thank me). It was just a matter of will, and work, and time.

six

The Great Church Council of Nowhere

On a dark autumn night in Belgium on a bus somewhere between Antwerp and Hasselt four local businessmen with a seedy bar-top church were engaged in one of the great theological controversies of their time.

Oh, shout out the names of the great church councils! Shout them out from the orange rooftops of Belgium! Don't hold back now, because you know them: Nicaea, Constantinople, Chalcedon, Constance, and Trent, then Augsburg, Dort, and Westminster, all the way to Vatican II! Bellow them out from your nethermost parts, send them soaring over the highest Gothic vault, then add to that hallowed list just one more: Four Local Businessmen on a Bus Somewhere Between Antwerp and Hasselt!

Shout out as well the great theological controversies the great councils were always going on about, and not just ordinary going-on-about but elite top-shelf going-on-about, involving some of the sublimest minds of all time, tearing countries and churches into so much fluff, and riling up heavily clothed and mostly unathletic bishops to the point that they started throwing things at each other when words were clearly not doing the trick. Shout out the great theological controversies too, because they're just as forever etched in the sacred annals as the great councils are! Was the Son consubstantial with the Father? Was the Holy Ghost consubstantial with both? Did Christ have a divine and a human will or just a divine one? How does grace go with works again? How many angels was it could stand on the head of a pin? Should a missionary kiss his girlfriend or especially non-girlfriend goodbye at the airport? Then add to that glorious pile the great controversy now raging at this latest and unexpectedly mobile church council in the middle of Belgian nowhere: which book of scripture should you use when reading the prayer over the Mormon Sacrament?

The tempest was precipitated by the four Hasselt-living missionaries not having attended the usual Sacrament Meeting in their bar-top church that day (Sunday). In fact no Flemish-speaking missionaries anywhere had attended any church meetings that day, which had to be another record, because missionaries never missed church. On this particular Sunday we'd all gathered together instead for a big Flemish choir festival, in Antwerp, 85 kilometers from Hasselt, where most of us had that day sung our missionary hearts out as part of the short-lived *Mormoonse Zendelingen Koor.*

We'd gone to all the trouble of joining the festival and rehearsing every Saturday and even unprecedentedly skipping Sacrament meeting today not because of some big passion for choir music, but because we'd hoped that if the large missionary-fearing audience could just see and hear a large group of friendly missionaries singing out friendly Flemish tunes in the friendly environment that was the hallmark of Flemish (and maybe all) choir festivals, then maybe that audience would despite the imperfect accents feel just a little less fearful the next time a couple of said friendly missionaries came inevitably knocking at the door.

It was the musical version of the local-businessman approach, with local choristers instead.

The results of the festival weren't as fear-dispersing as hoped, though, because even though all those missionaries together might've looked pretty friendly indeed standing in a distant choir instead of on the immediate doorstep, mission leaders were soon grumbling that there hadn't been a single convert out of all that singing and traveling and rehearsing and Sacrament-Meeting-missing. And that wasn't to mention all the hours of ordinary proselyting lost for 15 lousy minutes of heavily-accented singing. But I'd thought the festival a great thing, partly because I was already a wholehearted supporter of anything that gave missionaries a chance to show that they were too from planet Earth, partly because I'd gotten a big lump in my throat from all the songs performed by the missionary choir, and mostly because it'd been such a huge relief to get a whole day off from the ordinary proselyting we'd all thank goodness missed.

Oops. I wasn't supposed to think or even feel that last bit, and I'd felt really guilty about it all that choir-singing day. Sure, the proselyting business was turning out to be a lot less fun than I'd thought, but it still wasn't right to think that way. I'd felt so guilty about it that as usual I tried talking myself out of what I was actually feeling, saying for instance to Elder Downing, whom I'd sought out soon after arriving at the festival, that what I really felt like was that we should all be out proselyting in the rain instead of sitting here gabbing and singing inside this warm, covered, warm, indoor, warm, dry building. I was sure that a model guy like Elder Downing really *did* want to go out in the rain, and I wanted him to know that I shared the exact same sentiment (even though I didn't). But he'd surprised me by saying just to relax, there was nothing to be done, which was pretty much the sentiment I'd started out with that morning but which had required a declaration from Elder Downing for me to feel okay about.

It hadn't taken long for me to start feeling guilty again though, because after the festival was over and we four going-Hasselt missionaries had finally found our bus, I'd realized about halfway through our dark-and-stormy ride that we weren't going to make it home before 9:00. Which was too close to the official quitting time of 9:30 to go out and do any proselyting. Which meant that for the first time on my mission I'd have gone an entire day without proselyting. Which gave me another huge sense of relief. Which made me feel guilty. Which took away the relief and made me just ride along and fret.

There was nothing to see outside in the dark and almost no one else was on board, so we four local businessmen/choristers just started talking among ourselves. Casually at first, about the festival and who we'd seen, but it didn't take long for the conversation to turn to just how strange it was not to have attended Sacrament Meeting that Sunday and not to have taken the Sacrament, as we had our entire Sunday lives been wont to do.

But then one of us, the oft-talking and oft-smiling Elder Trimbo, lit up his eyes the way he was born to and — Eureka! — exclaimed that we could too take the Sacrament that day! We could just take it privately among the four of us in our apartment when we got back, instead of publicly among the usual throngs in the bar-top church Sunday morning.

In fact you could indeed do the Sacrament just about anywhere, at least if you were part of the church's all-lay priesthood, which almost-professional missionaries certainly were. It just involved reading a set prayer over a tray of broken bread, which was passed around and consumed, then reading another set prayer over a tray with little cups of water,* also passed around and consumed.

Settled then! Good idea! That's what we'd do when we got home. Pause. Quiet. Thinking. Ah, thinking. That's how the latest trouble started. While I was using the lull in the conversation to think about how maybe something holy like taking the Sacrament might help me feel less guilty for being glad about not proselyting that day, Elder Trimbo was remembering some important detail, something big, about doing the Sacrament on your own instead of the usual way in church. And as usual he felt like he needed to convince everyone else of his view.

Which was how this latest greatest church council on wheels really got rolling. In Dutch.

If we the Sacrament among us do, began Elder Trimbo slowly in his best passive-aggressive manner (raising his eyebrows innocently and lowering his chin humbly and pitching his voice even more kindly than usual, to suggest he was harmless, but in truth he was impossibly stubborn when he was sure he was right, like right now), *then President Jorgensen of the LTM has said that we the Sacrament prayers from out the Doctrine and Covenants must read and not the Book of Mormon, because the Doctrine and Covenants for the modern church written was.*

There weren't many set prayers in Mormondom, but the prayers over

---

* Even generally teetotaling Mormons had often used traditional wine until around 1900.

the Sacrament — a paragraph for the bread and another for the water — were two of them. And as suggested by Elder Trimbo they could be found in two different books of Mormon scripture: the Doctrine and Covenants, put together during the church's early days in the 1830s and 1840s, and the Book of Mormon, put together according to Mormons around AD 400. Way before the *modern church.*

Upon hearing this declaration from Elder Trimbo the other three local businessmen went into the same state as the target audience of Maimonides's famous *Guide for the Perplexed.* Why was he making such a big stink about this? We just wanted to go home and do the Sacrament, and *the prayers are written exactly the same in both books, so what difference makes it out as long as the words right are? Plus the Book of Mormon is a fine book, how would you can think that it wrong is a prayer thereout to read?*

The controversy got my mind reaching to the highest heavens now, as I thought of one dynamite objection after the next to Elder Trimbo's claim, like the fact that the Sacrament prayer was usually read from a printed card, not an open Book of Mormon or Doctrine and Covenants. What if the card had been copied from the Book of Mormon and not the D&C? Would the thousands of Sacrament prayers said from that card then not count? That might've been enough to convince the great Sacramentarian minds from Augustine to Zwingli, but they weren't even close to even millimeterly budging the exceedingly stubborn local businessman known as Elder Trimbo. He was politely adamant all the way home, repeating in various forms the sentiment, *well President Jorgensen has thus said and I for one shall against my leader not go.* Because of course the rest of the local businessmen onboard were just waiting for the slightest excuse to go crazy against theirs.

Now, Elder Trimbo wasn't the kind of guy who'd start yelling or throwing things when he didn't get his way. In fact I would've bet a cone of precious Belgian fries that he didn't even know how to throw at all, which was just one of the many things that bugged me about him. He was the definition of big and tall without the definition, was for some reason more interested in music than sports, modulated his voice a whole lot more than most local businessmen did, and when he was excited (often) he broke into a huge smile that made not only his eyes but his teeth twinkle. Also when he bore his testimony of the truthfulness of the church, which was something missionaries did often, he used the cheesiest phrases known to mice and local businessmen, so instead of saying the usual idiomatic *I'd like to leave my testimony with you today* he'd say with eyebrows raised higher and chin lowered lower than ever *I won't leave my testimony with you today because I'm going to need it myself, so I'll just share it,* followed by an exaggerated pause that gave everyone more than enough time to process his clever little twist, and making me want to yell *It's just an idiomatic and therefore not-to-be-taken-literally expression!*

Bugging me even more than all that was how Elder Trimbo always seemed to get his way, usually by breaking out his huge twinkly smile. On our usual day off (Monday),* for instance, Elder Trimbo the college music major appointed himself the expert on exactly what sort of music was proper for missionaries — a crucial subject, since P-Day was the only day besides choir festivals we got to listen to music at all. One P-Day he heard somebody quietly playing the Eagles and walked into the room to non-Latitudinarianly declare that even though mission rules didn't specifically forbid rock music, it obviously wasn't right. Only the Mormon Tabernacle Choir and *other church music* were *appropriate.*

That *other church music* clause turned out to be Elder Trimbo's secret stash, because five minutes after declaring the Eagles unfit for missionary consumption there'd come blaring from his own cassette player in the next room, where he was cheerily writing letters and ironing shirts, a loud sample of some of that *other church music:* the heavy brass sounds of the BYU Cougar Marching Band, of which he'd been a proud tuba-playing member (*We were a little crazy!* he warned). Wait, the other missionaries objected, why was loud and brassy music like that okay? Elder Trimbo was ready: even though the Cougar Marching Band's blaring sound was more blaring

* Once called Diversion Day but changed to Preparation Day when diversion came to be seen as something bad.

than the Eagles', even though the Cougar Marching Band sometimes even *played* the Eagles, it was the *BYU* Cougar Marching Band. Enough said: BYU was the church's school, ergo was the Lord's school, ergo the marching band was the Lord's Marching Band. How ergo could that band possibly play anything objectionable?

Music from *Saturday's Warrior,* the bafflingly popular Mormon musical, was despite its heavy pop sound also given the P-Day seal of approval by Elder Trimbo, because of its supposedly improving message. He even approved of *Saturday's Warrior* on other days, like when there were big missionary meetings, where during breaks he'd gather other *Saturday's Warrior* enthusiasts around a piano, and while he pounded out song after song at irreverent volume both he and the gathered enthusiasts would also sing at irreverent volume from the convenient *Saturday's Warrior Songbook* he just happened to have with him at all times — not for himself of course, but for his ever-changing cast of backup singers.

But again, despite Elder Trimbo's countless crimes against humanity I had to give him credit for never really getting mad, not even right now on the bus, where three people were saying less politely than he would have that maybe he was being just a little nuts about the Sacrament Prayer. While he waged his final eyebrow-raised defense on the subject, I looked into the darkness and gave a little eye-roll, for my own eyes only, forgetting that he might see the reflection in the bus's big windows. Still, no one, not even Elder Trimbo, was really upset or mad during the controversy, and the four of us church councilors/local businessmen/local choristers/ missionaries spent the remaining few minutes of the journey in congenial enough silence.

Reaching our apartment at last, we quickly made the few preparations necessary for our small Sacrament service, putting a piece of bread on one plate and a few little cups of water on another. But what about the prayer? Would it come from the Book of Mormon or Doctrine and Covenants? With the whole world watching, Elder Shepherd handed the BoM to me and asked me to say the first prayer.

Elder Trimbo was deep deep deep in the dumps by now, and not just

71

because the wrong book was being used for the prayer but because he was absolutely buried in guilt over having started our very little debate. In fact after I said the prayer over the bread and stood to pass it to the others, he just put his chin in his chest and wagged his head melodramatically no. Three little wags. He wouldn't take it. He wasn't worthy: he'd started an argument. All that without saying a word.

Now I gave a fully public eye-roll and mentally raised my hands to the heavens. It hadn't even been a big argument, not like at Nicaea or Constance or Dort where people were running in and out and yelling things and threatening each other with excommunication. But in Elder Trimbo's mind he'd broken the peace and he wanted everyone to know just how badly he felt about it, which I probably should have appreciated: it was better than someone being nasty about the whole thing. But I found it hard to appreciate, because it somehow felt in my own surely troubled and overly suspicious mind that those three little wags of Elder Trimbo's formidable head were just another way of declaring again his moral superiority.

Those suspicions naturally gave me something else to feel guilty about, for not loving my fellow missionary the way I ought. And when Elder Trimbo predictably turned down the passed-around water as well, I felt even guiltier still, and now so did the other two missionaries. Which meant that even though the Sacrament prayer that evening in the dark little apartment had been read against Elder Trimbo's wishes from the Book of Mormon, he'd still come out of the great church council as the pretty clear-cut winner: he'd out-righteoused us all. He wanted to take the Sacrament more than anyone, the whole thing had even been his idea, but then he gave it up because he cared more about offending his fellow missionaries than we grudge-holders cared about offending him. Maybe we were the ones who'd taken the Sacrament unworthily, we had to think.

This getting-along-with-other-missionaries stuff was turning out to be even harder than the cobblestones I sometimes fell down on.

Where were all the about-to-be-transfigured guys who were easy to get along with?

Elder Shepherd was a fine but not about-to-be-transfigured guy, not with his Discussions as sloppy as they were. And why did he get so miffed at my prompts and corrections during morning practice, which went something like:

> ES: *During the translation of the . . .*
> Me: *During the* translating . . .
> ES: . . . Book of Mormon, *Joseph Smith prayed . . .*
> Me: *Joseph Smith* and his secretary *prayed . . .*
> ES: . . . *constantly for understanding and . . .*
> (half-second pause to think what came next)
> Me: . . . *divine inspiration . . .*
> ES: *Just be patient . . .*

He seemed especially miffed by my habit of making corrections and prompts right out of my head, without even looking at the Discussion book lying in my lap, that's how sure I was about being right. But sometimes he'd just shake off the correction, like a pitcher shaking off a catcher, and proceed imperfectly on, exasperating me, because how were we going to convert anyone if we didn't get the words perfect? Elder Shepherd didn't like it either if at 9:29 am I started agitating because we weren't quite ready to go out the door at the white-book-decreed time of 9:30, or if at night after we got home I put too much jam on my bread (whatever *too much* meant), threatening the already paltry monthly food budget that was made even more so by all the travel to choir-festival rehearsals.

One reason the getting along was so hard was of course that I could be hard to live with myself, not to mention that my expectations for relationships were, as for most things, pitched a mile or so too high. But still another was that even though I'd grown up in a family of ten, and had spent a year in a college dorm and two months at the LTM, I like most others was long out of the habit of being around the same person for 24 hours a day, and now it was with a stranger instead of my mother. In all those other living situations since I was four, there'd been so many other people around all the time that if your brother or companion or roommate got under your skin then all you had to do was go a few feet away and talk to someone else.

But out in the actual mission field you were stuck all day long with people you hadn't chosen any more than your own family. Your companion and apartment-mates were all decided for you by the Mission President with the assistance of his two Assistants. Not even the Apostle Paul had to deal with a system like that, I thought. Paul seemed to sort of hand-pick his companions, or just go off on his own for a while when he grew tired of the whole companion business. But I couldn't do that. Modern missionaries had to work things out, or suffer, or hope for a transfer the next month. But only some people got transferred at the monthly transfer, and any replacement you got might not be any easier than the last guy, so the safest thing to do was to try to get along with the person/people you might be staying with for still another month or two or three. Some people couldn't or wouldn't fix things. Some suffered through. Sometimes, though — and here was the only genius part of the system — you might learn to like your Antagonist. Even Elder Trimbo.

Elder Trimbo was, to my profound relief, transferred away from Hasselt after I'd been there only a month, but I found myself living with him again a few months later in another town. I wasn't happy about it. What were the odds? Out of 150 missionaries in Belgium, I ended up roommates with *him* again! But this time Elder Trimbo became one of my favorites, and not because of any great virtue on my unenthusiastic part but because he just kept liking me and everyone else too. It drove you crazy at first, but then you came to realize that he really meant it, and all the *Saturday's Warrior* and non-throwing-ability just faded away. Plus except during his head-wagging at the Sacrament fiasco in Hasselt, he was almost always cheery, and it was nice to be around guys like that when no locals would talk to you, or especially when it started getting cold.

Maybe there was something to be said for compulsory living-with-people-you-wouldn't-ordinarily-choose-to-live-with (as long as it didn't involve Elder Furtwangler, who thank goodness was on the other side of the mission). Nuns had known that for centuries: living together with unchosen companions was the refiner's fire: you either burned up or forged some real virtues. And Mormons in general tried something similar: you didn't just go to church where you wanted, but according to where you lived, no matter who else lived nearby too. It didn't always work out, of course, maybe any more than it did for nuns, and of course like-minded people often tended to live in the same neighborhoods anyway, but there was still something to the theory.

In fact, the squabbles with Elder Trimbo over which book of scripture to read the Sacrament prayer from, or which music was right for P-Day, were the sort of petty but theoretically manageable squabbles that were a dime or actually a nickel a dozen in missionary life, the sort that were probably happening somewhere in the mission at just about any time of day. The sort that happened all the time in real life too. The sort that I therefore couldn't really complain about. The sort that I'd never ever bad-dream about.

No, that sort of squabble was still way up ahead.

seven

TO THE LIONS

When the door to the narrow row-house opened to reveal a vintage old Belgian lady standing in the hallway just two steps above street level, I was pretty sure I knew how the conversation was going to go, because no matter the neighborhood the neighbors always seemed to have gotten together in advance to practice what they would say on that great and dreadful day when the foreign-looking possible-CIA-guys they'd heard about finally showed up on their front step.

It'd been another rough morning of tracting,* and was likely to be followed by another rough afternoon and evening too. In fact even harder than always getting along with your fellow local businessman was trying to penetrate the well-coordinated front of local resistance confronting you at almost every door.

The defensive maneuvers usually started even before I and my new companion Elder Klein reached our first door of the day, because the vintage old ladies keeping watch at windows and the teenage boys standing or riding guard on the street would somehow spread the alarm that the possible-CIA-guys were in the area.

More than half the doors we knocked on wouldn't open in the morning

---

* The word no doubt came from all the religious tracts Mormon missionaries handed out wherever they could, but in missionary-speak it came specifically to mean going door-to-slamming-door trying to talk to people.

or afternoon, sometimes because people really weren't home and sometimes because they just pretended they weren't. At night maybe more than
half the doors would open, because neighborhood guards were off the
street and working-age inhabitants were back from work, except of course
in winter when it was dark by 4:30 and people were more alarmed than
usual by the knock of a possible-CIA-guy.

Any door that did open morning or afternoon almost always featured a
woman standing mostly behind it and poking only her uppermost extrem-
ities suspiciously around. Since Elder Klein and I had been trained to want
to speak to the woman's husband even more than we wanted to speak to
her (based on the questionable theory that if the husband/father converted
then everybody else in the family would follow), we'd say *Goede morgen Mevrouw, is your man home?* But that clumsy little question usually scared her
even more than her fight-or-flight eyes suggested she already was, because
what she often heard instead was *because if he home not is or you say that
you no husband have then shall we inside come and you hurt.*

After finally realizing just how ice-cold chilling that line of inquiry could
be, I switched to *Hello Mevrouw, my companion and I are Americans, here
in Belgium for two years as missionaries in order a message with people to
share, and we would very gladly with you and your man wish to speak.* If the
door-wielding woman didn't shut it at that point, then she'd usually ask,
What about goes it exactly? Which made things a little tricky, because if you
now said what church you were from, well the official name was so long
that the door was likely to shut before you even got it all out, but taking the
faster route of saying just the *Mormon Church* was usually worse, because if
she'd heard that word before then she was sure it was bad or she'd confuse
it with the *Moonies* who might've terrified her even more, and if she hadn't
heard the word *Mormon* before, well, that was reason enough right there
to shut the door.

So to avoid the whole name-of-the-church business we might finesse
the woman's question by asking her a question in return, usually along the
lines of *Have you any children?* Because if she said *Yes* then we could tell
her about a program we had for families called *Gezinsavond* (Family Home

Evening), which we'd be happy to present to her and her man, because who wasn't for families? But that question could be tricky too, because it could sound like the foreign-looking possibly-CIA fellows standing just inches away on the tiny step were maybe interested in stealing those children, especially since it was by now painfully clear that the foreign-looking fellows were foreign-sounding too. But if the woman was somehow still miraculously listening to your pitch then the missionary doing the talking (or if the pair was really smooth then the one *not* doing the talking) would in a single motion and to the accompaniment of still-running commentary pull from the recesses of the holster-pack beneath his overcoat a glossy brochure containing pictures of happy families doing happy things, and wouldn't she and her man like to learn how their family could do happy things like that too?

The door-approach business was even more complicated when your companion was as Canadian as Elder Klein, because if it was my door and I started out with the bit about us being two Americans, Elder Klein would turn his head sideways and give a little cough even though no doctor was probing him and telling him to, which was his little signal that right after the lady shut the door he was going to let me have it again: he wasn't a flippin' American, he was a flippin' Canadian! And I'd exasperatedly say again (still in Dutch) that *it takes too long to say* I am American and my companion is Canadian *because by the time that I that plus the name of the church say have they the door shut. Besides, it is true that we both* North Americans are, so *why can you not pretend that that is what I say?* But he'd just as exasperatedly say *Because when you* Americans *say no one thinks that you* North Americans *mean; ask any Belgian what of he thinks when he* American *hears, and it will not* North American *be. North American could also Mexicans include, but if your companion from Mexico was you would not say that* he American *was.* Which would just make me roll my eyes yet again, because Elder Klein knew perfectly well that no Mexican was ever going to be your companion in Belgium. Still, I'd conciliatorily ask, *Okay, what if we turns take? When you on the turn are, you can say that we Canadians are, and when I on the turn am, shall I say that we Americans are?* But it was no good; Elder Klein wanted the whole geo-political situation spelled out precisely every time, the way he did when it was his door and which always took so long, especially on cold days when he was really struggling to roll his r's, that the door was just as I predicted quickly shut. And I'd shake my head and think to myself, *Who anyway would a real American not want to be?*

But the geographical niceties weren't as interesting to vintage old Belgian ladies as getting the door shut fast was. Sometimes a lady would say that she'd talk to her husband about the *Gezinsavond*-brochure, and that we could come back to hear what he thought. Sometimes we'd go back and the couple would jointly say they didn't need a *Gezinsavond* program that was obviously invented for overly busy Americans, because here in Belgium people were home with their *gezin* every evening of the week, not just one. But whether the final no-no came from the suspicious woman alone that morning at the door, or from the now-informed suspicious man that night, it almost always included one of the following lines and accompanying actions:

(a) *No interest* (closes door quickly, eyes down, no smile).
(b) *No time* (same door and facial actions).
(c) *No thank you, I have my own religion* (implied Catholicism; closes door at regular or slow speed, eyes looking at you, no smile).
(d) *You have your religion, I have the mine* (implied Catholicism; closes door slowly with a tight smile, stops briefly when you talk again, closes a little more while repeating original answer with the same tight smile, stops again while you try rejoindering, closes further and further with tight smile still in place, while you keep talking until the last click).
(e) *I respect your religion, I ask you the mine also to respect* (implied Catholicism; same door and facial action as for c or d).

(f) *I admire you for your courage and that you to a strange land come and our language try to learn (because it is not every day that you that from an American hear), but I am Catholic born and will Catholic die* (henceforth same door and facial action as for c, d, or e, with maybe a bigger smile for this one).

(g) *I am Catholic baptized but go never to the church, but in the end all religion comes on the same down* (implying just let me stay nominally Catholic).

(h) *No thank you, I am Catholic.*

(i) *No thank you, I am Roman* (Catholic).

(j) *No thank you, I am Christian* (Catholic).

It didn't take long to see the common theme in all these supposedly different rejections, the same way folklorists can see just a few *Archetypes and Motifs* in thousands of folk tales and myths. Sure, Red Riding Hood might have 150 variations, but it was still Red Riding Hood. And rejecting Mormon missionaries in Belgium might involve 10 variations, but in the end they were just one big motif: *I am Catholic and therefore with you no longer about religion wish to speak.**

Once in a while the most curious or trouble-making local door-answerers might extend the conversation with the exceedingly popular question, *What is actually the difference between your church and mine?* But that bit of apparent curiosity faked us out every time, because we'd think people actually wanted to hear the difference and boy were we ready to tell them in *a series of Discussions* which especially I was prepared to deliver. But what people were really saying and not actually asking with that question was *I am already sure that you no difference can name that a difference to Catholic me will make.* And so they'd shut the door before we could even get going on our answer.

And once in an even greater while, a person would agree to make an

---

* There was a very occasional Rejection Motif 2 as well, consisting of *I am free-thinking* or *I don't believe in anything,* but you didn't hear either very often. Rejection Motif 1 reigned supreme.

appointment for a Discussion, or (if male) even say that we could come in right that moment to give one. Which'd make my warmed-up breast start springing eternally again.

After the conversation ended, you always wrote down the result. Depending on whose day it was, I or Elder Klein would whip out a little notebook from one coat pocket and a big fat orange-and-white four-colored pen from another and start writing. In code. A secret missionary code handed down solemnly in secret rituals from generation to generation, just as people looking out their windows suspected. The code wasn't as powerful as people thought — not enough to achieve world domination, for instance (though anyone intent on that would've been smart to start in Hasselt). It was mostly just a way to keep track of where you'd been and what people had said.

And you could do that with just a few little symbols and colors. $T2♀$, for instance, didn't mean *This house is ripe for takeover* but instead a disappointingly pedestrian *Talked to Woman* (with $T2♂$ an obvious *Talked to Man*). Writing either one in green meant *inconclusive conversation so go ahead and try again next time probably without any threat to your person,* but red (for Rejection) meant *do not knock here again because there might be (said threat).* If a woman even vaguely hinted that you could try again when her husband was home, then you wrote in happy blue $CB♀$, meaning *Call Back Said Woman,* but if she'd been negative in the real or imagined hinting you'd add a (-), even though that thin horizontal stroke of the fat pen was bound to raise eyebrows if not outright controversy, because how in the world could you pair a positive *CB* and a negative (-) on the same line, went the perfectly reasonable thinking. For some variety you could sum up a whole inconclusive one-minute encounter with an economical (and probably green) *AK,* for *Andere Keer* (another time), because the woman had maybe sort of said such a thing, or if you were desperate to write something else you'd resort to the championingly vague and decidedly green *BT* for *Backtrack(t).* Whether there was the tiniest sliver of demonstrable qualitative distinction between *AK* and *BT,* or for that matter between either of them and *T2* or *CB,* was anybody's guess. Absolutely definitive, though, were a blank space (for no one home), *Appt* (for if you actually got one), or a *Gave C* (for if you got in and gave the first Discussion) — the latter two, it went without saying, in blue. Black was reserved throughout the mission for writing street names at the tops of pages and numbers down the left side of the page. So you really did need every single color on that fat orange-and-white pen.

Of course you could add your own little touches to the standard code too, including writing out in full something like *absolutely bonkers,* or just *T2♂ Nuts,* in red. It didn't really matter what a missionary wrote as long as his companion and maybe his successors understood it, though it wasn't as if very many missionaries ever actually consulted the boxes of old tracting books stored inside every missionary apartment like they were holy writ.

Door-knocking and code-writing were what Elder Klein and I did most of the discouraging time, 50 to 60 hours a week, 9:30 to 9:30, with a lunch-dinner break from 2 to 3:30.* The experts at the Mission Home had said that we should spend half our 60 hours teaching Discussions if we wanted to make converts, instead of spending almost all our hours knocking on doors. But it didn't take long to see that in Belgium teaching even 10 hours a week was exceptionally good, and three to eight was more like it. No won-der hardly anyone got baptized, I thought. If we were going to get more converts, we had to get more teaching hours, and to get that, we had to have more faith. And of course work harder.

The Mission Home experts also said that almost any method of look-ing for converts was better than knocking on doors, a view that just about everyone wholeheartedly agreed with. But the alternatives suggested, like street-contacting, business-contacting (natch), holding street-meetings, starting a college-campus program, and best of all having local Mormons introduce you to friends and family, didn't exactly work here either. The first two could be as bad as tracting. The third was pure nostalgia for the good old days, because no one was going to stop and listen in Belgium to a street-preacher — in fact, they were going to swing around real wide. The fourth was great in theory, since 18 to 30 was the most likely age to convert,

---

* We had P. Day on Mondays off until 5:00, and Sundays during church services.

but colleges weren't thrilled about missionaries on campus. And the fifth, though clearly best by a factor of about 100, assumed that there were plenty of Mormons around willing to do the introducing, or that they still had any friends and family left after the introducing they'd already done.

You could invent your own methods too, like the Elder in Antwerp who stood on the town square and sketched big scenes from Christian history while his companion chatted up people who stopped to look, or like making the occasional presentation to schools and civic organizations, but most missionaries couldn't draw like that, and most school and civic presentations gave you the funny feeling that you'd been brought in as the entertainment. And so because we wanted to do *something,* we mostly just tracted, knowing things would go more slowly that way, what with the odds being one convert for every 1,000 doors knocked on, but at least we'd be getting closer to that one.

There were plenty of days when we didn't make a single firm appointment or get inside for a single Discussion, but just wrote down 100 or so $T2\female$'s in green (bringing the supposedly 1 in 1,000 conversion-ratio pretty rapidly into question). On good days we'd get a few *Call Backs,* and even a firm appointment, but even that had at least a 42 percent chance of falling through. On the best days we'd have an evening appointment or two, and maybe even one during the day. But most days we spent our time engaging in really short conversations that required a pitifully small range of vocabulary and a really strong understanding of the negative.

All this was why I was pretty sure I knew how this latest conversation with a Belgian lady, even a vintage little old Belgian lady, would go.

Even though she stood two steps above us in her hallway, I could look her almost levelly in the eye as I started my pitch, but before I could get out even a sentence she defied all expectations and experience by opening the door up wide and inviting us in.

Stunned and disbelieving, we hesitated, like Lancelot in the legend, but not for the same reason as that bravest of made-up knights. Old Lance was afraid of what his noble neighbors might think if usually-horse-riding he stepped into a lowly wagon, while we feared for our persons if we entered a home where the admitting resident(s) didn't understand exactly who it was they'd just admitted.

The rule of thumb and forefinger too was that you were supposed to be sure the admitting resident(s) did understand who you were, to protect yourself against people who were dying to do some behind-doors dirty work on Mormon missionaries. If you stayed on the outside step until your identity was clear, went the thinking, then you at least had a chance to run away if someone got mad. Usually you didn't need that red-alert level of caution: probably no Belgians were lying in wait for missionaries. They were a million times more likely to peek out through a curtain in the window or a peephole in the door and pretend they weren't home than they were to let you in and ambush you.

But there was always the exception, ergo the rule. Still: at this house? With this sweet vintage old lady? Maybe the word *church,* or *missionary,* had persuaded her, I thought, except hmm: those were usually the flashing yellow lights that warned people to shut the door faster than its quality of hinge usually allowed. Had she heard right? Had I even said those words? I tried to remember the flow of conversation but it'd ended so quickly that I was still a little stunned.

Or maybe she'd invited us in, I thought in a flash, because we looked like — the payoff at last — friendly local businessmen come to deliver product!

But even that wasn't enough to silence my nagging and soon-to-be-confirmed doubts that the woman had any idea in the world who we were. But she was so kindly and little and vintage, and an invitation to come inside so rare, that just this once we decided to throw caution to the stiff Belgian wind and cross the threshold unsure.

I was happy to step across, because although still fresh-faced and optimistic I was also showing early signs of door-shock, to the point of losing some of my smile, which though never as constant as Sebastian St. Croix's had still always been one of my defining features, and now going across the threshold it perked again a little.

The vintage old lady motioned us to follow her down the straight hallway so typical of Belgian homes built between the wars. Just inside the door stood the coat-rack-and-umbrella-stand-in-one. All down the hall stretched the yellow and brown linoleum older Belgians couldn't live without. On the walls hung the brown-patterned wallpaper and brown woodwork and brown much else that I would later think of as Catholic brown. Hanging in turn on the wallpaper were lots of pious pictures of pious people, some of them no doubt family but the bluish-greenish figures looking heavenward in pain probably saints — blasted saints. And in the air for atmosphere the already-familiar aroma that you got when you blended mildew from an old water-leak with several decades of roasting coffee plus the occasional indoor cigar plus sewage pipes not quite firmly attached to the small toilet room that was almost always located at the end of the hall.

Passing a door to the left that almost certainly opened into a narrow living room featuring brown furniture and assorted crosses that still scared me, then passing the narrow staircase on the right that led to mysterious parts upward, we followed the vintage old lady through a second door on the left and found ourselves in the kitchen. There the vintage look just kept on coming, as the floor was one big greyish sheet of something, the sink boasted the latest in 1940s faucets and knobs, and a big black iron stove dominated all, including the walls, where it'd left big smoky marks.

The lady seated us at the Formica table and went to fetch her equally vintage husband. I happily pondered that all we'd written in our tracting book so far today were dozens of $T2\male$s in vague green, but at this blesséd address we already had a blue $T2\female$ that just might turn into a *Gave C.*

The lady returned with the fellow we were after, all 5'2" of him, and nattering away even before entering the room. He was around 70, but his waxed hair, tight suspenders, trim physique, alert eyes, straight posture, and overall chattiness gave him a 60-ish vigor.

After uttering several smiling mostly incomprehensible sentences he finally stopped long enough to ask what he could do for us *fine young men.*

We started introducing ourselves as *representatives of the Church of Jesus Chri*... but that last i was the last vowel or even letter we fine young men ever got out in that house, because that was all he needed to go berserk. *Absolutely bonkers.*

What happened next happened too fast for me to do any real thinking, but I did manage to put together the thought *I knew the vintage old lady hadn't heard us right.* The vintage old man started shouting a lot more words I couldn't understand, then grabbed the both of me and Elder Klein by the arm, from behind, and commenced shoving us toward the front door.

In just a couple of short, staggering, off-balance steps we were noisily back in the narrow hallway, going single-file now and looking for all the world like a lead-out line in the Tour de France that the vintage old man surely loved. Unfortunately for me, the surprisingly strong vintage old man had flung Elder Klein to the front of the line, leaving the VOM free to now grab both of my arms and shove me even harder than before. While Elder Klein moved without let or hindrance across the hallway linoleum, I suffered the full extent of the VOM's shoving and arm-twisting repertoire. Elder Klein didn't wait for his host to open the door, as good manners required, but opened it himself and ran out as fast as he could. This cleared the way for me to follow, which I did in impressive fashion, thanks to the VOM, who not only gave me a final furious push across the threshold, but while I was still airborne also managed to land a small but powerful dress shoe to my backside. Then the VOM slammed the door, still shouting, maybe at his wife now for having let in the wrong sort of local businessman.

The persecutions had begun.

Oh sure, I knew from browsing around in Foxe's fantastic book that having Ricky O'Connor chase you with a bottle of whiskey or even having a VOM kick your behind wasn't nearly as bad as the sorts of treatment real martyrs usually got. But for just a split second while suspended in the air, maybe from the millisecond that the VOM's well-polished shoe hit my bottom until the millisecond that I caught my balance on the sidewalk outside, I was right there with all of them — stoned with Stephen, chained with Paul, tortured with Origen (self-castration wasn't enough for him), scourged and pierced with Perpetua and Felicity, shot up with Sebastian, grilled with Lawrence, stretched on the rack with Vitalis (the person), strangled with Ludmila, thrown to the lions with Blandine, and tarred and feathered and killed with some early Mormon missionaries.

A few minutes later I came to my senses and we started laughing at what'd just happened. We hadn't even gotten out the whole name of the church: how did the vintage old man know we weren't going to tell him he'd won something? Or maybe we should have stopped mid-name and left him hanging, dress-shoe in air, to hear the rest. Or maybe we should have opened the mail slot in the door after our ignoble expulsion and yelled through, *Would it be more convenient if we at another time back came?* As it was, we just laughed and wrote *T2 angry* ♂ in the tracting book, in red.

For all my laughing, though, I was glad that the persecutions never really got any more vicious than being on the business end of a kick from a vintage old man who could barely reach his target. Because it wasn't fun. And it didn't feel as glorious as I'd thought it might. In fact it felt completely humiliating and horrible to be disliked by someone who didn't even know you.

A few months later a guy would wave a shotgun at me and yell *If you back come will you this see!* (What code to use for that in the tracting book?) Another guy would come to the door twirling a handgun, but maybe he just thought that as an American I'd have a natural affinity for guns. There was also the guy who let his German shepherd circle my companion for several frightening minutes before calling it off. And of course there were all the teenaged boys yelling *CIA!* and all the people laughing in cafés when we rode past. But during my almost two years in Belgium, that was as violent as it got.

So I had to admit I wasn't in the same league as the real martyrs after all. Most of the time I was just in the Rude, Indifferent, and Dismissive (RID) league, and sometimes in the Funny or Polite league. But in some ways

RID persecution was actually harder to deal with: at least when you were being stoned or tortured in public, everyone from locals to girls back home could admire you for standing up for your faith. But nobody was really even watching RID sorts of persecution. Plus with RID persecution you hardly got a chance to say what you were standing up for, as almost no one wanted to hear the details or even an entire sentence. If I'd been asked to give my life for my religion like the olden martyrs had, well, I would've in theory gone gladly along, because that just sounded so heroic. But RID persecution was just about killing me.

I blamed it mostly on local Catholics of course, confirming I'd been right after all about how wicked Belgian Catholicism was likely to be. And that was confirmed even more the day I wandered out of curiosity into one of their churches and saw people kneeling before some bronzed saint, and could hardly believe that anyone could be brainwashed into something like that. It was strange enough that everyone belonged to one religion here, but if they were going to choose just one, why in the world would they choose this one?

Other parts of local culture were killing me too. For all my fluency in the Discussions I hardly ever gave, I still made plenty of grave errors in Flemish-Dutch when free-styling, like when I thought I was saying *change my clothes* but was really saying *take off my clothes,* or thought I was saying that I would *take my companion along* but was idiomatically saying I was going to *seduce my companion.*

Or how about negotiating the thundering herd of bicycles that whooshed down city streets twice a day, blown in and out with the wind from the North Sea or the frozen plains of Siberia? Where was I supposed to jump in with my own purple bike, and where exactly had the bike path gone? Everyone seemed so sure about the proper location and etiquette, and I got a lot of stares and wagging index fingers when I rode wrongly.

And then all the diesel in the air was just so different from all the good-old-regular gasoline fumes back home. In fact for the rest of my life the scent of diesel fumes would take me right back to some narrow street in Belgium crowded with diesel-spewing trucks and busses and legions of scooters darting like flies and whining like vuvuzelas, their high-pitched sound amplified to ear-splitting volume by canyon after canyon of row houses and their breakneck speed, the result of some teenaged girl clinging onto some leathered-up teenaged boy.

Or how about the pain-in-the-butt cobblestones that took the self-winding right out of your watch? And what about the food, of which sure the fries and chocolate sprinkles were as spectacular as advertised, but the cow tongue and witloof (chicory) almost made you pass out — and don't even mention the sterilized-not-pasteurized milk that you could get down only if you mixed in enough corn flakes and raw oatmeal. And where did they hide the public bathrooms and why were they called, of all things, toilets? And why did local males sometimes just skip the toilets and pee right outside in a bush, or against a wall in an alley, and why did girlfriends or wives just stand there waiting, bored, instead of mortified? And if you couldn't see the toilets then how could you smell them all the time, maybe even more than the diesel fumes? Not smelling like toilets was another way America was a world leader.

And why was everything so olden here? Why didn't women shave their legs and armpits? Why did everyone including fellow local businessmen shake hands so limply and fishily instead of firmly and boldly? Why didn't people wash and comb and brush everything a little more carefully? And especially why was it always so cold and rainy and windy, with the wind in your face like a good defender no matter which way you rode?

But as hard as all those things were, and as hard as it was to always get along with fellow local businessmen or to be kicked in the butt by a vintage old man, I was sure that the hardest thing of all was putting up with almost constant Rude Indifferent Dismissive (and only sometimes Funny and Polite) rejection.

Okay, maybe the cold and rain and wind were close.

eight

FIVE-SENSE GRAY

It's 9:15 in the morning in the very late autumn in Belgium.

It's barely and unenthusiastically light because the sun has just come grudgingly up (if you call ten feet above the horizon up), and because the heavens are so blanketed with clouds that whatever rays manage to get through are homogenized pronto-like into gray. Belgian towns aren't colorful in any sort of autumn or winter light, but in this flannel-gray sort they may as well go ahead and admit it: *we are thoroughgoingly monochrome.*

You'd be crazy to try shooting color film in light like this, because everything will just come out gray, even the orange busses and blue cars. And forget about the train station, which is always the grayest thing in any Belgian town: even though it's painted some optimistic color, even though the time schedules stretching along the platforms are printed on bright yellow posters surrounded by blue frames set on top of red poles, any picture you take of that will just come out as one big shade of gray with no definable shapes at all.

On a day like today you can not only see the gray but touch it, hear it, smell it, and taste it too.

The touch happens because as usual it's raining, and emphatically gray Belgian rain is not only above you but all around you, like the blanket of clouds has dropped down low enough to wrap you wetly up, or like the blanket is so saturated that Zeus himself is standing up there wringing it out onto everything down below.

The crazy thing is that you can hear the gray, when the rain hits your window at just enough of a slant to make just enough of a noise to let you know that it's waiting just for you, or when you hear through the dark window the long whooshing sounds cars and busses make as they splash through the shimmering puddles that have formed in the settled parts of the asphalt.

Or maybe the really crazy thing is that you can smell the gray, not like the dusty smell you get out in some country field or on an urban blacktop in the rain, but a more-intense-than-usual diesel smell, the fumes of which you might've thought the rain would dilute or beat down to the ground, but you'd have thought wrong, because instead they just regroup at street level then defy gravity and every other law of physics by rising back up stronger and grayer than ever until they find your unwelcoming nose.

And finally there's maybe the craziest thing, tasting the gray, because even if you have the nifty plastic raingear all the real locals seem to have, you just can't keep the water off your mouth forever.

The gray is everywhere, even in your bones.

Upstairs in Albrecht Rodenbachstraat number 3, fittingly named for an idealistic young man, you and your fellow local businessmen are about ready to head outside.

You got up at 6:30 sharp in the darkness of your dismal little afterthought of an upstairs bedroom, which has only a giant awful lumpy mattress on the floor and an armoire that is actually a cool piece of furniture but that says to American-suburban you *why don't they i.e. all Belgians have real closets?* You every-other-day shaved in the tiny cold-water-only sink in your dismal room (which water felt even colder than usual), maybe washed a little more thoroughly in the one true bathroom downstairs, shiveringly put on your suit-pants and white-on-white shirt and *Hello Handsome* tie, and then finally prayed in private, until 7:00.

At 7:00 you prayed with your companion, then until 8:00 you rehearsed an entire Discussion together, under dim lights that on a day like today not only made your apartment look starker than usual but made you feel lonelier than usual too — something about those lights and the old furniture in tandem made it impossible to imagine that you'd ever feel joy again. Even though you knew by now that you almost never got to perform very many of your well-rehearsed Discussions live on stage in someone's home, you keep rehearsing them all anyway, just in case, and also because you've worked so record-settingly hard to learn them that they're sort of your trademark by now. That you and your companion and the other two missionaries in the apartment were the only ones in the whole town working in the darkness of morning on these words of life and death and salvation weighed especially heavy on a day like today, like the gray helped you sense more than usual that you had a special responsibility to get the words just right for the sake of everyone out there who was dying to hear them but didn't know it yet. That you spend almost all your time trying to convince people to hear those words, rather than actually letting them hear them, had weighed heavier than usual too, because on a day like today you knew it'd be even harder to convince people to hear them. You didn't stop to think about it for long though, because if you did then you might feel like you were drowning and fall unconscious right there, so instead you just focused on getting the words perfect, as usual.

From 8:00 to 9:00 you studied on your own, going back over Discussions that needed polishing, then reading in the scriptures, and it was during this hour that you thought the sun might've come up, but you weren't sure because on a day like today it was always hard to tell.

Then from 9:00 to 9:15 you ate breakfast, which on a day like today is always hot oatmeal with apple slices and cinnamon tossed in — but since there are so many days like today the slice of variety that the slices and cinnamon used to give seem a little common.

And now here at 9:15 you and your companion are gathering 'round with the other two missionaries for your daily group hymn and prayer before you head out. You take turns choosing the hymn, all three or four or five verses of which you now enthusiastically sing to get your spirits up, and also maybe to delay just a moment having to go out, maybe dreaming even what it'd be like just to stay in for once for a whole day, especially on a day like today, and just read and stay warm and rest. Elder Shepherd asks someone to pray, which that person sincerely and lengthily does, and when the prayer

is finished just before 9:30 you all shake hands and look each other in the
eye and say as convincingly as you can with each shaker *Success!* At last you
go down the flights of stairs and out the door, stick your supplies in the bike
bag that you hope will keep out the rain, jump on, and ride away — two in
one direction, two in another.

No one says anything about the weather, because that would mark you
out as a whiner or even a slacker and you don't want that, but on a day like
today you're definitely thinking about the weather before, during, and after
the prayer — and maybe before, during, and after everything else too.

You don't have any appointments lined up, or any hope that the rain
will stop, because the sort of rain coming down on a day like today doesn't
go away while you're watching but only when you're asleep, and even then
it doesn't really go away but just reorganizes itself for another attack some-
time soon. You'll be lucky today if someone invites you in for something
warm to drink, and if you're really lucky even for a Discussion, but that
doesn't happen often because when it's as wet as today people seem even
more anxious than usual to shut the door, like they're the ones getting wet,
not you, or like they're afraid you're going to drip all over everything.

On a day like today you feel even less hope than usual going out, because
even though Elder Klein your new senior companion is a good-hearted fellow he hasn't been in Belgium much longer than you, but was made Senior Companion ready-or-not-here-he-comes because of the glut of young
missionaries (including you yourself) recently arrived. His good heart isn't
enough to give you the security you'd felt with Elder Shepherd, who always
seemed to know what to do even on days like today, and who probably could
have calmed down the butt-kicking vintage old man even before the butt-
kicking vintage old man went into action. Elder Klein is struggling with
Dutch about as much as you are, not so much with the words, because he
knows a lot of those and writes new ones down religiously in a little book he
keeps, but with trying to say them, like he's the walking proof that you really
can't change your mouth muscles after you're seven even if you practice
heroically like he does every morning, in the bathroom so as not to bother
others, but he just can't get his r's to roll no matter how long and excruci-

atingly he tries. Because the bathroom isn't quite as quiet as he thinks, it takes only about 15 minutes of unsuccessfully rolled r's to make you start feeling like fingernails are scratching on a blackboard in there. You know you can't expect Elder Klein to make the tricky French r at the back of his throat, the way Flemish people speaking Dutch seem to do, because most missionaries can't make that, but you have to at least do some sort of rolled r so you don't sound like a total foreigner instead of just mostly one.

Missionaries are supposed to be the weak things of the earth, that's what Mormon scriptures say, but with Elder Klein you feel incapacitatedly weak, because he's not making up for your own natural weakness the way Elder Shepherd might have. Instead you and Elder Klein are just two hyper-weak things together, and on a day like today that's just accentuated (if possible) even more.

Your new tracting area #9 that you thought would change everything is far enough away that there's no way you can walk to it. On a day like today you think about taking the nice and dry bus, but that costs money and it's a little complicated to figure out. So you just ride your bike as usual, even though you know that the *waterproof overcoat* you'd been happy about not having to buy (because you'd inherited it for free from your recently deceased uncle-in-law) won't live up to either one of its names and you'll be soaked through in less than an hour. When you're riding, that so-called overcoat isn't over your legs at all, but keeps separating, so your legs are the first things soaked, and you can't afford or don't have enough initiative to figure out where to buy all the nifty plastic rain gear all the real locals seem to have, that stretches out over your handlebars and protects everything except your face. But even the nifty plastic rain gear wouldn't stop the water coming at you from below, thanks to the splashing cars, some of which if you're not mistaken or if you're feeling especially martyr-like seem like they're actually trying to splash you, like on purpose. You can try riding along with an umbrella open over your head, but that's usually more danger than it's worth, because your hand brakes don't work all that well to begin with in the rain and using only one of them feels just a little suicidal, especially if you have a cheaper Belgian bike that makes you lean way forward when you ride instead of a more expensive Dutch bike that lets you sit straight up. And if it's as usual windy then an umbrella is useless anyway, whether you're Belgianly leaning or Dutchly sitting straight. You try at least to protect your head, with a hat, which the mission rules say you have to wear during cold months, but it's a cheap hat made of corduroy and it'll be drenched as fast as your not-even-close-to-waterproof overcoat is.

When you finally reach your area #9 that you thought would change everything and lock your bikes to a tree and start tracting, there's usually only one umbrella for the both of you. That's because one of you has inevitably lost his, but also because one of you has to write in the tracting book, and it's too much trouble to write when you're holding an umbrella, or to say every 10 seconds *Here hold my umbrella while I write.* The large problem presented by only one umbrella is that it's almost never built for two: there aren't any big colorful golf umbrellas here, because the official color for umbrellas in Belgium is black (to give a little variety to the gray tableau), and the official size is medium (to avoid poking too many passing people in the eye). So your outside arm and its accompanying shoulder are guaranteed to catch a lot of rain because the black medium is hovering over only part of you, and it doesn't help that your black medium always has a broken spindle or two from the wind that turned it inside out the day before, so the water runs off at that pretty much collapsed part of the umbrella even faster than it does elsewhere, so that not only your outside arm and its accompanying shoulder get soaking wet but some of the contiguous regions on your back as well, and then anything contiguous to them too.

You'll spend most of a day like today casting suspicious glances sideways to see whether your umbrella-holding companion has found true center over the both of you, or has allowed a little natural drift to occur toward his own side, or has failed to notice that the wind is now blowing the rain at a severely slanted angle almost exactly the opposite of the severely slanted angle of just a few moments ago, thus requiring radical repositioning of the umbrella; you politely suggest a new angle of defense against the rain, because by all means you the custodian of the tracting book for the day must keep it absolutely dry. You don't think of going to buy a second umbrella, because they cost money, and you'd rather just share your companion's, at least until his breaks completely or is lost.

It's not easy to write in the tracting book on any day because of all the people watching you suspiciously from the windows, but it's even harder on a day like today, because people are still watching from the windows and now your ink isn't flowing either, so that the pen slides scratchily across the page without making a single mark or maybe making barely one, which means you're standing there even longer than usual trying to write in it. And if horror of horrors the book does get wet because of radically miscalculated umbrella-positioning or a shift in the wind then the page will likely run with the ink that was already on the page, and several pages will mash down before drying out and then plump up and stick together when you try to turn them.

Your worries about the little tracting book would seem a tad excessive to outsiders, but if it gets wet, well, how will you know where you've been or where to go? And the odds of it getting wet are even better in area #9 than they were in old area #5, because so far not one person in area #9 has even once let you in the door, meaning you're probably going to be out in the rain the entire livelong day today too. You'd thought that area #9 would change everything and finally give you some *Success!* because it'd hardly been worked by anyone before, and because the missionary who'd hardly worked it before had been none other than your favorite LTM teacher, the legendary Elder Fisher, the thought of which when you'd realized it had so filled you with a burning in-side that you'd been sure the burning was telling you this was the area where people were just waiting to hear you, and besides, area #9 consisted almost entirely of a village named Godsheide, which in Dutch meant *God's heath,* and that just had to be portentous, because in fact this village right outside of town and right out of a Bruegel painting was beautiful enough that God may have indeed chosen to dwell there at least part-time. But so far you've passed through Godsheide almost five times and haven't gotten in a single door or made one single appointment, but you've felt that burning inside about it so you aren't going to give up. It's probably better on a day like today not to know that it will end up being the only area during your entire two-year mission where you won't get in a single door to give a Discussion.

Sometimes on a day like today you might not ride all the way out to area #9 that you thought would change everything, but try instead one of the big apartment buildings in town that you always say you're saving for a rainy day, where you stand in the lobby like some NASA engineer in front of a huge grid of doorbells and start pushing one at a time, even though you know pushing those bells is even less effective than appearing at a door in person. It always gets really awkward when some resident walks through while you're standing there pushing bells, and looks at you suspiciously as s/he opens the second inner door to go truly inside and then shuts it as fast as Mrs. Dinkel back home used to so that you can't piggyback on in behind him/her. Your flustered companion might even ask one guy coming through, *Which bell are you?* Which will almost certainly result in the guy saying back without the slightest hint of humor *Me? I am no bell!* then going on past in a huff. Your best hope in front of those bells is that the person who answers on the intercom will as usual not be able to understand you through the static and so will buzz you up to see what you want in person, but most non-understanders aren't curious enough to buzz.

Or instead of riding out to area #9 on a day like today you might be desperate enough to try *business contacting,* but despite all the things you supposed you had in common with the fellows at such places, most of them don't have time for you while they're working, even when it's raining. So mostly you, as usual, just tract, and since you like to be systematic about it that means, even on a day like today, area #9 for you.

After a morning/early afternoon of no-luck tracting, you walk wetly back to your bike just before 2:00 to make the long and wet ride home for lunch-dinner, which you merge into one big culinary event because then you don't waste time riding home and back for each, but on a day like today you wouldn't mind riding home and back twice, just to get out of tracting in the rain, even though riding home even just once is almost certain to get you even wetter than staying out in the rain with your partial umbrella. The other two missionaries go home a little early to make the meal, but it takes only 15 minutes or so to boil some noodles or potatoes or fry some oatmeal with egg and an Oxo cube and on really special occasions with hamburger too. You eat and clean up as fast as you can so that you have some time to relax, which you do by reading scriptures or a letter you got this morning or yesterday morning, especially if it's from the girl you're writing, especially if it's from Rachelle, because if you got one from her then the rain beating against the window is just a little bit easier to bear. Or maybe you take a short nap, but it's hard for a 19-year-old to take just a short nap so you usually avoid the nap thing altogether and just read some more.

Then 3:30 rolls around faster than you thought it might and a little dread sets in. Not a dread of telling people about your religion: you actually like doing that, especially if it means teaching a Discussion. Instead it's a dread of all you have to go through just to get to that point, especially on a day like today, and also that you don't like feeling like you're twisting their arm to get them to listen, what with all the techniques you've learned to counter objections and all the boldness you've mustered up to approach people. But you remind yourself that all your countering and approaching is for people's salvation, and you also think about the poor and the orphaned and starving and permanently wet and cold people who are worse off than you are, so you keep trying.

To steel yourself to go outside again on a day like today you avoid looking out the window and you say another prayer together, even though you just said one together over the food an hour before and probably said one on your own too a few minutes earlier, and maybe to pass a little more time you even take time to sing another song together, all four of the regular verses and if there are any extra verses, well then those too. Finally you all make it out the door around 3:30 or maybe 4:00, about a half hour before the sun goes conclusively down, which means you've got about five or six more hours of tracting in the rain to go and only five of those hours in serious darkness. At least it'll only *feel* gray when it's dark, instead of looking gray too. And at least at night you'll find some men home, but then you realize that that's not necessarily good, because the men seem even less sympathetic about your standing out in the rain than the women usually do.

Sometimes you argue with yourself on a day like today about what's worse: the rain or the bitter cold.* Your inherited non-wind-resistant non-waterproof overcoat and your soaked gloves are about equally useless in either sort of weather, you reason. Since there are more rainy days than bitterly cold days, maybe rain is worse, you conclude. But, you retort, the cold just about disables you and sinks your spirits maybe even faster than rain. It's a tough choice, you admit. But finally you give just a slight preference to the cold, because except for the little icicles forming on your face at least you're not totally wet then, and also because if it's absolutely inhumanly cold then not even other missionaries will expect you to stay outside the whole day, and you can say without the slightest prick of guilt *Maybe ought we inside to go because this cold dangerous is.* You couldn't really say that about the rain.

And despite all the gray you have to try to be at least a little cheery or you will die. It's a necessity to be cheery now, not just something optional for the cheerily inclined: you have to be cheery or be beaten down. Have a little hope or be crushed like a kernel of wheat in a millstone. But the missionaries with a bigger natural dose of cheeriness do best on a day like today, no doubt about it: *Fantastic day for missionary work, Elder!* they say. And if it's a bitterly cold day they rub their gloved hands together and say *Let's around the block walk and up warm!* instead of *Maybe ought we inside to go because this cold dangerous is.* And you don't even mind these cheery guys on a day like today, in fact you're glad to be near them as long as they don't expect you to be naturally cheery too, or act like being naturally cheery is just a matter of will. Because again even if you can't be naturally cheery you can appreciate cheeriness, and so do people at the doors, because they're not dying to talk to a couple of foreign local businessmen on any day but they're especially not interested in talking to a couple of sullen and drippingly wet foreign local businessmen with a beat-up umbrella, which has an odd way of making you look beat up by association. In fact if you can manage a cheery smile on a day like today it might just be incongruous enough to make you curiously attractive at the door — unless people think you're crazy for being outside in this and smiling.

* Rain is just ordinary cold.

If you're working on a day like today alongside an easily cheery twinkly-smiling missionary like Elder Trimbo, then you have a chance to make it through in decent shape and even have a few laughs about it afterward. You can also get through by remembering that you've made it through days like today before: *Look,* you said at the end of the last day like today, *you're still here, you didn't die, the clock did move, the day did end.* You can also get through days like today by remembering how the clouds looked from up above when you flew into Belgium, which reminds you that everything up there is still light and sun and bright, which you want to believe is the natural state of things even in Belgium. And you can also get through by remembering that some days like today have actually turned out okay: you had appointments. *You got in.* Not all days like today made you wish you were unconscious or that this was just a bad dream and you would just wake up and it would all be over.

But then you remember your friend in the mission who didn't get in a single door for six weeks, which is bad enough, but even worse is that you know most of those weeks looked just like today. You also remember that even when it's sunny and warm it doesn't last long, because the clouds get together to move back in and drive away the light, like they're telling the sunshine *You are NOT the natural state of things, not here in Belgium!* And if your companion isn't cheery either naturally or artificially, and you aren't any sort of cheery yourself, and you don't get in all day, or the evening appointment you've so been looking forward to ends up falling through, then you'll be wondering just what in the world you're doing here, and how you'll ever get dry, and how will a day like today really ever end?

What did Vince Lombardi say? *Fatigue makes cowards of us all.* The missionary version is a little less poetic: *a gray day like today makes rejection hurt even worse than it already did.*

At around 7:00, or 8:00, if you still haven't gotten in a door for a Discussion or spoken with a friendly person, and you're really feeling the wet and starting to shiver, you'll be tempted to turn in early, like that one night when something about the lights on the treeless street shined so harshly on the row houses that they looked like a scene straight from an Ayn can-I-alienate-

you-even-more Rand novel, like they were saying *no one will ever open to you.*
The wind howled down that barren canyon of a street with lots of noisy cars
and five people in a row quietly refused to open the door and a sixth looked
out the window and explicitly shook his head *No* without even bothering to
find out who you were, and that was when you'd just had it. You couldn't go
to another door, even though you'd always pushed yourself playing sports
to the point that you thought your heart and head and lungs would burst,
even though you'd stood bravely in the dumpyard from hell, even though
you'd already sloshed through a lot of rainy days in Belgium already. Maybe
if you'd had a letter from Rachelle that day then you might've been able to
keep going, because you would've been too ashamed for her to think that
you'd given even a single thought to turning in early: what kind of a husband would that make? Maybe a letter from her would've helped you go to
one more door, or ride to another friendlier area, but there hadn't been a
letter and so instead you'd just said to your companion that you didn't feel
well. Which was true, but not the way your companion was thinking you
meant. And even if he didn't want to turn in himself you knew he'd have to
take seriously the health-needs of his companion and concede, so you went
home at 7:30, ashamed about the two whole hours before quitting time. But
at least on that night even you were numb to guilt.

Most of the time, though, on days like today you won't officially turn
in early, but just go visit one of the precious old ladies who can be found
in any city where Mormon missionaries have been, because if you go visit
them then at least it doesn't look like you're turning in early even though
you might as well be, because you're not going to find any converts among
precious old ladies. They were once among the legions who stood at windows looking suspiciously into the street, but they were also among the few
brave enough or lonely enough to let missionaries in and even to hear a few
Discussions. After a few of these they said to just come back for a regular
chat, or dinner, or to drop by for some *peperkoek* and bubbly water,* but no

---

* *Peperkoek* simply means way-too-spicy cake. Bubbly water is hard enough for North-
American you to get down, but with *peperkoek* it is even harder. In fact bubbly water is arguably the worst possible accompanying beverage in the world with *peper-*

more talk about religion, okay? And so on days like today you'll sometimes take them up on their offer and go by to visit.

If you've already visited the precious old ladies in the last few days though, then you might look for a little warmth and welcome instead at one of the three houses in town where actual practicing Mormons live, because they also are likely to give a friendly welcome to missionaries just happening to drop by in the rain or cold. The problem with going to see actual Mormons, even unpracticing ones, is that you can't count most visits to them in your total proselyting hours because you can't proselyte someone who's already Mormon, and so you go there only when absolutely worn down, or your statistics will suffer. But if worn down enough you might on a day like today go anyway, and ride several miles out across the mammoth Albert Canal and its cold steel and concrete bridge, where the horns of the boats moan through the dark and the wind whips across the bridge and chills you even deeper as you ride across, and impresses into your smallest little cells just what a desolate and inhuman place this canal is at night and how hard it will be to actually convert anyone. But you keep riding through the cold and rain that makes rejection hurt even more than usual, because ironically you're trying to escape cold and rain and rejection, and the road that runs across the bridge will take you eventually to the warm government-subsidized Mormon home of the De Smet family, who are always home because *Mevrouw* De Smet is too sick to go anywhere.

And oh what luck: you can count a visit to them as proselyting hours, because *Mevrouw* De Smet and the two children haven't converted (yet)! You're glad about that tonight because even though you're not getting any teaching hours just sitting there talking and drinking herbal tea and munching *koekjes,* you're at least still piling up the proselyting hours, which in the absence of teaching hours show that at least you're trying. *Mevrouw* De Smet has actually had the Discussions several times, and sure, she's never been rock-solidly alert during any of them, but you can at least feel

---

koek. But if you don't drink coffee, the usual accompanying beverage, bubbly water is often the only other non-caffeinated or non-alcoholic beverage in the house, so you accept it to be polite.

like your just being there might increase her chances, or even those of the two teenaged sons who like to try out their new American (mostly swear) words on you. You also like to make *Broeder* De Smet feel appreciated for being sort of the lone man in the bar-top Garden of Hasselt, you really do, which the very act of your visiting shows. But mostly you just want to get out of the cold, and it's too early to ride home already.

Even though you've got some good motives mixed in with your gray-escaping ones, you feel guilty going to see the De Smets or one of the precious old ladies, because you're supposed to be spending your energy finding *quality converts,* not seeking refuge from the elements among friendly old ladies and fellow-believers. You feel even guiltier if you happen to run into the other missionaries at one of these places, who apparently had the same idea you did. If you do run into them, then you'll both leave as soon as politeness allows, then do some half-hearted tracting for the last hour or so of the night to make up for your guilt at having been seen by the other missionaries among precious old ladies. But if you don't run into the others, then you might stay even longer than politeness allows, and you probably won't say anything about your visit to the others after you all get home.

At last the day ends, as it always unbelievably does, and you ride back home, getting soaked yet again in the Belgian now-really-dark gray. You lock your bike outside the front door, climb the three flights of stairs to your apartment, take off your wet outerwear (mostly everything), put on your pajamas, grab what's left of the slightly stale Belgian bread on the kitchen counter, and if you're all getting along you all sit down at the table and eat numerous slices of it ravenously together, with butter and (not too much) jam. Then you get ready for bed and hope that it won't be gray like this tomorrow.

But as you fall into sleep on your giant awful lumpy mattress smack dab on the floor of the dismal upstairs bedroom, you know the odds are good that it will be. And that you'll try again. And that you'll wonder again how much try you have left in you — maybe enough for another day or week or month, but 21 months? You don't believe the calendar nearby, which says that those months really will come.

And you sleep at last.

nine

AN ANTHROPOLOGY OF BUTT-KICKING

So what happened was that in a living room that looked more like a shadowy Rembrandt interior than the twentieth-century-space-with-incandescent-light it barely was, there came a flash of hope, and not from any dim bulb or even the crackling fire but from the glorious fact that Elder Klein and I were giving a fourth (F) Discussion to someone(s) besides ourselves.

We'd never gotten this far with any investigator before. But even more exciting was that the F Discussion was the big moment when you invited/challenged your investigator to convert.*

I *knew* the conversions would start coming, because that was how The Missionary Story always went. First came pitchforks full of difficulties thrown at you by the devil. Check: we had that. Then came fighting through them all, until finally at the last door on the last street at the last hour of the day, someone opened and gratefully declared *We've been waiting for you.* Check: we had that now too, thanks to Maria and Martha, sisters like in the Bible, who though not quite the last house in old area #5 had been close to it, and who though not actually saying the exact word *waiting* might as well have, just by getting all the way to this fourth Discussion. Then finally came

---

* Strong missionaries preferred to say *baptismal challenge,* which was what most English-speaking Mormons said too. But locals and milder missionaries said *baptismal invitation,* which probably said a lot about how American and Belgian and strong and mild people thought you best motivated someone to do something.

the conversion itself, which would make all the rain and rejection just go away. Almost check: if we could just get this F right tonight.

That morning we'd practiced it purposefully instead of just routinely, and practiced the short baptismal invitation/challenge G too, which was separately lettered because you could throw it in at a lot of places, including during a C, D, or E Discussion. But the classic or maybe just last moment to throw in a G (because it's hard for *classic* to refer to something rarely done) was right after F-9: *It Is for Our Salvation Absolutely Necessary That We in the Right Manner Are Baptized.* And it was the post-F-9 throw-in we'd prepared that morning. I would give the odd-numbered concepts and Elder Klein the even, because he as the Senior was going to issue the invitation/ challenge right after I the Junior gave a presumably flawless F-9. All the cold day we'd looked forward to this appointment, and we'd prayed that Maria and Martha would keep it.

Not that M&M would be going anywhere. The sisters biblical were respectively 84 and 76 and didn't get out much, especially in the cold, and Maria was only half-lucid, even in the warm. But what if they didn't answer the door? Like that 42 percent of the time already mentioned? People would say *Sure, come you on Thursday for a Discussion,* and you'd mark that time in your agenda and show up on the dot all excited, but then no one would answer, because they'd (a) forgotten, (b) changed their minds and were gone on purpose, or (c) changed their minds and pretended not to be home. And even though you'd steeled yourself to stay calm in case any of a, b, or c happened, you'd be devastated anyway, because you'd really wanted to give that Discussion, and because when you gave one you felt like you were doing what missionaries were supposed to be doing, and also because you'd be in the great indoors instead of floundering around in the cold outdoors trying to figure out what to do next, which floundering was especially hard on winter nights.

But any worries had proven baseless because Martha opened right on cue, thus about five minutes after the bell rang, and seemed as happy as ever to see us. After a little small-talk, and after Martha had biblically and Belgianly brought her guests something to drink, I started in with a flawless

F-1, Elder Klein followed with a slightly labored F-2, and then finally came my flawless F-9, the lead-in for Elder Klein's invitation/challenge.

The sisters had to know the invitation/challenge was coming, I thought, after all the hints being dropped in the F. They had to know that we weren't just there to eat *peperkoek* and drink bubbly water, the way real precious old ladies (unlike M&M) thought we were. And they had to say *Yes!* Because even though M&M probably couldn't get up the steps to our local bar-top church and so probably weren't the ideal candidates to start a run on it, their conversion might start other people running. It had to mean *something* that Maria was 84 years old, my magic number of converts, like maybe a sign that she'd be the first.

My throat constricted and my knees shook as I trembled through the last words of F-9 and turned my head toward Elder Klein,* waiting for the magical opening words of the baptismal invitation/challenge, words that I'd never before heard live: *Meneer de Brown (substitute M&M), during the translation of the Book of Mormon. . . .* But wait . . . Elder Klein wasn't saying that. He was obliviously saying instead the non-magical opening words of F-10: *Meneer de Brown (substitute M&M), you are sincere in your desire yourself to prepare for your membership in Christ's Kingdom. . . .* What the fetch was he thinking? You couldn't start F-10 unless you'd already given the baptismal invitation/challenge and the investigator had actually said *Yes!(!)* Because F-10 and everything that followed assumed a said *Yes!(!)*

I couldn't believe it, and so needed a few seconds to orient myself. Even though it was cold out and even though the fireplace wasn't of the efficient persuasion, sweat started running down my back and forehead anyway. I knew I should have done the invitation/challenge myself and not just handed it over to Elder Klein just because he was the flippin' Senior. He had gone Pavlovally on to F-10 because that was how we usually practiced, moving right from F-9 to F-10 without throwing the G in between, because except for this morning we usually practiced the G separately. So when El-

* You were always supposed to look at your companion when he was talking, but it wasn't always easy since you knew what he was going to say, so you'd start focusing on the unpleasant features of his face or start looking at what was on the wall behind him.

der Klein had started feeling pressure he'd just gone with what his memory dialed up by default when it heard the end of F-9. How were M&M going to convert now?(!)

Finally I threw an elbow at him. I hoped the sisters wouldn't notice, but I was on extremely safe ground there. Elder Klein grunted and looked at me in total confusion. I whispered in English, *the baptismal invitation/challenge!* He was horrified. After all our practice! I motioned to indicate that I could go flawlessly ahead if he was too dazed to do so, and he indicated with a pale-faced nod that he indeed was, so I started in, hoping to rescue the situation. Because surely whether the knitting Martha and the half-lucid Maria said *Yes!* to the invitation/challenge depended on my getting the words just right. And if I did, then they'd not only be saying *Yes!* in a couple of minutes but would for years afterwards — I could hear it already — gratefully be uttering our names in reverential tones to their equally grateful descendants, even though neither M&M had ever come close to actually having any descendants (so far, anyway — remember Sariah!*).

I made my way through the invitation/challenge as smoothly as ever, and finally came to the big question at the end: *Meneer de Brown (substitute M&M), may we you (and your family) then invite yourself to prepare for your baptism, through which you at the same time a member become of the Church of Jesus Christ of the Saints of the Last Days?* My heart was pounding and pinging like a cobblestone-hammer slamming its target.

But there was nothing. Just silence. Had M&M heard? I wasn't sure. I had to admit I wasn't always sure whether the sisters knew exactly who we were, much less what we were saying, but I'd tried to ignore stuff like that and refused to think that M&M were just another set of precious old ladies who'd let the missionaries in for a little company and *peperkoek.* After all, they (at least Martha) were all the way up to the F Discussion and Martha had read all the way up to page 293 in the Book of Mormon, which on both

---

* The wife of Abraham who according to the account in Genesis was 90 when she bore their son Isaac.

counts was a lot farther than real precious ladies or any of our other investigators ever got. But then I had to admit that it'd sometimes been a bit of a problem to convince the sisters that we weren't *Catholic* missionaries, and that the Book of Mormon wasn't a Catholic book, because Martha was always nodding her head and saying *Right, that believe we,* when we'd say something, like we were all already on the same team. Oh, she wasn't dumb, she knew the Book of Mormon was something new for her, but I got the feeling she read it near the fire while fingering her rosary and happily clucking her tongue, thrilled at the discovery of this fine Catholic book she hadn't known about before. Still, I'd been willing to overlook things like that, unlike some missionaries who wanted to work only with *dynamic fathers* and other supposedly totally together people.

When the sisters finally responded, Martha was as usual the mouthpiece. She looked up from her knitting when she realized I was waiting for an answer, and asked me to repeat my question. When she grasped that we were asking her to join a new church, she chuckled and kept on knitting and rocking and said she and Maria were too old for something like that. We were always welcome to come back for some *peperkoek* and bubbly water, but no more talk about religion, okay?

And that was it. Rejection Motif 1-something again, even if it took four Discussions to get to it, and even if Martha didn't actually say *We are Catholic.* Plus Motif 1k too, even if she didn't say that either: *And by the way we're precious old ladies, not serious candidates for conversion.* That was how our big baptismal invitation/challenge ended. No F-10. No H, I, or J Discussions. No conversion.

But just when hope seemed lost for good again, it suddenly appeared again, as it had a habit of doing among hard-to-keep-down local businessmen. Because from off to the side there came another voice in the room: that of the sisters' young caretaker, Margareta, who'd sat in on every Discussion to make sure M&M weren't being taken advantage of. The voice was saying she was interested in learning more. And maybe attending church. And maybe converting.

We'd been directing our Discussions to the wrong person(s) the whole time. And she'd been listening a whole lot closer than either M or especially M had. We swiveled our heads to Margareta, happy to tell her more, but maybe a little worried that she was only interested in learning more because in 1975 young American boy-men like us were still potentially exotically attractive to certain Belgian girls of a certain 18-19-year-old age that she was. But I was overestimating my powers of attraction, because Margareta was a serious person and seriously interested in religion. Maybe she could even handle a bar-top church.

Martha volunteered that Margareta could even follow the rest of the Discussions at their home if she wanted, and not just so the sisters could chaperone her as she'd chaperoned them, but because Martha knew that Margareta's parents and sisters didn't want any local businessmen coming into the family home with a foreign religion.

So a couple of days later we went back to M&M's and started teaching Margareta, directly. Soon she accepted a smoothly delivered baptismal invitation/challenge. Soon she came to the bar-top church and actually liked it, as she got along great with Emmalina, who in turn was happy to see someone her own age and gender there, which made our hearts burst with pride. Soon Margareta was all the way through an unprecedented H Discussion, the tough one about Mormon commandments like not smoking and not drinking and not having illicit sex, all of which she seemed positively eager to keep. But then Margareta had to take a break because her exams were starting. And then she disappeared.

Maybe she didn't like the Mormon commandments after all. Maybe Tristan or more likely Willi scared her away from church. But most likely was that by the time her exams were finished her sisters and her parents had found out what she was up to over at M&M's and on Sunday mornings at the bar and ridiculed her into not going back. She'd mentioned before that her sisters already knew she was meeting the missionaries and were teasing her about us. But we didn't know where she lived, and M&M weren't exactly sure either or they didn't want to tell us, so we couldn't go find her. And so just like that we lost her, which was even harder than losing M&M.

But again hope died hard, and just after losing 3M we found some again at the truly last address in area #5. The blind man who opened the door was unusually kind from the start, inviting us in immediately and playing the piano and introducing us to his wife and three young kids, then having us back for a *Gezinsavond* the next week, during which we were treated to a feast of Bruegelian proportions while the kids showed off their formidable *Gezinsavond* musical talents, and after which the whole family eagerly invited us to come back again for a first Discussion, which also went exceptionally well, everyone listening with exceptional interest and the room full of exceptionally good feeling, the likes of which Elder Klein and I had never known before and which just had to have been the Holy Ghost, especially when the blind man prayed at the end for more enlightenment about the message they'd just heard, all of which made us jump up and down on our bikes with excitement all the way home, thinking that this was the start of things for sure, and it was a whole family this time, not two precious old ladies or a possible missionary-liking girl.

But then the blind man got an answer to his prayer that we hadn't counted on, because when we showed up all eager and optimistic and smiling for the next (D) Discussion, the one that was about eternal family togetherness that this obviously together family was sure to love hearing, well, the blind man barely opened the door, handed us the books and pamphlets we'd left, and said with a voice even colder than this cold Belgian day never to come back again. Then he shut the door.

It was a classic throw-over (and here the word *classic* was entirely apt). He must've heard something bad from someone, we guessed, most likely from a priest. No wife or kid had been in sight this time, even though at every other visit they'd all crowded around the door smiling at the back-smiling Elder Klein and me. I'd be rejected thousands of times in Belgium,*

---

* A retrospective estimate is 6,700: ten rejections a day (which can of course be only too low) times the number of days I was in Belgium (around 670).

but being thrown over like this when you actually had some hope for someone was the worst — worse than having doors shut in your face or being kicked in the butt by little old men or being told by people that they were already happy and didn't need anything new (which always made me write in my journal *the problem here is that people* think *they're happy!*), and even worse than losing 3M. Because no one had ever been as enthusiastic and lucid and familial as the blind man and his family.

The disappointments and rejections were piling up like the bodies at Agincourt. And they were coming in even more varieties than I'd ever known. Barely a day or so after the blind man shut his door, we also learned that there were 35 official Mormons in town. *Thirty-five?(!)* There were only six at church most Sundays, 14 if the two over-qualified families showed up. Who were the others? Missionaries had been in town only a year or two, so these couldn't have been names lingering from the 1950s like a lot of old European branches had.* No, they all must've quit the church recently.

We went out to investigate, and lo and behold discovered that the missing 20 or so were real and recent indeed. Behind almost every barely opened door we knocked on was someone who might have briefly been officially Mormon (they weren't all exactly sure) but who now just wanted to be left alone. Turns out most of them had been converted a year or two before by my legendary LTM teacher Elder Fisher, who'd promised that it really was possible to baptize in Belgium because he'd proven it, but Elder Fisher hadn't told us how fast all of those baptized people had left, hadn't issued any follow-ups to his original heroic story.

And finally there came the most disheartening news of all: not only briefly-Mormon people were quitting, but now some of the top top stalwart few as well. Including the local Lambrecht family.

---

* Before the new Antwerp mission was born, Flemish Belgium was part of the Netherlands Mission, so it wasn't that missionaries hadn't been in Belgium before, it was that there hadn't been very many of them, maybe 20 to 30 in a few major (non-Hasselt) towns. But with the new mission, there were now 150 in 13 towns.

I couldn't believe it. *Broeder* Lambrecht was one of the most impressive Mormons in Belgium, a teacher who at the last bi-annual conference of Belgian Mormons had given one of the most inspiring talks I'd ever heard. *Zuster* Lambrecht was just as impressive. Together they'd constituted a big part of the walking proof that it was possible to be both a respectable Belgian and a respectable Mormon. But now they were gone.

Hearing that, Elder Shepherd took me with him the next Sunday on a 30-kilometer bus ride to visit the Lambrechts. But when we finally arrived *Broeder* Lambrecht didn't want to see us: he was lying down in the back room in a crisis, his wife said. Elder Shepherd and I rode back home in silence, unable to believe he wouldn't come out of it smiling and Mormon. But I never saw either of the Lambrechts again. Neither did most any other Belgian Mormon.

There could be only one explanation for all this rejecting: the devil. Working against us as usual, and as usual through the Catholic Church. By now I was mentally shaking a fist at every Catholic church I rode past, and I was sure that the dull red light barely gleaming through the stained-glass windows at night was nothing less than a little tête-à-tête going on inside between the devil and the local priests.

That (the devil working through the Catholic Church) was my big Univariate Theory of Rejection, a sort of corollary to my big Univariate Theory of Conversion (the Holy Ghost working through us).

I didn't know about the possibility of a Multivariate Theory of Rejection (or Conversion). I didn't know that there might be a hundred reasons why a person might leave, stay in, or join a church. I didn't know about all the studies showing that the biggest visible influences on someone's affiliation or non-affiliation with a church were what you could call social and familial structures, not theological ones, or in other words that people left or joined or stayed in a church mostly because of the people they cared about most (their family), and partly because of bigger social ties even beyond their family (their friends).

So there was no way in heaven I could've understood what people in a mostly-Catholic place like Belgium were really saying when they said their particular variation of *We are Catholic* to me. It wasn't that they necessarily loved being Catholic, or that they were thoroughly-believing Catholic, or even that they went around thinking about being Catholic, but instead something like *Catholicism isn't just another religion here, like a religion in America is, but is part of the whole social structure, and even though most of us are indifferent Catholics and cultural Catholics and lapsed Catholics and even anti-clerical Socialists, we at least have a place in that structure, and Mormons don't, so if we join the rival and feeble structure of Mormonism, then we're not just leaving Catholicism, but we might as well be kissing goodbye our whole society too, including probably a lot of family and friends, which will make us feel like total oddballs, which is a heavy thing to bear, and why would you want us to leave our family anyway, which you Mormons say nothing is more important than?*

I couldn't understand that in a mostly-Catholic place like Belgium, Mormonism would remain a rival and feeble structure until it became at least a small part of the main structure, which was only going to happen fast if people started converting in biblical-proportion numbers (like 84 converts per missionary), but given the postlapsarian tendency of people to convert to a religion because they know somebody in it, this made for a classic chicken-and-egg type problem: there weren't very many Belgian Mormons for other Belgians to know, so most Belgians wouldn't convert. The few who would were those who had no place in the main structure yet (like recent immigrants and the lonely and maybe the poor and maybe some students), and those very few within the main structure who'd had an experience so extraordinary with the new faith that they were willing to leave the main structure anyway, despite the real costs.

I couldn't understand that in a mostly-Catholic place like Belgium, people weren't necessarily slamming doors and kicking me in the butt and handing stuff back to me on doorsteps or quitting Mormonism as fast as they had joined it because they were evil and blind or had been tricked by the devil, but because they were thinking in their mind and feeling in their heart about their family and defending their bigger social and moral order. Just like people in most other one-church cultures did, including mostly Mormon Utah, when coming face to face with some rival church.

I couldn't understand that in a mostly-Catholic place like Belgium, longtime longsuffering Mormons like the Lambrechts also quit the faith because they were just tired — of living outside the main structure, and of having to do so much in their new faith because there were so few other people to help them.

And I certainly couldn't understand exactly what I was asking people in a mostly-Catholic place like Belgium to do when I asked them to convert, even though I thought I did because I had friends back home who'd also lost family and friends after converting. But what I didn't see was that those friends back home had all sorts of new relationships to look forward to in their new full-fledged Mormon congregation, and those friends weren't also quitting American society by converting, at least not in theory, because in theory Americans were committed to a religiously mixed society, even if once in a while someone like Big Ricky O'Connor put a big fat question mark on that commitment. And I didn't see that while I myself was theoretically going to go home someday in a presumable blaze of glory, home to a fully functional comfort-giving church with a gym and gigantic metal curtains and lots of family and friends who would all slap me on the back for going so foreignly and heroically on a mission, I was asking local people, most of whom I would pretty soon forget, to move themselves to a bar-top church and the fringes of society. Maybe if you already were on the fringes you could go along with an invitation/challenge like that, but if you weren't, well, that was asking a lot more than I could have ever gotten my head around without knowing the Multivariate Theory of Rejection (or Conversion).

So it might have helped to know that theory. But at school I hadn't had any anthropology or sociology or history really. And in my missionary training I'd had only the non-Belgian water-bottle game and some lessons on

Charity to help me make sense of stuff like this, because word was that our missionary teachers and the people teaching the teachers didn't like any talk about anything even resembling the Multivariate Theory of Rejection (or Conversion), didn't like any talk that structures might play a role in rejection or conversion or especially that those structures made conversion harder or easier in some places than in others, because teachers and people teaching the teachers were afraid that if they said something like that then maybe missionaries in hard places would quit trying or just give excuses for not converting anyone. But maybe those missionaries just would've tried differently.

Yet it was also entirely possible and even highly probable that even if I had somehow heard the salient bits of the Multivariate Theory of Rejection (and Conversion), I would have ignored them anyway, thinking just like my teachers and the people teaching the teachers that a theory like that wouldn't have fit into my heroic dream of a mission, and that it would've been an 84-killer for sure. Because any Multivariate Theory of Rejection (or Conversion) is about probabilities, and odds, and the heroic theory of a mission was always about heroically defying both.

And that of course was what I'd always had in mind, and heart.

ten

YOUR OWN PATHETIC SELF

Against the usual weather-patterns and all the literary clichés in the book(s), the crisis did not come on a gray and rainy day with thunder rumbling in the background oh so precisely on cue.

Instead it came on a glaring day in winter, with the stark and severely angled rays of rare late afternoon sun piercing the little window of the dismal upstairs bedroom where I'd gone during lunch-dinner to be alone. I was kneeling on top of the giant awful lumpy floor-top mattress with unmade blankets and rarely washed sheets, not upright at-attention kneeling but beaten-down butt-on-feet kneeling.

I often headed upstairs around 3:20 to say a short prayer, trying to muster some courage to go back outside again at 3:30, but today some sort of despair with no I.D. pushed me up there earlier than usual, a despair that made me feel like I just could not go back outside today, even though it wasn't raining or even really very cold.

I'd never ever felt like this. Sometimes I hadn't wanted to go back out but then had anyway. Yes, on that one cold windy Ayn-Rand-like night I'd turned in a couple hours early, and on more than one night I might as well have turned in early by going to visit precious old ladies. But I'd never ever at 3:00 in the afternoon had the feeling that I couldn't see myself going back out that day or maybe even ever again.

And I'd never ever been unable to start the words of a prayer.

Oh, I'd expected a mission to be tough. I'd even begun to expect that it might be tougher than I'd expected. But in The Missionary Story and my working model and my good mission dream the tough stuff wasn't really all that tough, because you knew it would vanish once *Success!* showed up and started throwing its weight around. But *Success!* hadn't been doing any throwing at all or for that matter even showing up, at least so far. Usually I put the emphasis on *so far,* because even though hope might spring eternal in most human breasts it sprang especially so in the breasts of local businessmen. But today there was no springing at all.

I'd kept fighting, kept going over the top like countless soldiers in World War I coming out of the trenches, thinking that I'd be the one to beat the odds and get through. But like most of them, I hadn't.

I'd even tried joking the hard stuff away, making myself say *Hey what a great day!* when it pretty unanimously wasn't. Or saying *Hey it was a good day even though we in no doors got!* Or *Hey we have fun had even though we soaking wet are!* I said it because I'd heard top top missionaries say it, and it would work for a day or two. But then it would wear off.

And now I had nothing.

I'd never had the classic crisis of faith over whether God existed, or even the classic Mormon crisis over whether the church was the True Church or not, because there hadn't been any thought of such thoughts growing up. But today maybe I was having both, without even knowing it. My conscious feeling was along the lines of *Where are you God after everything heroic I've done?* Or *What's taking You so long?* Or *Why isn't my mission going the way I'd dreamed it would go?* But what I was actually feeling was more like *Are You there period?* Because what'd happened so far on a mission made me feel like God and the church not only weren't playing the way I'd imagined they would, but maybe weren't even in the ballpark at all.

I didn't know Anselm's or Aquinas's* or anyone else's sophisticated proofs for the existence of God, but I did have a few personal and un-

---

* Famous medieval theologians who tried really hard to develop rational proofs of God.

sophisticated proofs of my own. But today not even the very best of this sort were coming to the rescue — not the time I got lost as a boy in huge Roeding Park and first experienced the big void and then about a half-hour later also the big rescue in the form of my big sister running up to save me; not the time I almost passed out from ecstasy singing Handel's Hallelujah chorus in the big youth choir; not the countless tear-rolling testimonies at youth meetings that always made me feel as heroic and swelled up inside as singing Handel did and that always made me swear again never to sin again; not the comfort I felt from what I took to be God after yet another disappointment with my non-girlfriend; not the dumpyard that negatively proved God, partly because of the stinking layers of grass and partly because of the gatekeeper who took your dollar while hacking and chain-smoking and looking like he could turn into a skeleton and fly right at you from inside his tiny little booth plastered with pictures of naked girls all day long, all of which just had to be hell; not the record-setting Discussions I praised-be-God-and-not-my-name-for-it memorized; not my vision of 84 converts; and not even Rachelle, whose status as a proof of God was after all still decidedly provisional. I just felt nothing.

Maybe my all-star lineup of proofs wasn't quite as stellar as I'd thought. Maybe what I'd taken to be God burning in my bosom and making me almost pass out and giving me comfort was just a stomach ache, the way Chopin had said it was just a stomach ache and not any divine inspiration that inspired Beethoven to write his Funeral March. Maybe I was just fooling myself into feeling God, the way I was pretty sure Sister Hanson back home fooled herself when she thought anything she found on sale was a miracle from God. Maybe especially some of those big heroic feelings I'd thought were from God, like say opening area #9, were maybe just the result of getting all riled up by the big crowd around me, the way big crowds in the footage I'd seen of old Nazi rallies got all riled up and which I was pretty sure couldn't have been from God.

I wasn't actually thinking any of this in consecutive or even thought-out thoughts, because again I wasn't in a state to think, but it was all there in

119

the emptiness I was feeling, the sort of emptiness I'd felt in Roeding Park as a boy except bigger.

Maybe this was the sort of emptiness the mystics said you had to feel before you could really feel God — thus that you had to clear out all the clutter inside, including your notions of who you thought God was and how He worked, and only then were you in a state to let real God in.

Or maybe the emptiness was all there was, rather than just some sort of lead-up to being filled by God. Maybe the void was it, period.

Probably everyone who felt the void felt it differently, but for me struggling on top of the giant awful lumpy mattress for what seemed like forever but was really only the 15 or 20 minutes it took for the last of the sun's rays to go almost completely horizontal, the emptiness wasn't so much filled as reduced to something smaller and smaller and quieter and quieter, until finally it took the form of a totally silent thought/feeling that calmly but overwhelmingly entered the emptiness inside, and it was just this: *Just be yourself.*

If I hadn't been down there already, I would've been floored. Of all the thoughts/feelings in the universe that might've been lightning-bolted down to me, this was it? Of all the gems I might've found in church councils and scriptures and sacred history or God Himself, this trite 1970s thing was all I actually got? No new magical proselyting techniques? No new dose of heroic resolve to get the faith necessary to make 84 converts?

The biggest obstacle to my saying *Yes* to this unexpected thought/feeling was that I'd never really stopped to consider who I was, had never even stopped to consider that I even *needed* to consider it, because who I was supposed to be or more accurately supposed to become had already pretty much been laid out for me, my whole life long. I was supposed to become and in fact desperately wanted to be the guy I was sure the people at church and God Himself expected: a guy like the great Mormon missionary Wilford Woodruff, or the Book of Mormon hero Ammon, or any of the other big heroes held up to me for as long as I could remember. The idea of just being plain old myself, if by that was meant being myself as currently constituted in the form of still mostly English-speaking me, just sounded so weak, like God was giving up on me as someone who had the potential to become *really* special. If the thought/feeling *Just be yourself* really was coming from God, then it had to be referring to the *yourself* I eventually would become, my *true* still-dormant self, not the *yourself* I was right now.

But I was disturbingly getting the distinct feeling from the thought/feeling that oh yes it was trying to tell me something along the disappointing lines of being content with who I was right then. I should just be my own self, not my special self. That thought/feeling wasn't just a big disappointment but a big surprise too, because all the church councils and scriptures and sacred histories seemed to be about *not* being content with yourself, but to be(come) what God wanted you to be(come), to lose your (presumably ordinary) self in order to find your true (presumably great) self, all of which was pretty much the whole repetitive point of Augustine's *Confessions* too. *Just be yourself* sounded like some syrupy Hollywood idea, like Good Witch Glinda telling Dorothy that what she needed to solve her problem had been right under her nose the whole time rather than behind the magical curtain in Oz she'd worked so hard to reach. What a crappy ending, I'd thought watching that on the neighbors' color TV. What a cop-out. And then Oz himself turned out to be a guy who didn't really have much more on the ball than anyone else. At least the Wicked Witch of the West drew big words in the sky!

All that running through me in just a few seconds made me doubt again that the overwhelming thought/feeling *Just be yourself* could've come from God at all. Besides, wouldn't God have sent it out King-James style, like *Verily be thyself?* And what about those chills and thrills and heroic feelings I'd had in recent months while pondering just how big Flemish-speaking going-foreign me could be? Those feelings had been way bigger than this quiet little wimpy thought/feeling. Maybe *Just be yourself* was the stomach ache. Or maybe the devil was up to his usual tricks of turning himself into an angel of light, trying to make me think something was from God when it was really from the cagey old devil himself, because if that didn't sound like something the devil would say, *oh you're good enough already,* then I didn't know what did. I'd already heard at church (and the very first Jesuit, Ignatius Loyola, had said the same thing centuries before) that there were three influences working on you when you prayed: your own self, God, and the devil. That meant there was only a one-in-three chance that what I was thinking/feeling right now actually was coming straight from God Himself, and a two in three chance it was from somewhere bad.

But *Just be yourself* was so strong and clear and calm and persistent, and I was so sure that I never on my own would have invented such an inglorious answer to my emptiness, that even though the thought/feeling went against most everything I'd learned or wanted to be, it finally sank in deep enough for me to take it seriously, and thus to go into actual thinking mode.

Now that I thought about it, it wasn't exactly obvious what *Just be yourself* meant. You'd have thought it would be. You'd have thought that just being yourself was about the easiest and most natural thing in the world, and that someone like Paul Tillich was just wasting his time writing his famous book, *The Courage to Be,* because why in heck would you need courage to just be you?

But it turns out you don't always want to be you, because you know very well all the spectacular failures and character flaws lurking around inside, and you think that maybe it'd be nicer to be someone else instead, who obviously doesn't have all those failures and flaws. You also know that God knows all about your lurking failures and flaws too, and you suppose He doesn't like them and wants you to be a much-more-acceptable-to-Him you. And you especially know that the people around you, a.k.a. your culture, don't really want you completely to be you either, but only the parts of you they approve of, especially the parts that are most like them, because that's what they're basically telling you all the time: *be more like us, or at least the way we imagine ourselves to be.* Oh, the culture gives you some structure, and direction, and mooring, and other helpful metaphors, it does, but it can also give you some pretty heavy ones too, like a taskmaster, or even, say, a steamroller. And especially with that last metaphor rolling around it's easy to feel like in the end maybe no one is really all that interested in standing up for oddball idiosyncratic three-dimensional just-the-way-you-are you, so you end up trying to be someone else instead.

Maybe it's only when that doesn't work out so well that you finally and mostly out of desperation get enough nerve to let out that teeny tiny oddball idiosyncratic part of yourself that actually might make you most you, the part that might allow you to make your own particular and possibly impossible-to-replicate contribution to life. But isn't it just a little absurd that you are now having to *learn* to be you, which is about as absurd as a fish having to learn to swim? With all that going on, you can see why Tillich put *Courage* and *Be* in the same title, or why it might take a thought/feeling from heaven to get you to do what you'd think would be as natural as waking up: to just be yourself.

But I still didn't know what that meant, and at the moment all I could come up with was what it probably didn't mean. Like it probably didn't mean just blurting out whatever I was feeling at the moment, or just doing whatever I felt like doing: not even Rabelais's famous old abbey of Thélème with its world-famous motto *Do as you will* meant that.* It probably also didn't mean never trying to get better at something. But that was all I could think of.

Actually that wasn't a bad start, because *not* being something is how all sorts of people and cultures start trying to figure out who they are. Adolescents start out *not* being their parents. Churches start out *not* being Catholic or *not* Protestant before they are positively Protestant or Catholic. Even theologians hoping to define God might start with the *negative* or *apophatic* way, trying to pin down first what God is not. Hindus are maybe more apophatic than anyone, so it's only fitting that they should have invented the best apophatic chant of all time, a chant that could work either in the quiet of a calm mountaintop or in the racket at Soldier Field:

> *Not this,*
> *not this,*
> *neither this,*
> *neither that.*

This is what Bears fans are yelling, with slightly different words and a lot more gesturing and beer than a Hindu holy man would use, when they see

* Described in his very non-abbey-like *Gargantua and Pantagruel* (1530s).

something on the field they don't like. But a guy could chant the same thing in private too, when seeing something in himself that he wasn't.

In fact even though *Just be yourself* was technically a positive rather than negative way of putting things, I was pretty sure that in my case it was meant to be understood as purely apophatic — i.e. to *not* be the grandiose guy(s) I'd been trying to be and that I imagined others and God expected me to be, to *not* think of myself as the savior of Belgium, to *not* secretly think myself superior to other missionaries, to *not* think Flemish-speaking me was my true identity instead of just a language mode. And more. And given the low spirits the grandiose guy(s) had brought me to, I was at last and maybe unbelievably willing to at least *consider* not being him (them).

But it was still hard. In fact not three minutes later I was mistrusting the *Just be yourself* yet again, because once again I started worrying about who in the world had given me authority to do such a radical thing.

It would've helped to know that, contrary to what I'd assumed, there was in fact some actual authorized authority, including in church councils and scriptures and sacred histories. You could read Jesus's *The kingdom of heaven is within you,* in Luke, to encourage looking inside yourself, but a reading like that was beyond me at the time. You could say *Just be yourself* was implied in the great commandment to love others as yourself, but I didn't yet understand the implications of *implied.* And you could argue *Just be yourself* was what the Gnostic Gospel of Thomas meant when it said *If you bring forth what is within you, what you bring forth will save you. If you do not bring forth what is within you, what you do not bring forth will destroy you,* but I knew even less what a *Gnostic* was than what *implied* was, and if I had known I would've been scared off by all the times the Gnostics had been condemned. And so to me *Just be yourself* was still hanging out there pretty much by itself with no comfort-giving authority to support it, as though I was being reckless and defying everything sacred around me, maybe even God Himself, even by entertaining the thought.

But lo and behold there was even precedent in church councils and scripture and sacred history for defying what previous church councils and scripture and sacred history had said. Saint Peter had to be one of the most defying of all, having a dream in which God told him to go ahead and eat things that he and everyone else in his culture had supposed God and church councils and scripture and sacred history had declared unclean. Or there was the big Book of Mormon hero Nephi, who against all the church councils and scripture and sacred history went and cut off the head of someone because a thought/feeling he took to be from God told him to. You couldn't get much more reckless than that.

There was even support for the idea of being yourself in Mormon theology. Mormons believed God was the literal spiritual father of everyone, so if there was something of God already inside of you then maybe His will for You sometimes was to follow your own already divinely informed will. Maybe His will was even for you fully to be the oddball idiosyncratic self He'd presumably created you to be, rather than to be something else. Maybe losing yourself the way Jesus said meant losing the Handel-loving adolescent heroic self you thought you were supposed to be and being the self you actually were. And not just for some selfish reason but because the full version of yourself was the one that could love and live and help others and honor God best.

And there was support for being yourself in the famous Buddhist idea that the way to happiness was just through being, right now, rather than through focusing on what lay ahead — but wasn't that maybe what Jesus was saying too, with his famous *Take no thought for the morrow?* It wasn't that the morrow wasn't going to come, but that it'd take care of itself. Maybe that's how being and becoming were too: if you were focused on *becoming* (say, the Greatest Missionary in the World) then you weren't *being* (say, Whatever Sort of Missionary You Were), and if you weren't being then maybe you weren't living.

But again, almost all of those ideas were beyond me at the moment. What really won me over to entertaining even longer the theory of just being myself was how persistent and calm and assuring the feeling behind it was, even through all the doubts and worries still whirling inside. The *Just be yourself* thought/feeling not only felt better than any of the doubts and worries I still had, not only felt more likely to be from God than from me or the devil or other people, but even felt more likely to be from God than all of the big heroic feelings I'd had in the past. It was the best proof of God I'd had so far, it seemed to me, even if it was the calmest, even if it did seem to go against church councils and scripture and sacred history that all claimed to be from God too.

But of course one thing for dang sure was that someone as heroically inclined as I wasn't going to learn to be himself overnight, either negatively or positively. Even later that same afternoon I was already telling myself that maybe this whole just-be-yourself business was a temporary thing, a way to survive the hard times of the moment until my truly great still-dormant self actually emerged. But the basic thought/feeling was at least planted inside now, and gave me something to hang onto for all the times when I'd most assuredly go all grandiose, and thus be most assuredly beaten down, again.

Elder Klein knocked on the door to say it was time to go back outside: he knew to knock because I'd hung a sock over the outside doorknob, as Belgian missionaries always did when they were praying alone, to alert others not to walk in so you could have some privacy for a few minutes, in a day full of no other privacy at all.

I got up, opened the door, grabbed the sock, threw it over on my unmade bed atop the giant awful lumpy mattress, went downstairs, and put on my coat. After a song and a prayer we all headed outside again into the stark winter afternoon.

eleven

SNOW WHITE

If on Christmas Day of 1975 you happened for some harebrained reason to be outside on the frozen snow-covered Belgian tundra near the small town of Zichem, and you squinted up your eyes against the shiny white landscape to look east, then you would have almost certainly noticed in the distance the unlikely sight of four overcoated and possibly harebrained local businessmen trudging along on a slippery, messy path near a big field.

They weren't exactly sure where they were going or even whether the person they were going to see was interested in seeing them, but they kept trudging anyway because Christmas was a time to try extraordinary things.

They'd actually begun trying the night before, on the plush mauve carpet of their new living-room church in Hasselt, where they hosted a combination housewarming-party/Christmas-pageant extravaganza to celebrate not only the season but their joy at being out of their bar-top church at last.

It'd turned out that the local businessmen had been more joyous about the party/extravaganza than anybody else, as the four of them made up four entire fifths of the audience that came to watch a few of the few local Mormons act out the parts of the Christmas story that required only a very very few characters. It'd also turned out that the other member of the audience, the mother of the person playing Mary (Emmalina), happened to have some very strong feelings *against* acting out the Christmas story, and she decided to stand up and express those feelings just as her daughter was dramatically making her way with Joseph across the mauve-colored Egyptian desert: *this story,* insisted Mary's mother at unnecessarily high volume, *is too sacred as a common skit performed to be.* This caused Joseph (Tristan), walking alongside Mary in an ancient terry-cloth bathrobe, to do the unthinkable and break character. Turning to look right at Mary's mother instead of stage left and forlornly into the desert-distance the way he was supposed to, he started moving his scarf-covered head back and forth and raising his voice in return. This only made Mary's mother raise her voice even higher, this time in her native German, her more natural yelling language, but Joseph knew that language well enough to yell in it too. Mary just veiled her face hoping everything would be over soon, while Elder Shepherd broke character as an audience-member and intervened. In the end, the German-speaking scene in the Egyptian desert set in a living room in Flemish-speaking Belgium calmed down, the Holy Couple finished their journey to Bethlehem (the kitchen), and the evening ended surprisingly well, with everyone apologizing to each other for so many offenses freely given and taken in the spirit of the season.

Christmas Day had started out better than Christmas Eve, not least because the local businessmen were giddy at the thought of not having to tract, which would've been too much for Belgians whose patience was already stretched thin by bell-ringing at other sacred times, like dinner and Sunday afternoons. Today all the four of them had to do was attend a Christmas dinner and go around bearing gifts like local magi, which gifts they quickly realized endeared them a lot more to people than appearing on doorsteps empty-handed did.

Their first stop that morning had been at the home of precious *Zuster* Jans, whom they called *Zuster* even though she'd never been Mormon and never would be. In fact the local magi liked to call all the precious old ladies *Zuster,* not so much because the POL liked the title but because it made the local magi feel like they were still sort of doing their job while visiting them, subtly reminding the ladies that the invitation to convert was still out there, even if they were as old as Sariah. *Zuster* Jans was even lonelier than Maria and Martha because she had no family at all, so the local magi had brought her a card and a tart from a good bakery, which like all Belgian bakeries was open Christmas morning and Sunday morning because especially on special days did fine-dining Belgians want things fresh. The local magi prayed that *Zuster* Jans would dish up some of the tart itself to them rather than some of the endless *peperkoek* and bubbly water she always had in the house and supposed they loved. The prayer was partly answered, because she brought out a tray filled with both *peperkoek* and tart, which the local magi managed to get entirely down.

The four filled-up local magi had then taken another tart to their next stop, Christmas dinner with the Jaspers. The family wasn't close to rich, but like most Belgians they brought out their best today, starting with such feast-day favorites as shrimp cocktail, moving on to tomato soup with little meatballs, then *Koninginnehapje*,* then the main course(s) of potato croquettes and pork roast adorned with peas and carrots, or/plus meatballs topped by a heavy sweet sauce of half-apricots, then dessert of tart and herbal tea (coffee for most Belgians), then cheese, and then capped at last in most homes but not here (unless Willi was sneaking something in the other room) with cigars and brandy. How salvific it'd been for the four local maji to taste real food after a week of eating stale Christmas treats sent from home and after months of way too much oatmeal boiled and fried and maybe even poached.

They'd had to leave the dinner a little early and a little embarrassingly around 2:30 in order to get to their third and final destination of the day, which turned out not to be local at all: a house out in the countryside near Zichem, Flemishly named after the old Canaanite town in the Bible, and about 35 kilometers from Hasselt. In that country house lived a woman they'd just learned was officially on the membership roll of their little branch but who'd never even come close to showing up for church. The four of them decided that they'd go introduce themselves and wish her Merry Christmas by bearing the gift of yet another (surprise!) tart.

* The *Queen's Dish,* or in French *Vol au Vent,* a fluffy round pastry smothered with a sauce of chicken, meatballs, and mushrooms, which in most places and times was a more-than-satisfactory main course — but not at Belgian Christmas.

How in the world had this woman become Mormon, the local magi had wondered as they sat on the slow (and only) train to Zichem? All they knew was that she was poor, and that her house stood about five or six kilometers from the station, but they weren't exactly sure of its location because it didn't have an actual street address and so all they had from their torn-at-every-fold map were a few clues.

After arriving at the station, the local magi had pinned down the location a little more precisely, thanks to the help of a few chin-scratching locals, which led the local magi to realize that any bus they hoped to take to get themselves closer to the mysterious house did not exist, and not only because it was Christmas but because the roads leading to that home were nothing but dirt paths. If they wanted to reach the mysterious house, they'd have to walk across some fields and through the woods and maybe over a river as well.

Which was why anyone outside would've been able to see them in the distance today, looking like hunters in a Bruegel landscape.

While walking along I felt more content than an informed observer might've expected, given my recent troubles and the frosty circumstances.

Maybe it was because walking along a country road in the snow was still a country mile better than (sub)urban tracting, or maybe it was because I'd started being just a fraction less grandiose lately, thanks mostly to another unpleasant event I'd experienced while tracting. Just hours after my big calmness in the dismal upstairs bedroom a few weeks before I'd gone full-tilt grandiose again, this time on an atheist couple who'd been kind enough to let Elder Klein and me in from the cold and listen to a Discussion as long as they could take it, which to be precise was the moment when I'd boldly told the couple that no matter what they said or thought, God really did exist! That bit of what I'd supposed was pure heroism had gotten us thrown right out into the cold again and left even Elder Klein thinking that maybe

I'd been a little hard on the couple. In fact on reflection (at last), I realized I'd felt more mean than heroic in saying what I'd said, and had even felt something inside saying *not this, not this.* I'd even felt that maybe if it was important for me to be myself, then maybe it might be just as important to let other people, including atheists, be themselves too, and that I could do a little better job finding the line between offering my view of a subject and telling someone that if they didn't agree with it then they couldn't be happy, because really the line that ran between those two positions wasn't even a fine line but more like a four-lane double-divided highway. But at least I'd sort of found that line recently, and felt better when I decided to at least try respecting it.

The farther our little band of local magi trod through the frozen and half-frozen mud in our wing-tips, without seeing any houses along the way, the more we wondered whether the chin-scratching locals at the train station had given us wrong directions on purpose, the way people sometimes did to us, for a laugh. But we decided to trust them and just keep going, hoping that we'd get to the house before dark (around 4:30), and thinking that if we did, then we could find our way back to the station just fine, even in the dark.

The totally unexpected and unsought-after latest epiphany came around dusk. I didn't know exactly where we were on the road/path, and I'd never be able to find the spot again in my whole life even though I'd try, but I knew that when it happened I was looking to my right (west) down into a slight valley with slightly rolling ground and rickety-fenced fields that stretched all the way to the horizon, where the sun was probably just setting behind the white-gray clouds. And what I saw most of all when I looked was a white puffy mist stretching all the way across the little valley, a mist so white I couldn't always tell where the snow-covered ground ended and the mist began, or where the top of the mist ended and white-trending-gray heavens began, especially since the puffiness moved up and down as the ground moved up and down. But the valley and the puffs were low enough that I could see over them all the way to the slightly raised horizon. And suddenly from my own slightly raised angle looking across the valley into the last remaining light, the scene was no longer a frozen field bordered by rickety fences but something ethereal. No one was saying a thing, and so except for some occasional sloshing where the snow hadn't entirely frozen it was completely silent.

I didn't know whether the other local magi were seeing what I was seeing, or maybe just happened to be turning their heads to the right like I was, but I was smitten, overcome by not only the sort of calm I'd felt in the dismal upstairs bedroom but an unexpected joy too — at seeing all this, at being in this place, in this land. This beautiful, gray, occasionally bright white land.

The French writer André Gide once stood near a meadow in summer as a boy and saw a young girl move into it: suddenly the whole place was magical. Anyone else walking by at the moment might have seen some scientifically defined geological formation and a young humanoid. But Gide saw a vision. That's how it was for me near Zichem in winter: I saw a vision where someone else might have seen clouds and freezing mist and partly-sloshy snow. And not because I was more perceptive than anyone else but because I was made to see this place this way.

Just as darkness arrived, we found the woman's home. Maybe. There was no other house in sight, but there wasn't any nameplate or identifying address hammered up on this one to declare it as absolutely the right place. But this had to be it, didn't it? It sort of fit the vague description we had from our files, and the vague coordinates on our torn-at-every-fold map, and the especially vague directions from the chin-scratching fellows back at the station. The house stood at the edge of a bluff, which was unusual enough in flat Belgium, so again, this had to be it. But no one answered our knock, and not because they were pretending not to be home. Like at least half of Belgium today, they were at someone else's home. We hadn't called in advance because the woman didn't have a phone, so we'd just taken a chance. And lost. And now what to do with the especially big Christmas tart in the extra-large bakery box that we'd taken turns carrying all this way?

We couldn't leave it on the unsheltered porch, we decided, because there were wild animals around. The only shelter nearby was the chicken coop. That was it! The obvious place to put a fancy Belgian tart was inside a chicken coop — obvious if you were a city/suburb boy. We reasoned (sort of), well, the chickens were inside cages so they couldn't get at it, and there was a door to the coop that could be latched so no other animals could get at it either, and someone from the family would have to come home pretty soon to take care of the chickens, and so even though the tart might stink to at least mid-heaven before the woman and her family found it, even though it might taste like the stink too, even though it might be completely stale by the time they got home, at least it wouldn't get rained on or snowed on or eaten by the wrong creatures.

And what a shock it must have been for the family if/when they discovered the fancy tart in the chicken coop with an unsigned note on top that said only *Vrolijk Kerstfeest*. We'd decided to give our gift anonymously, supposedly in the spirit of pious giving but probably to avoid the embarrassment of being identified as the idiots who'd left a tart in a chicken coop. Real locals might've talked about that for weeks if they'd found out. We never knew though what the family thought, because we never went back to see the woman again, and she never came to visit us in Hasselt, which meant that we'd sort of defeated our purpose for going all the way out there, which was to identify ourselves. And which also meant that the woman would forever be oblivious to what a sublime experience it had been for at least one of the magi, even though the official purpose hadn't been achieved.

The four of us headed back toward the train station in the dark now. We couldn't see any misty field anymore or much of anything else either, because everything had faded to black, but unlike Gretel in the fairy tale we'd at least marked the path in our minds. Still, there was at least one more surprise for us on the way back, something we'd somehow missed the first time we passed by. Off to the right we now saw the ruin of a massive but crumbling brick tower that looked unimaginably old. Someone had a flashlight so we all went through the doorless doorway inside. Even though the place was empty, the flashlight shining on those interior bricks brought all sorts of images to my mind, not very well-informed images, mind you

— images of soldiers fighting and ladies swooning mainly, as those were the only things I could imagine people doing inside towers like this. But the main outcome was that I got an unforgettable impression of Belgium: that a lot more life had gone on here than anywhere else I'd ever been. As of this moment, all that life was no longer dead but breathing out right there on the crumbling-tower spot. Someday I'd actually learn what'd gone on in that tower, which was part of a big fortress and the site of a lot of bloody struggles that were a lot less romantic and a lot more horrible than I on that Christmas night could have understood.

Even though when we finally reached the station we had to wait almost an hour for our train, it felt good to at least have tried something extraordinary that day. But mostly what I felt inside was the transformation of the formerly obscure and mysterious land known as Belgium. Once I started seeing Belgium for what it was, instead of what I thought it should have been, it was more beautiful than I'd ever imagined it could be. Maybe that's how it was for any place. Or thing. Or one.

It was the best Christmas I'd ever had. Maybe the best I'd ever have. But when I finally flew back home from my mission, and people asked me as they always asked newly returned missionaries to tell a Christmas story, it didn't turn out so well. Because even though people said *Tell us a Christmas story from your mission,* what they were really saying was *Tell us a conversion story that happened at Christmas,* Conversion Motif 1m or so, which included the usual finding of the convert at the last door on the last street on the last hour of the day, but added the seasonal touch of some holly and ivy and good cheer, all of which made everyone listening feel even better than they did when listening to an ordinary conversion story. *Make us feel even better than usual!* was what people were really saying when asking for a missionary Christmas story.

The reason I knew this was that the one time I tried to tell my Christmas story I got a lot of blank and confused looks. Oh, my story was a conversion story all right, but not the sort that the clamoring crowd was expecting. It didn't have a baptism, and I couldn't come close to getting across what I'd seen in the landscape, and of course I left out the most personal bits that really gave the story its meaning — and bowdlerized like that, even I had to admit it sounded like a dumb boring story. The smiles of anticipation that accompanied the start of my story, the knowing looks of knowing for sure what was coming, just kept fading and looking more and more puzzled as I went along, and then at the end totally screwed up into absolute confusion. That was it? No baptismally white Christmas (you wore all white at baptisms) but only a landscapey white one? Just a pie in a chicken coop for some people you never saw who never came back to church and who might never have actually seen the pie and who come to think of it might not even have lived there? And just a crumbling tower ruin with no magic investigator in it? What kind of a Christmas story was that? What kind of missionary (eyebrows furrowing) were you? Next story from someone else! I never told it again.

But the story always meant everything to me. Seeing gray old Belgium in a new way got all tied up with seeing myself and people around me in new ways too. All the things that'd bugged me about Belgium started either not bugging me or became interesting and perfectly acceptable, started being not necessarily the wrong way to do things but just another and potentially interesting way, including the bad-tasting *witloof* and the gray and the whiny motorcycles and the sometimes closed-mouthed people.

I started understanding that people shook hands like they were offering a dead fish because they didn't want to come across as aggressive.

I started liking the huge horses I saw pulling plows instead of thinking they were so backward, started liking the old farms instead of thinking they were smelly, and started liking the lumpy pastures with rickety fences instead of thinking they were messy.

I started seeing the benefits of serious cloud-cover as opposed to the 105-degree heat of my hometown.

I started waving in a friendly and not sarcastic way to the old ladies who never ever let missionaries in and therefore never became precious, but just kept watching forever fearfully from the window.

I already liked the predominantly-non-butt-kicking old men on the street who we mostly out of affection called *bubs* and who would stop and talk to you about the wars anytime you wanted, all you had to do was say *14-18* or *40-45* with a question mark and off they would go, but now I liked them even more.

I started liking the funny dialects people spoke at me instead of thinking they were just bad Dutch.

I liked the food even more the more I understood how things went together and what food meant here, and without even trying I started learning the names of a lot of the 300 local beers I didn't drink.

I started seeing how kind people in general were once they got over their suspicions, even if they rarely wanted a first Discussion much less a second or third, like the angelic lady on the non-electrified farm who one night let Elder Klein and me inside her farmhouse and said she didn't want to hear any talk of religion but gave us some warm cow's milk and told us in all sincerity that she saw halos around our heads, which wasn't just the result of the dim firelit room, she assured us, which made us feel surprisingly good.

Of all places, Belgium was now firmly inside me, more like something I discovered was already there instead of something I had to learn, because when I later saw Flemish art and read Flemish history they weren't the only art and history I liked around Europe or even the world, but they always felt the most familiar, and not just because I was partisan but because they somehow already fit me, just like the Flemish language did, or the Flemish landscape, especially the landscape with snow on it near Zichem. Okay, Belgium wasn't the most famous of countries, even with all its great art and food. It wasn't exactly the country you'd expect a guy to pick as his favorite. And it wasn't always highest on the hygiene meter. But it was perfectly suited to me, and maybe was even a lot like me too.

Of course helping my mood too that Christmas was the new mauve-carpeted-living-room church we'd just moved into, a move made possible because the Mission President had visited town and gotten a taste, or more accurately a whiff, of the bar-top church and even though we hadn't filled that church with converts he told us to look for a better one anyway. We joyously complied, and this semi-detached brick house in a newish neighborhood was what we'd found. The living room was the chapel, the upstairs bedrooms were the Sunday School classes (class), and the modern kitchen was the modern kitchen. We couldn't live in the bedrooms/Sunday-school-classrooms upstairs, said the rules, but we could live in the little spare room just off the kitchen, which was separate from the rest of the house/church, and so the four of us had gladly fled our apartment with the dismal upstairs bedroom, and squeezed two bunk-beds and one armoire into the little room off the kitchen and called it a bedroom. We could at least use the rest of the house for study in the mornings.

But what changed my view of Belgium even more than pile carpeting and efficient heating did was my epiphany just before Epiphany while walking unsteadily alongside a misty field somewhere in the frozen environs of the once-sad town called Zichem, where everything suddenly seemed familiar.

It all said *this, this.*

twelve

STONED AGAIN

I peered out the window trying to see whether the station my train was slowing down for was the one I wanted, because there were a lot of stations in Brussels, and the blue-and-white signs saying *Schaarbeek/Schaerbeek** told me that yes sir this was definitely it.

I grabbed my giant green mostly-cardboard suitcase and caromed out the train door, looking left and right along the platform for the baggage car, where my purple bike was supposed to be emerging, and looking also for my new companion, who wasn't just any old new companion but none other than the guy I'd from the start dreamed of being companions with: Elder Downing.

Oh, I'd been happy about my twin epiphanies in Hasselt, but I was even happier about being transferred to the most cosmopolitan city in the mission with the most ideal missionary I could imagine. The unfortunate little incident with The Stone back in the LTM hadn't changed my glowing image of Elder Downing one bit, because the more I thought about it the more I was sure that me myself and I had been entirely to blame. And now I had

---

* Public signs in Brussels are by law written in both Dutch and French. In other parts of Belgium public signage is in the prevailing language, but things like cereal boxes and soup cans are labeled in all three Belgian languages (there's a tiny German-speaking corner too). All that multi-lingualism on so many writing surfaces keeps a lot of translators and copywriters happy, and probably makes up around 83 percent of GNP.

a chance to prove to Elder Downing what a humongous aberration that whole thing had been.

Who'd have thought?(!), I excitedly thought. Your odds of being companions with any of the 149 other missionaries were really long, but your odds of being companions with the person you most wanted to be companions with were almost infinite. The only thing better would've been if we'd been sent to open a new city together, because from what I'd heard there was nothing more heroic than opening a new city.

Ah, heroic. Maybe the only little blemish in this big lovely picture was that going to Brussels with Elder Downing was the perfect recipe for me to break my promise and go all grandiose again. Just ten minutes into the train ride I'd even started forgetting what I'd learned in the dismal upstairs bedroom and snowy white field about being content with myself and my surroundings, not to mention about accepting limits and accepting that I even had limits, because I was already seeing stars again and thinking that finally my mission was going to go the way I'd always thought it would. Sure, short non-r-rolling Elder Klein was a nice guy who tried hard and all that, but Elder Downing was tall and could trill his r's like an Arab woman in mourning, among many other talents. Put those together with my talents, and wow. I'd even on the train started soberly pondering whether it'd really been all that wise for the Mission President to put two all-stars like Elder Downing and me together on the same team. Wouldn't it have been better for the mission to spread the talent around a little more?

I wasn't thrilled about still being a Junior companion, of course, but Elder Downing himself had just been made Senior this very transfer, so I couldn't complain. Instead I just focused on what an honor it was to be his first Junior. I imagined that he'd be glad about the situation too, because really how much training would he have to do with a guy like me? We'd be more like equals than Junior and Senior. We wouldn't be Jew and Gentile, or bond and free, but full local-business-partners. And we probably wouldn't be together that long anyway, because both of us were almost certainly going to be promoted soon, I was sure of that.

I'd run myself ragged and gotten myself respiratorily sick while putting things together to leave Hasselt and trying to say goodbye to all the precious old ladies I was sure would miss me, but I was so thrilled about my new situation that as soon as I spotted Elder Downing himself in the glorified flesh I forgot all about my sickness. If the hilarious inside jokes and silly handshakes he greeted me with were anything close to reliable barometers, then just as I suspected he was giddy about the transfer too.

They do things differently in Brussels, Elder Downing started explaining when we both finally arrived at our new apartment on the western edge of the city, in a suburb called Dilbeek (Elder Downing had hauled my giant green suitcase by bus, while I'd ridden my bike alone through the terrifying traffic, glad that it at least wasn't raining or snowing).

The apartment was classic Mormon-mission style, and thus a huge let-down from the modern semi-detached I'd enjoyed during my last weeks in Hasselt. It was more like my first apartment, featuring three drab rooms on the top (third) floor of a really narrow row-house on a noisy highway. The four beds of the four missionaries who lived here all lined the walls of the least cold room, each bed covered with red wool blankets but not necessarily sheets. Each companionship had one of the other two rooms for storing clothes and getting dressed and studying. There was also a small fourth room that'd once been a bathroom but that'd since been divided into a tiny kitchen and an even tinier bathroom, the division proclaimed by an opaque plastic accordion-style sound-enhancing door.

Still traffic-shocked, I was inside that bathroom now, easily hearing everything Elder Downing said about why Brussels was different, but finding it hard to concentrate since the toilet was located beneath the lowest part of the bathroom's sharply slanted ceiling, a strategy that brilliantly optimized floor space but that almost entirely eliminated the equally crucial air space you liked to see right above a toilet too. Anyone brave enough to use the thing while standing had to lean the upper half of his body backwards at the same angle as the sharply slanted ceiling, twist his head sideways, and then show the sort of balance, endurance, flexibility, and aim usually seen only on a biathlon course.

For one thing, Elder Downing was saying, I could say goodbye to the bike I'd just parked downstairs, inside the landlords' garage. Missionaries in Brussels didn't ride bikes, because it was so dangerous (couldn't disagree with that), and also because Flemish-speakers were spread so thin around this big mostly French-speaking city. So missionaries rode trams and busses instead. Now there was the finger of God, I thought, realizing immediately that this would mean a lot less time in the rain.

For another thing, Elder Downing continued as I now took a seat on my new bed, missionaries here — hold on to your corduroy hat — did *not* tract. Both of us burst out laughing at that revelation. Flemish-speakers were so few and far between that tracting was an even bigger waste of time in Brussels than usual. What you did instead was ride trams and busses to busy pedestrian areas and find Flemish-speaking people right on the street. Then in the evenings you'd go look those people up who'd been willing to write down name and address and have you over some night for a chat. That had to be better than tracting.

In fact during those first tracting-free days in Wonderland it was, as we hopped from one bus or tram to another, flashing our new laminated metro passes and being dazzled by all the lights and posters of local stars and products. If we didn't know who the French singer Sylvie Vartan was before arriving in town (we didn't), then we found out fast, because her picture (along with those of a lot of other barely dressed ladies I tried not to look at) was everywhere. It was a lot easier not to look at posters of the local singing superstar Will Tura, a sort of Flemish Wayne Newton.

Even the trams were dazzling, from the spanking new modern yellow versions with a live conductor and automated ticket-takers, to creaky old models with a creaky old live conductor at the front and a creaky old live ticket-taker at the back, who at what seemed to be totally random moments suddenly both started turning creaky old wooden cranks for all they were worth, in order to stop and start and for all I knew maybe exfoliate the tram too, because sometimes absolutely nothing happened from all that turning, as far as I could see. The busses were more dizzying than dazzling, in all that traffic, especially on the long flimsy elevated road we took almost every day into town and back — four skinny lanes with two skinny rails on the sides and occasional skinny pillars beneath to hold the whole thing up and no shoulders whatsoever but only a 20 foot drop over the rails if one of the honking speeding cars accidentally or purposefully bumped into you.

But most dazzling and dizzying of all were all the chic places we went to with all the chic names, like Avenue Louise, or Boulevard Anspach, or Rogier Square with its Sheraton Hotel and Martini Building featuring a huge martini glass, olive and all, blinking on the front.

But it didn't take long, like about four days, for the bright lights of Brussels to start fading as fast as bright lights anywhere, because not even the lights and fancy names could hide the fact that proselyting in Brussels was not only as hard as it was anywhere else but maybe even harder.

Just about every morning we got on the M bus right outside our door, nodded at our nodding driver, and rode all the way to Rogier Square, where we stepped off in the middle of a busy pedestrian area and went to work. Usually we started walking south, down Boulevard Adolphe Max, toward the next big Square over, De Brouckère Square, where the name of the boulevard changed to Boulevard Jules Anspach, which we'd walk down too. All along the way we'd talk to every guy we could, stepping slightly in front of them and asking, *Excuse sir, speak you Dutch?* Most men weren't used to being spoken to on the street by a stranger, especially one in a stainless-steel suit like Elder Downing's, and so they were usually stunned enough to stop momentarily, look you quizzically up and down, say *No,* and keep on walking. Even if they said *Yes,* the men'd usually start walking fast again as soon as one of us started explaining what we were doing there, most of the time using the recycled language we'd learned from the bad old days of tracting. This'd go on for an hour or two, Elder Downing talking to one guy, I the next, and once in a while someone would give us name and address for potential future conversation at home. When we reached the end of the

143

boulevard, we pulled out our fat book-map of Brussels and caught a tram or bus somewhere else.

But it turned out that this fancy new method of full-time street-contacting was just a movable form of tracting. In fact in Brussels full-time street-contacting was maybe even worse than plain old tracting, because having to establish whether a guy spoke Dutch made the whole epically inefficient process even more epically inefficient than usual. What did go faster now was rejection-speed, which rose to levels never even contemplated in plain old tracting, which I'd always assumed was the gold standard for rejection-speed. Regular tracting could yield one rejection maybe every two minutes, but bouncing from one guy to the next on the streets of Brussels could raise it to one every 20 seconds. And if you and your companion divided up (still within seeing distance of each other) so that you could talk to even more people, then your aggregate rejection-speed hit world-record levels.

Compounding all this was that of the few people willing to give you name and address, at least 37 percent (or maybe 73) told us something fake. Had the guy made an honest mistake when he'd written down the address of an empty field, an abandoned warehouse, his mother-in-law, or some unsuspecting citizen? Or had he been half-smiling? It could take all late-afternoon and evening to look up maybe six or seven such addresses, and not just because the city was big but because we spent a lot of time making sure a fake was a real fake, thinking that we ourselves must have it wrong, because no way would the nice fellow we'd remembered talking to have given us a fake address. So we'd look in the map again and try all streets with a similar spelling, even if they were all the way across town, or we'd try number 18 on the street instead of 81, only to have some angry French-speaking person we'd never seen before start yelling at us that it was too late to be knocking on especially French-speaking doors.

The only good thing about all that wandering at night was that it slowed down the overall rejection-speed for the entire day. And maybe one other good thing was that it gave Elder Downing and me a lot of time to get to know each other, and to talk about school, and jobs held, and careers con-templated, and the girl he was writing and planning to marry, and the girl

I was sort of writing and distantly hoping to marry, and of course all the *Success!* we wanted to have here in this unusual city. And that sort of talk and camaraderie were just fine with me.

Except all that sharing, and all that spending of time together, didn't necessarily keep on boosting camaraderie the way I'd hoped. In fact just as difficult as the proselyting part of the picture in Brussels was, to my absolute astonishment, the companionship part, and each part just kept aggravating the other.

I was already fully aware by now that constant companionship was almost money-back guaranteed to bring out things that'd surprise and yes even alarm you about the person usually only inches away from you most of the day. But something about the vibe with Elder Downing was proving to be more troubling than usual.

The first sign of trouble came just a few weeks in, when I was writing in my journal that *we need to work on our relationship,* mostly because the devil's favorite trick was to cause contention between companions, because where there was contention there was no Holy Ghost, and where there was no Holy Ghost there wasn't going to be any converting going on.

The trouble might've started with the latest huge theological controversy missionaries just couldn't get enough of, this one over whether our fellow teenaged Mormon, Donny Osmond, should go on a mission. I was with the Nay's, insisting that he would obviously stir up too much fuss wherever he went, and that he'd do more for the church by singing and dancing in Hollywood than by knocking on doors in Japan: *we have ourselves referrals gotten, thanks to Donny Osmond,* I reminded. But Elder Downing sided firmly with the Yea's, because the prophet had said that *every* young man should go on a mission and did you hear him say *except for Donny Osmond? You can believe what you want,* concluded Elder Downing, *but the prophet said everyone.*

What made this more than the typical squabble, though, was the way Elder Downing tilted up his head while making that last declaration, tilted it up at an angle that said *there's no chance in the world that you're right or that your view is even valid but Senior Companion I will put up with your wrongness until Junior Companion you figures things out.* And that just four-alarmed me. It opened my eyes to the impossible possibility that there might be some serious rifts between us on other subjects too, some of them possibly even important, and that we might not actually be the full equal-share partners I'd imagined we were.*

My ever-lingering mystery illness didn't help things either, the illness that'd been lingering since the day I'd arrived in Brussels and that probably not coincidentally just kept getting worse the more these little conflicts with Elder Downing kept happening. Multiple visits to the doctor turned up nothing, with each visit seeming to exasperate Elder Downing and me and the doctor a little more, and finally the exasperated doctor said for me not to work more than six hours a day, and even better to do like most tired Belgians and go to Spain for a month to recover, which I laughed at in public but in private actually hoped the Mission President would okay. He didn't, so I settled for working shorter hours, which on the one hand was a relief but on the other just absolutely stress-inducing. Because if you wanted to become the Greatest Missionary in the World, as I and Elder Downing too wanted to become, then sitting around inside reading books and listening to tapes from home wasn't going to do the trick. Oh, it was nice for a while, but it wouldn't get you to the top of the missionary heap that we both were very much interested in getting to — and I was to blame. Elder Downing was polite about it, and maybe even as torn as I was sometimes about the shorter hours, but after a couple weeks of six-hour days and even less teach-

---

* Many years later, I saw part of an interview with Donny Osmond on his 50th birthday, during which he explained that he hadn't gone on a mission because church leaders had advised him not to for the very reasons I'd suggested to Elder Downing. Which made me remember the old dispute and chuckle. But when the more recent teenage Mormon heartthrob David Archuleta announced that he was indeed going on a mission, Elder Downing would have had grounds to chuckle himself.

ing hours than usual I felt guilty enough to ignore the doctor and just up my working hours to eight, then nine, then 10 a day, just short of the usual 10½. Maybe that was still enough to help us both get where we both wanted.

But the little incident that convinced me we had more than a routine problem here was my horrible unlawful letter.

One day we had a Discussion with a man who broke down crying over the fact that his 21-year-old son wouldn't speak to him. This made me start thinking that maybe I hadn't spoken to my own father as much as my father deserved. That very night I had a dream that filled me up with all sorts of hitherto unexpressed affection that I wanted to express before it went away. So when I woke up the next morning, I decided to write my father, even though it wasn't P-Day, the official (and only) day for writing letters.

Oh, I knew very well that technically I was breaking a rule, but I was also already familiar with the notion that sometimes two good things clashed and that when they did then you might have to choose one over the other. In this case I was sure that writing this good letter outweighed the good rule about not writing today. So when Elder Downing went into the bathroom to get ready, I took out one of my really lightweight light blue aerogrammes and wrote my letter in 10 efficient minutes.

But he finished what he was doing before I did, and when he came back into the room he was horrified to see an aerogramme out, and sternly said so. I explained that I respected the rule, just like I did every other rule, but it wasn't like I was writing some girl, and today it was very important that I write this note to my father. Which a scoffing Elder Downing took as just the biggest bit of self-deception or devil-listening he'd ever heard, because the rule in the white book was clear as the glass on the Martini building: *write your parents once a week on Preparation Day.* If I thought it was okay to break it then I was pretty obviously being misled, and by the way which rule would I decide I could break next?

There was no need for anyone to state what was really being argued about here, because both of us knew that perfectly well. To convert people, and to therefore rise to positions befitting the Greatest Missionary in the

World, it wasn't enough to get the Discussions perfect: you also had to be practically perfect yourself, with perfect here understood to mean *flawless,* rather than the word's more classic and sanity-saving meaning of *finished* or *complete.** And the way to determine whether you were practically perfect in every way (beyond the Discussions) was to measure yourself against the rules engraved in the official white missionary book.

What Elder Downing was expressing, in other words, was the highly popular missionary view that if you didn't obey 100 percent of the rules 100 percent of the time, then you couldn't be worthy of God reaching down and blessing you with converts, or maybe even Discussions. Not in Belgium at least. Maybe in Brazil, where converts were supposedly running up to missionaries and begging to convert, you could slip up a little. But not here. One false step and God would seal up the heavens, just like he'd sealed them up from the Israelites for breaking the rule about that golden calf, and no one would listen to you. And you'd never be the Greatest Missionary in the World.

I knew this was Elder Downing's fear, because I had it too. I already believed in the Univariate Theory of Conversion (and Rejection): that the Holy Ghost alone caused conversion and the devil non-conversion. But I was more convinced than ever from what leaders said that my own personal worthiness was the real key to the conversion business. *I* was the one who really determined whether the devil would be locked out and the Holy Ghost let in. That was why I'd thought hard and carefully before deciding to write my technically unlawful letter: I didn't want to risk offending the Holy Ghost, and so I didn't go ahead until I was sure I wouldn't. But Elder Downing was just as sure or even more sure that I had offended, and that my nefarious sin would be on his unwilling head too, just like the sins of one person in a medieval village threatened everyone else. Sure, we were giving a pretty fair number of Discussions, especially for Brussels, but as far as Elder Downing was concerned we weren't going to get to that next

---

* *Finished* or *complete* was what *perfect* meant in Matthew 5:48, for instance: *Be ye therefore complete/finished,* which gave that thought a whole different meaning than it'd come to have in modern Mormon English. But I didn't know that yet.

step of actually converting someone if either one of us (certainly not him) was breaking rules.

I didn't know what to say to Elder Downing's stern reminder, beyond what I'd already said. If I'd been the sort of guy who always had all sorts of clever responses on the tip of his tongue instead of just smart-alecky ones, I'd have said that the point of the rule was to keep us from thinking too much about home and especially girls, and writing to my father for 10 minutes was not making me homesick but was actually helping me to feel better about my work. And I'd have said that I could've written in my journal or study notebook exactly the same words I'd just written on a cheap blue aerogramme and he wouldn't have batted an eye, but somehow because they were on an aerogramme then I was ruining all our hopes for conversion (and promotion) for at least the next week? And if I'd really wanted to twist the knife, I could've said that whenever he got a letter from his girlfriend, he usually spent the first 20 minutes of our work day reading it, and then rereading it at a bus stop or at lunch, and in my estimation he was breaking the rule about thinking of home in firm half-hour segments two or three times a week.

But I didn't say any of those things, because (a) those thoughts were just unsprouted seeds tumbling around inside me, and (b) he would've just said that the rule didn't say anything about not *reading* letters on non P-Days. So I just sat there tongue-tied instead, and fuming at being chewed out for a decision I felt responsible enough and equal enough to make, but now here I was being reminded of my Junior status, which by the way I didn't like being reminded of now that two people in my LTM group (both way behind me in memorizing Discussions) had just been promoted to Senior companion themselves while I so ignominiously had not.

I recovered enough to engage in some brief dark-clouded exchanges with Elder Downing on the way out the door, now in English (always a bad sign), and then all the way to the bus stop too, and then dragging on during the ten minutes we waited for the M. At one point, he calmly but condescendingly said something that made me feel particularly powerless, and that did it for me: now I raised my voice and to my own horror started bawling in frustration, blubbering out something to the effect that despite my Junior status I was just as much a missionary as he was and therefore had just as much standing to decide about a flippin' letter. Causing Elder Downing to just shake his head, look away, and say *Grow up.*

Grow up?(!) Again?(!) Just like with The Stone? This was what my model missionary was saying to me? Again? This was what he really thought of me? That I was not co-equal or consubstantial after all but just another Junior? A baby? A child who spake as a child? That we were just Jew and Gentile? He'd said it as calmly as he said everything else, of course, but his whole dismissive manner hurt me a lot more than yelling did. In fact if there'd been some contest where I had to choose between someone dismissing me and someone yelling at me, I'd have chosen the yeller every time.

When I was a boy and spake as a boy I sometimes bawled to get my way, but during my mission I'd never bawled once in front of anyone, not even when I'd felt like it. And now here I was, embarrassing myself in front of Elder Downing and also a local Belgian who'd just walked up to the stop too and who heard everything, and who because of that and only that would probably never become a Mormon.

I'd never felt this alone my whole mission.

Maybe Elder Downing hadn't either.

Here was the serious getting-along stuff, the serious sort of squabble. The sort that was way worse than arguing over the Sacrament prayer, or P-Day music. The sort that just like gray weather could make all your proselyting rejection seem even worse than it already was. The sort that made you feel like not even trying at all.

And we weren't even to the horrors at De Brouckère Square yet.

thirteen

Big Ol' Jed Had a Light On

When things with your fellow local businessmen had ebbed to their lowest ebb, when converts were still nowhere to be seen, when the whole mission business felt like it was about to go eternally bankrupt, you could always just look at the sky.

Especially in spring you could, when the rays of the weary sun were finally enough to push through the clouds for at least part of the day. Oh how joyous those occasional partly-sunny not-quite-halcyon days were for Belgians, who threw off their usual reserve and ran joyfully outside in search of a seat at one of the open-air cafés that popped up like dandelions across town and countryside whenever the weatherman uttered the nowhere-else magical words: *a possibility of sun tomorrow but I'm not promising anything.* And how joyous for local businessmen too, because suddenly your troubles felt a little lighter, and the vapor trails across the sky were a lot more clear.

The vapor trails were the real reason you were looking at the sky, see. In fact you and your suddenly aviationally-inclined fellow local businessmen looked at vapor trails way more than ordinary people did, even way more than you yourself ever had before arriving in Belgium. And no one had to tell you why: the long white plumes and the tiny little planes at the front of them somehow said *home.* They were your promise that someday, even though you couldn't believe it, you really would go back there.

Hopelessly giddy missionaries about to go home might spread their arms out wide and zoom around when they saw a vapor trail, but the more respectable visible response was to start quietly whistling or singing something like *Leaving on a Jet Plane,* or more likely (except for Elder Trimbo) the Steve Miller song *Jet Airliner.* Even if you didn't know what that last song was exactly about, even if you got most of the lyrics catastrophically wrong, like the guy who even though he knew the song's title kept insisting that the chorus was saying *big ol' Jed had a light on,* it didn't matter, because you always heard right the part that mattered most: *carry me to my home.*

Now, it wasn't like you wanted to drop everything and hop on a plane that instant. Not usually. There'd be too much shame in that. Besides, the world still seemed too big to organize something that complicated on your own. And besides that you actually wanted to accomplish something first, like convert multitudes and become the Greatest Missionary in the World. No, it was that vapor trails got your mind off the disappointments for a while, and numbed your hurt, and gave you some tangible if vaporized proof that one day you wouldn't have to stop people on the street any more, that one day somebody really would be glad to see you at their door, that one day you really would stop having stupid arguments with your companion, and that a plane would somehow play a big role in making it all possible, just like Steve Miller said.

Even though you yourself might pretend not to notice vapor trails, because you wanted to be known as a burner not a slacker, you noticed them all right, just like almost everyone, including even the real burners, like your rule-stickling companion, who despite all his stickling didn't even pretend not to look up at the sky. In fact he looked up longer than you might've expected, maybe thinking, you guessed, about running down the ramp to his girlfriend when he got home, because that's what you'd have been thinking if a girl had guaranteed she'd wait for you. You didn't mind him thinking about stuff like that sometimes, or even thinking about it yourself, because you just didn't have the time or energy or honesty to meet your individual and collective troubles head-on all the time, e.g. to have an all-out crisis in a dismal upstairs bedroom, or to totally lose it at a bus stop, whenever your world threatened to fall apart again. It was a lot more workable on an everyday basis to take the more classic approaches to problem-solving: pretend they weren't there, or better yet distract yourself from them and hope they'd go away.

That's what even you and your rule-stickling companion did most of the longsuffering time too: instead of going at each other's throats every chance you got, you mostly just let underlying things lie, and looked at the sky, and did other things like unto it.

Like thinking of just one more errand you had to run before you could start proselyting. Or maybe being glad you missed a whole day of proselyting because of a choir festival. Or maybe being secretly delighted that at the rare dinner you were invited to there was no way in the Belgian world you could stay only an hour, like the white book insisted, because you'd barely be getting the soup by then and it'd be rude to leave, spoon in hand.

Or maybe like playing Damnation Baseball when you proselyted, getting a single when you heard answer A from someone, a double when you heard B, a triple when you heard C, and a home run to hell when you'd heard them all. Or maybe doing like Elder Gabberd and just for a little fun walking up to guys eyeing girlie magazines at a kiosk and say, *Excuse meneer, but my friend and I are a survey making to learn why men at pornography look; would you a few questions can answer, please?* which'd chase the guy away and send Elder Gabberd into hysterics.

Or maybe like quitting a whole half-hour early on Friday nights to go meet the other local businessmen in Brussels at Zizi's Italian ice cream parlor, where you'd bond by ritually devouring a nine-scoop wonder called the *Coupe Americaine,* invented with the young overeating North-American male in mind. Or maybe like meeting up even on a non P-Day for a heavenly Liège waffle at Cave Man's, which you called the place because it was a hole in a recessed wall near Rogier Square and because the guy didn't speak any Dutch or possibly anything else, so you'd just exchange happy grunts and local-businessman-hand-signs to express how much you loved his product.

Or maybe like suddenly discovering how much you loved studying, or of all things going to church and other meetings, especially meetings with other missionaries, especially ones that lasted all day.

Or maybe like not minding as much as you said you did about being sick, or about your companion being sick so that you'd have to stay in with him, and maybe if there were four in your apartment you'd trade off staying in with the sick guy, arguing on the surface over who'd get to go out and who'd have to stay in but really arguing over who'd have to go out and who'd get to stay in, and what a relief if that last one was you, even though your apartment was sometimes cramped and fetid and moldy and alternatingly sweltering or freezing.

Or maybe like getting some relief by stumbling across someone famous, like the thoughtful bearded sunglassed fellow you stopped one day, who after a half-hour of talk finally pulled out his wallet to get 40 francs to buy a Book of Mormon and there in the wallet was a picture of him running, and you asked who he was, and he said his name was Ivo van Damme and he ran for the national team, and even though you hadn't heard of him you remembered that name when the guy won a silver medal in the 800 meters at the 1976 Olympics, and also when he died in a horrible car crash soon after.

Or maybe like even getting relief by talking to a Welsh *pig shepherd,* as you so cluelessly called him, who scammed you out of 60 whole francs (two whole dollars) by sobbing a big story about how his leg had just been crushed by a pig in France and could you give him just a little something to help get him on his way home, and those 60 francs were all you had, and giving them to him made you feel supremely virtuous, at least until you talked to Elder Gabberd and found out that six months before he'd had exactly the same conversation with exactly the same guy in Brussels. But you got some relief anyway because you could laugh that you'd both read things so wrong, just like the guy hearing the Steve Miller song so wrong.

But certainly the best relief of all, better even than the relief you got from looking at vapor trails, was in the form of a letter from the girl you were at least somewhat seriously writing.

Oh, getting any letter was a fine thing, even one of those cheap blue aerogrammes that tore in all the wrong places so you could hardly read it. But a crinkly onion-skinned thing in a real envelope on real stationery with loopy handwriting and nice smells and your name on it could keep you going for days.

Your rule-stickling companion might get an unbelievable two or even three good-smelling letters a week, but what else could you expect when he was writing the founder and president of a Waiting-for-Missionaries Club? What a lucky guy, you'd think jealously, writing a girl who'd not only promised to wait but who'd built a whole flippin' impregnable structure around herself to make sure she would. Run-of-the-mill Waiting-for-Missionaries-Club members might give in and start heretically dating someone while their guy was away, and even get booted out, but no way would a founding president do something like that: you knew she'd still be standing at the end, going to meetings all by herself if necessary. She was the Greatest Waiting Girlfriend in the World, which was only fitting for a potential Greatest Missionary in the World.

Every few weeks or so you'd get a neutral-smelling letter too, from the non-waiting Rachelle. Your heart would start pounding, then you'd hold the letter like a relic for a few seconds before opening it up, wondering what new clues of affection it might hold or whether it might instead be a heaven forbid Dear John, then you'd go into a room by yourself and subject the thing to an exegesis worthy of a Talmudic scholar.

You'd pore over the Salutation (how formulaic or heartfelt was this particular *Dear?*), ponder the hidden meaning in her Introductory Statements (*I really liked getting your letter* was promising but ruined by *because I enjoy getting letters*), mostly skip her Recounting of News (*I got a job at the gas station!*), thrill at her expression of Religious Sentiments (*I really needed the talk I went to hear on Repentance!* which was fantastic not because Rachelle was some big sinner but because it showed she was humble, which mattered because there was no way someone that beautiful was going to like you unless she was humble too, not to mention kind), jump for joy at her Near Declarations of Affection (always near the end of the letter, which you knew because you structured your own letters exactly the same way, Near Declarations like *I think you're a pretty neat guy! Your letters have really impressed me!* or *I'll bet your wondering why it's taken so long to write again! I hope you don't think it's because I don't care about you! Because I do! I think about you a lot! It's just that I write such corny letters!,* all of which, despite all the exclamation points, you'd taken as very good humble signs), and then you'd absolutely seize up in anticipation of the Signing Off.

Would it be *Love* or *Love ya?* you/ya wondered. She'd signed her first letter *Love,* which was a stunner, because you'd assumed you only wrote that to family or people you really loved and *Love ya* to people you didn't. But from then on she'd swung back and forth, throwing you into total confusion. She'd sign *Love* after a weak Near-Declaration-of-Affection, like *I'm out of things to say so I guess I'll go,* and then *Love ya* after a really strong NDOA, like *You've got me for an admirer!* And her *Love ya lots* didn't help, because was the *lots* or the *ya* the operative word? Since *Love ya* was casual, *Love ya lots* could mean you were liked more casually than ever.

And it still wasn't over, because there was still the all-important P.S., the thought of which was making you almost pass out, because here at the end was her final last chance to say what she'd maybe been wanting to say the whole time. Like *P.S. Maybe we can get together in a year or so and talk about your mission.* What joy! That was even better than *P.S. You wore braces too? Maybe we can get together and share notes.* And it was at least as good as the P.S. that asked you to give her a thrill and send another picture of yourself, although that panicked you too, because how were you going to get another picture of yourself that flattered you as much as the last one you'd sent?

When you were finished, you folded the letter back up, put it back in the crinkly envelope, and stuck it in your suit pocket in case you wanted to read it again on the bus for possible new meanings, when you got tired of staring out the window or didn't want to watch your companion read his own crinkly letter again, which outnumbered yours at a rate of about 9 to 1.

Maybe you liked those letters more than you should have, but if you did then you weren't alone. Even your rule-stickling companion was knocked off balance by such a thing, going into full-tilt happy mode when he got one but slamming the mailbox shut when he didn't. But you had to admit that you probably thought about your letters even more than he thought about his, because you didn't have the sure thing of a Greatest Waiting Girlfriend in the World waiting for you and so you had to wonder about things more. There was no way Rachelle was going to write two or three letters a week to you, or you to her even weekly. And since it took a week for a letter to go each way, then it was usually at least three weeks between letters, and sometimes more, causing all sorts of anxiety in between, until the next one arrived and you'd be relieved again.

But *relief* wasn't actually quite the right word with Rachelle, and neither was *distraction*. Watching vapor trails and going to Zizi's were distractions, Isaiah's tinkling brass was a distraction, but a letter from Rachelle was on a way higher plane than anything like that, including the planes. Oh sure, a girl could be a distraction if you thought about her too much, but unlike a *Coupe Americaine* or an Air France jet that just took your mind off things for a while, the girl you were writing somewhat seriously could motivate you to work harder than before. She might keep you going and trying even when you didn't want to, because you couldn't be unworthy of her when you got home. A letter from her was more like a religious experience than a religious distraction.

So even though the white book said to put out of your mind all thoughts of home and girls and worldly things like that, not only you but rule-stickling others found that sort of out-putting not just impossible but maybe even unnecessary. How could you put out all thoughts of home? You were supposed to write your parents every week, for one thing. For another, how could you lump in girls with *worldly things* or banish them out of your mind when they were mixed up with your fetchin' everlasting salvation, and when you were supposed to go home and marry one (soon) and propagate (soon), and when you were telling people all the lovesick time just how world-historically important marriage was? You had to think about marriage some, even though you were a non-dating out-of-practice letter-writing-only missionary who wasn't supposed to think too much about girls.

You and your fellow local businessmen didn't dislike girls, like Augustine did. You usually didn't want to castrate yourself either (there were stories), like Origen actually did. You didn't usually want to run into the desert with that other ancient Christian, Anthony, to get away from girls forever, because just like him you'd have still dreamt about girls anyway, probably dancing girls too, the way he did. You even officially thought that celibacy forever was plain bonkers. In fact some of your nineteenth-century predecessors had actually spent good chunks of their Mormon missions *looking* for (sometimes polygamous) wives, which was one of the things that'd made Mormon missionaries terrifying to so many people for so long, and that'd finally caused the church enough headaches to just say, that's it, no more looking at all, everyone just wait till you get home. By now missionaries had basically forgotten the practical reasons for the ban on girls, so that sometimes you felt like there was something inherently unspiritual about them, but it was still okay to write them, which meant you had to sometimes think about them too, which meant you'd sometimes end up talking about them, and not just on P-Day but at night when your work was done, or when you were sick, or when you were lost in the country or even city and had a long way to walk and talk with your companion, at least until one of you said *Okay let us on our work think.* But even though you felt a little guilty when you thought about girls, you didn't necessarily think about them in bad ways, and sometimes even felt like thinking about them was saving your mission.

In fact if you'd later tell your missionary story and hardly mention Rachelle in most of it, well that would just be full-on misleading, because she'd been there in your head for just about every moment of your mission, from your first wing-tipped step in Belgium until the very moment you flew back home.

When you woke up in the morning, she was already on your mind, which helped you get up and get ready. When you were reading scriptures, there she was in breathtaking Kodachrome, which made you want to study harder. When it was cold and gray and rainy outside and gloomy inside, or Maria and Martha and the blind man threw you over, or the vintage little old man kicked you in the butt, or your companion told you to grow up (again), well you'd have been embarrassed for Rachelle to see you in some of those moments but it was mostly the thought of her that kept you going, you had to admit, even more than the thought of God directly.

And when you fell asleep at night she was usually the last thing you thought of, and sometimes you dreamed in a part of your mind that only God knew about whether you might be lucky enough to someday fall asleep next to her instead of in this sheetless scratchy bed all alone.

Now of course you'd only think about her sacredly in all of this, and not too often, because those were the keys to thinking about a girl on a mission. If you thought too often, or carnally, well you were almost certainly hurting your chances not only of converting people but of having things work out with that girl in the form of say marriage, because God wouldn't help you then.

So you tried never to think about Rachelle carnally, though it must be said that this wasn't just because you were so supremely virtuous, but also very possibly because what you knew about carnality was pretty spectacularly incomplete. Oh, your parents explained as bravely as most parents of their generation could about birds and bees, but one conversation wasn't going to suffice for someone as clueless as you and as euphemistic as they. What you mostly knew on the subject were the things you remembered from that single nervous parental presentation full of hushed tones, the things your church leaders repeatedly but vaguely said not to do (mostly unspeakable), all the things a lot of your friends kept saying you should do (which sounded suspicious and involved a whole new set of euphemisms), and some of the things your biology teachers taught you (which mostly sounded like something happening in a lab), which all still added up to only part of a bad-fitting puzzle. Oh, you knew enough to be interested in the lesser manifestations like kissing, and of course there'd been the touching of those (three) girls, but even that last subject had shown just how spectacularly incomplete your knowledge was, because when you'd sheepishly told the bishop what you'd done the bishop had about knocked you off your seat with this completely unexpected question from nowhere: *was this above or below the waist?*

Below?

That question had thrown you for such a loop that for a few seconds your confusion overwhelmed your humiliation. Who'd want to touch below, you'd thought? Wasn't it obvious that the place where you weren't supposed to want to touch a girl was above? You'd managed to get out, *above,* and the bishop had nodded kindly. But wait, you'd thought to yourself: the bishop wouldn't have asked about above or below unless it mattered, as in one being worse than the other, which was when it'd hit you that maybe this whole line of questioning had something to do with the heavy and light petting stuff your church leaders had sort of but not quite sufficiently spelled out over the years. *Don't engage in either heavy or light petting* was what they'd said with really clenched jaws but very little detail, and you'd nodded your head soberly like you knew what they were talking about. But this talk with the bishop had finally done the trick: the difference between heavy and light, you realized, didn't have anything to do with intensity, the way the words suggested, but geography. On one side of the Mason-Dixon line was heavy petting, and on the other light. And heavy was worse. But you *still* weren't sure which one you'd done. The bishop hadn't clarified it for you, and you hadn't wanted to look stupid by asking. He'd mostly encouraged you and patted you on the back and didn't have to say not to do again whichever one it was that you'd done. Naturally you'd assumed you'd done the worst, or at least assumed that if you hadn't then whoever'd made up the terms had gotten them seriously backwards.

The point was that for myriad reasons you weren't going to do a whole lot of carnal thinking about Rachelle. Which was maybe one of the advantages of a little ignorance on that score: all the psychology books said that a male your age should've been tormented all the time by thoughts about sex, but it was hard to be tormented if you didn't know the details of what to be tormented by. Maybe you were tormented in an unaware sort of way, but in an aware way you were tormented only by wanting, like a young Augustine or millions of other young fellows before and since, *to love and to be loved* — and you didn't mean by that your parents or siblings but a particular girl.

You'd liked plenty of girls, but the ones you'd like most hadn't liked you back (the Cyrano de Bergerac syndrome), or some girls had liked you but not the ones you'd wanted (the Lifetime Movie syndrome), or some girls that you might've liked you'd stopped liking once you knew they liked you (the Groucho Marx syndrome*), all of which showed plenty of disturbing trends going on in your head. But with Rachelle there seemed at last to be a chance of a meeting of (pure) hearts, which was why you didn't want to lose her, and thus why you had to sacralize her and be worthy of her.

You didn't make any rude jokes any more about girls. You didn't (like some missionaries) rate in the tracting book the looks of local girls who answered Flemish-speaking doors. You not only put Rachelle's sacred picture in your scriptures, but when you accidentally-on-purpose let someone else see that picture you did so reverently, without any testosterone-laden chuckles or leering looks or elbows in the ribs. When you thought about finally sacredly meeting her and being sacredly near her it wasn't rolling around in some meadow full of wavy grass and fluttering butterflies, but more like sitting on a bench in that meadow and holding hands and reading the Book of Mormon together, with a lot of gazing and hand-holding, and okay maybe some very soft kissing, while you oh-so-benevolently instructed her in all the special mysteries you'd learned on your mission, all this seen through a soft-filtered lens.

And when you oh-so-occasionally allowed yourself to think in a little more thought-provoking detail about her beauty, you did so in the authoritatively canonized terms known to every Bible-believing smitten teenager for centuries: the love-dripping words of the Song of Solomon. You liked how the young Palestinian woman there (the Shulamite) loved staring at her Beloved and memorized all his features. Not that you wanted lily white skin and bushy black hair like his (you still insisted you were trending to blond), or eyes like the *doves by the rivers of waters, washed with milk,* or cheeks like *a bed of spices, as sweet flowers,* or *lips like lilies* full of sweet-smelling myrrh — just that you wished Rachelle would pay that level of attention to your own vague features in the overly flattering pictures you'd sent her. The Beloved paid even more attention to the Shulamite's features

* Referring here to his famous quip that he wouldn't belong to any club that would accept him as a member.

than the Shulamite paid to his, which gave you even more material to think about Rachelle with, like that her cheeks were comely and that her lips *dropped as the honeycomb* and that *honey and milk* were under her tongue and that her head was like the *beauty of Carmel* (you understood that because you'd been to Carmel yourself, right there on the California coast). You weren't sure why having hair *as a flock of goats that appear from Mount Gilead* or *teeth like a flock of sheep which came up from the washing* might be flattering on a girl, but you liked how it sounded. And you read fast over the part where the Beloved said the Shulamite's breasts were like *clusters of grapes,* or *two young roes that are twins, which feed among the lilies,* or where the Shulamite herself said that her *breasts were like towers,* or that her Beloved was like *a bundle of myrrh* that lay *all night betwixt my breasts,* or you might pass out. But if it was in the Bible then it had to be sacred, even if some people thought it shouldn't even be in the Bible or should just be taken metaphorically and not literally. All you knew was that the words had the same sanctity-giving gold-leafed page-edges that also edged Matthew Mark Luke or John, and the same King James English that God spoke. And besides you understood even then that a metaphor wasn't any good unless it had some sort of basis in reality: someone must have tried out actually and not just metaphorically all the things mentioned by Solomon and still thought they were holy.

Now it was possible that all your effort to dream about a girl sacredly was maybe for all of your good intentions still not necessarily the best thing in the world to do, because when people and especially you sacralize something they/you tend to make it better than it is or ever can be, and the superhuman image that you with lightning speed had developed of Rachelle, which was even speedier and easier to do than usual because you'd never actually met her, was probably just as doomed as the superhuman image you still mostly had of yourself and that you'd once had of your model companion Elder Downing too. But believe it or not you still weren't an absolutely complete idiot about Rachelle. You never allowed yourself to think, for instance, that marrying her was a sure thing. You'd been rejected so often on your mission, and by so many girls you'd liked, that expecting the least desirable outcome had sort of become your default mode for most everything. Of course you were hoping for a happy ending, as a sort of reward for all your hard work, but you knew it was no guarantee. In fact you couldn't let it in your mind become a guarantee, because if you did and then it somehow didn't work out with Rachelle (in the form of say marriage) then you might start blaming God, or even wonder whether all those inspiring feelings you'd felt about her and that'd gotten you through so many rough patches on your mission really were from God, which could make you feel like maybe you'd been even more alone on your mission than you'd thought, and start you wondering whether God had maybe even been there at all. You didn't want to go to that last place so you didn't go to the first place either.

So instead you just sometimes felt like the stern God was saying to you about the whole Rachelle thing, here is your chance to make a big sacrifice (stop thinking about her) and reap great rewards (baptisms) — but you are blowing it. If you'd just give up thinking about her except on P-Days, then you'll make all those converts you hope for. But you aren't. So you won't.

But other times you felt like the kindly God was saying to you about Rachelle that He was working with you through her, the way He worked with a lot of humans who were just too dense to hear Him directly most of the time. Sure, you were pretty sure you'd heard Him Personally in the dismal upstairs bedroom and in the snowy field near Zichem, but most of the time if He wanted to get through to someone like you on a more regular basis then He'd have to do so through one of His visible and comprehensible creatures, until you figured out a more direct way to let Him through. Now in thinking like this about the kindly God you might've just been doing some big-tent mental acrobatics to save your view of Him and of Rachelle, but it also seemed to you that God wasn't above doing some pretty high-flying acrobatics Himself to get His human creatures to listen to Him once in a while, like talking to Balaam through Balaam's usually non-talking ass.* So maybe God wasn't above speaking to you too through another creature, one who was a lot more plausible and desirable than Balaam's ass.

* Famously told in the Old Testament in Numbers chapter 22.

So maybe God was saying to you, *Look I love you enough that I'll speak whatever the fetch language you need at the moment, through whichever the fetch creature you might listen to, because sometimes even your Mormon God-with-a-glorified-body is too distant for you, and you need something you can understand right now, which in your pretty clichéd case is something like a beautiful girl. Because like those fellows in the Renaissance and maybe a lot of other fellows too, you'll pay attention to outside beauty, and not just because you're hopelessly shallow but because you're also convinced that outside beauty reflects an inside beauty that you also way down deep are interested in but that you tend not to see in non-beautiful people (like yourself) and also tend to make secondary to outside beauty. You'll have to get over that nasty little habit someday, but in the meantime I get that for the moment you're not in a great position to practice relationships with girls, or to learn to idealize certain of them less, so I'll stick for now albeit very briefly with that pretty predictable go-between of the beautiful girl, because at times that'll be the only way I can reach you on a regular basis. And when you go back home, if things don't work out with this one (in the form of say marriage), don't be tempted to think that what you were feeling wasn't from Me, because it still was: it was just what we in the religion business call an expediency.*

Of course maybe you were imagining all that too, because would a serious God really want anything to do with supplementing one already overdone ideal you had (your own perfect and heroic mission) with another (the perfect and heroic girl)? What an ungodly way to communicate. But again maybe it wasn't any more ridiculous than the whole Balaam's ass thing, or the big fish going after Jonah. In fact it was less ridiculous.

And at least as effective, because you knew for sure that at least in the aggregate your thoughts about Rachelle motivated you more than they distracted you, and kept you going more than anything else did. Which was the next best thing to actually solving your individual and collective troubles — especially if, as you increasingly suspected, said troubles were not actually solvable. Not in the way you hoped anyway. And not by you as presently constituted.

fourteen

Kyrie Flippin' Eleison

Lord have flippin' mercy, specifically on me, because You know why: transfers are coming up again next week and I really need one.

I know, I said that last month too, and the month before that. And I know that my chances get better every month, because I've been with Elder Downing almost four months now and that's a long time to be with anyone. So maybe a transfer will just happen on its own this month and I won't need any (extra-)special intervention. But I can't take any chances. I can't do a fifth month here, and today is maybe the last moment to get Your help in all this, because today is Saturday June 5, and transfer letters go out Wednesday June 9, so transfer decisions are being made right now as we speak. That's why I'm saying this (extra-)special prayer today, during lunch-dinner. That's probably why Elder Downing is saying one too, in the room next door, which I don't know for sure but there's a sock on the doorknob there just like on the doorknob here. With both of us asking for help You're bound to hear one of us maybe.

I'm always a little nervous asking You for something specific like this, because whenever I do it seems like Your answer is exactly the opposite of what I'm hoping for, which I'm sure is because I'm not asking right, thus according to Your will, and You're teaching me a lesson or something in how to do that better. But today I'm hoping that I can get not just another lesson but for once the actual specific thing I'm asking for, like the fourth

Nephi in the Book of Mormon, who was in such a pure spiritual state that he never asked for anything that wasn't already Your will and so his prayers were always answered. I know I'm not to his level (yet) of being so pure that I can move the whole heavens, but maybe I'm ready to nudge a little corner.

I know that hoping for a transfer is the chicken way out of solving problems, but I've tried facing them for almost four months now and I'm worn out. Things just haven't gone the way I thought they would. Again. We're still not converting people and we're still not getting along so great. I got some hope from those two new revolutionary programs that were money-back guaranteed to improve our *Success!* because usually the more *Success!* we have the better we get along. But the revolutionary money-back-guaranteed programs just haven't made all that much difference.

In fact the first new program, ATAP, talking to anyone around you Any Time Any Place, is the hardest thing I've ever done, because striking up a conversation back home with a stranger is hard enough, but here it's like you're committing a crime. If you try talking to someone in a cultural no-talking zone like the line at the bakery or the post office, or on a bus or tram, you might as well be pulling a fire alarm, because the person plus anyone nearby practically goes into shock and almost starts running for help, and one look at your suit and one listen to your accent tells them pretty fast who you are, which makes them like you even less than they already did if that's even possible. And ATAPping is harder in Brussels than anywhere, because here you're *always* next to someone you can talk to, so you never get a break. Bike-riding missionaries in every other place at least get a break when they're riding, and we used to get a break just riding along sitting on the bus, looking out the window, but now we're supposed to talk to people the whole fetchin' bus ride long. I keep making myself do it, because I know You're not happy with anyone who won't open his mouth, and because everyone needs a chance to hear the truth even if it is for only five seconds, and because some guys have it way harder than I do, like Elder Legrand who just rides trams and busses around all day without talking to anyone because he's so shy, but ATAPping is still the worst thing ever, sorry for my attitude. In fact plain old tracting might be better, because at least when you're tracting you can't see people praying that you won't talk to them, like you can when you're ATAPping on a bus.

But even if ATAP's been rough, I really did think the other new program would fix things. In fact it sounded so good that everyone just called it The New Program, like it was the only one we'd ever need again. But trying to apply the secrets of top top insurance salesmen to missionary work hasn't worked as great as you might think it would for guys who are trying at least to *look* like salesmen. Sure, everyone was really happy to hear that we should stop all our random street-contacting and tracting (but not our random ATAPping), because it was *inefficient,* and that what we should do instead was to start looking for people who were in *big transitions* — like say maybe they've just had a baby, or gotten married, or moved, or had a loved one die. Doing that was supposed to bring our contact-to-sale (conversion) ratio down from 1 in 1,000 (which it's never been) to at least 1 in 100. So we've spent months looking in newspapers and at town halls for the names of big-transitioners, and we even ask everyone we ATAP whether they know anyone who's recently had a baby/marriage/move/death, making sure to ask the right way of course, not *whether* they know anyone but *who* they know, because they really do all know someone and just have to be reminded, but most ATAPped people who've just told us to keep taking a hike aren't usu-ally then dying to give up the names of their friends. The guys at town halls aren't either, but most of the names there are usually French anyway. The newspapers were also tricky at first, because we didn't know which ones to use and didn't want to poke around too much at kiosks to find out, what with all the pornography there, but then we finally learned about the parish newspapers that had all sorts of big-transition names. And in fact the names in those parish papers usually do want more religion than they had before, but come to find out they just want more of the sort they already have, which of course is Catholic, which is why they're in the parish newspaper to be-gin with. Plus when you do find big-transition people they're always a little alarmed at the sight and sound of two strangers standing on their doorstep calling them accentedly by name and congratulating/condoling them on their recent baby/marriage/move/death.

Now, if we just keep working maybe it doesn't really matter what program we use, because there are always a few people who are polite enough or curious enough to listen, and who invite us over for a Discussion, and we do pretty well that way, but really our Discussion hours are about the same as they were when we were just street-contacting. And we're still not converting anybody.

Of course part of that might be that some guys are just better at ATAPping and The New Program than others are. In fact a little while after we started The New Program, we got that checklist with 60 Proselyting Skills, where each missionary is supposed to check whether he *Always, Usually, Sometimes, or Rarely* does each particular skill. I had way fewer checks than I thought I would under *Always.* Like I Always give the Discussions word-perfect and Always ATAP, but I only Usually use the over-the-shoulder method to show a visual aid, and only Sometimes watch apartments to see where young families live (people get suspicious if you stand there too long), and only Rarely have investigators to church. But I've gotten better and even though I really don't like doing some of them, especially the ones involving any serious boldness, now I can check off almost all 60 skills at least somewhere on the line between *Always* and *Usually.* Maybe that's still not good enough, but at least being that close to so many *Alwayses* makes me think that maybe something else besides not enough Proselyting Skills is my problem.

Like that maybe I still don't have enough faith, because as we know, if we have enough faith we can do anything. Sometimes I start thinking, oh, it's good enough just to try my hardest, or oh, maybe since I haven't converted anyone after all these months I should just lower my conversion goal from 84 to something more *realistic* like 30, which would still be like 300 in Latin America. Or I think, oh, it's not entirely up to me whether people convert, because they have their free agency. And sometimes a high church authority will even come through and say every one of those things I just said, and tell us just to do our best, and that we only have control over preaching, not baptizing, and pat us on the back for planting seeds because you can't have a harvest without planting seeds first. But somehow none of those things ever feels like they're the *real* message, but just temporary ones to help us feel better for a while. And sure enough that's confirmed when even more authorities come through saying the *real* real message, which is the same one I've mostly heard my whole life, which is namely that this is a time of harvesting not of planting, and that Jesus commanded go into all the world not just preaching but baptizing, and He wouldn't have commanded that unless it was possible, and He didn't mean just baptizing one piddly person, like you missionaries in Europe do, but lots. My friends on missions in Latin America or real America write me the same real real message all the time, because all their converts are living proof of just how much faith they have. Even my friends on missions in Europe believe the real real message, even if they don't actually have the proof. And of course I believe the real real message too, because that's what a mission is really all about. I know You told me not to act bigger than I am, but I don't think that means I have to think *It's not realistic to baptize (much) here,* because accepting an attitude like that isn't accepting reality, it's accepting a lack of faith. I don't think I've done that, but if I have well then no wonder I'm not baptizing.

But again I think I do have more faith than I used to, so maybe the real reason things aren't going the way they're supposed to — in fact I'm suspecting it big-time now — has more to do with some worthiness issue. Maybe Elder Downing was right about my unlawful letter to my dad, because I can see now that the whole worthiness business was more complicated than I thought at the time. There's not just the white book now to follow and the 60 Points of Proselyting Skills but also the other checklist with 53 points of Personal Spirituality. And on that one too I didn't have as many *Alwayses* as I thought I would, and it's the *Alwayses* that matter most, like the bottom line says: *The number of checks you have under* Always *will determine the degree of your Success!* At first I had maybe 15 *Alwayses,* in easy things like Always staying in my assigned area, and Always writing my parents every week, and Always paying bills on time (which I hadn't realized was such a big point of spirituality). But for most things I just had *Usuallys* and *Sometimeses,* like Usually or at least Sometimes serving with all my heart, mind, and strength, or keeping dinner appointments to one hour, or looking neat (my shirt collars are starting to do funny things), conducting myself in quiet dignity, having an attitude of *Success!,* not thinking about home and girls, being grateful to be a missionary, being strictly obedient instead of merely obedient, and things like that.

Well, I got better at all these things too, so that I'm once again mostly on the line now between *Always* and *Usually.* Maybe *mostly* is good enough for Proselyting Skills but it can't be good enough for Personal Spirituality, because Jesus didn't say *Be ye therefore mostly on the line between* Always *and* Usually, He said *Be ye therefore perfect.* Sure, Paul says it's impossible to keep all the rules perfectly all the time, or King Benjamin in the Book of Mormon says that even if you do manage to do everything you're supposed to do you'll still be an *unprofitable servant.* Or people say, well you don't have to be perfect to be worthy, you just have to do your best. But then the same people who say that also say that you have to be strictly obedient to be blessed, which gives you the impression that if you really are doing your best then you'll be strictly obedient and actually do everything you're supposed to. So in the end it's hard not to conclude that being worthy really does mean being perfect and that when Jesus said perfect He really did mean flawless.

In fact all the stuff my high-baptizing friends elsewhere in the world are sending me is saying that too, and is even making me feel like the 53 things on our Spirituality checklist are basically the minor league of worthiness. This other stuff says that to be worthy of being a big baptizer you also have to be a big sacrificer, like my friend in Japan who is an Assistant and who doesn't just write letters only on P-Day but only *reads* them then too, and what a difference it has made in his conversions! Or like my friends who say they're sacrificing lunch and dinner *all over the place,* or working 91-hour weeks, or praying eight times a day instead of just three or four, and what conversion rewards they've gotten! Then another friend who's an Assistant sent me a sheet called *Devotion?* which asks lots of questions to figure out just exactly how much you have, like do you use *all* your time wisely, or let local Mormons *mother you* instead of give you the names of their friends, or do you avoid casual conversations especially with girls? And one really popular book going around actually proves that baptizing is a matter of faith and worthiness, not location, because (let's see if I can get this right) since You God have commanded us to baptize You are *obligated* to help us do just that, as long as we do everything You say, so if we're not baptizing it means we're not doing everything You say, and if that's the case then how can we possibly say we're doing our best?

Now sometimes it gets a little confusing, like when I notice that some pretty slacker missionaries, who probably don't know a single Discussion word-perfect and who I know for sure get up late, baptize people. Or when some of my missionary friends in Latin America while writing about all their conversions just toss out the N-word like it's nothing, referring to some of the people there, but maybe that's not on their Personal Spirituality checklist and so is okay in their mission, or maybe it's somehow not as bad as thinking unsacredly of girls. But instead of dwelling on confusing stuff like that, I just started digging even deeper inside to see what other sins I could root out. And I thought okay maybe I do think about Rachelle too much or too unsacredly, and maybe I should fix my shirt-collars. But then I remembered something else, something big: all those times I danced too close to Lori Peterson. That had to be it! Maybe if I'd confessed that in the Mission Home, right at the start, I'd be baptizing by now, but all I could do at this point was write her a letter asking her forgiveness for the usual *anything improper I might have done,* and she wrote back just a week or two ago and said she wasn't exactly sure what I meant but if I felt like I needed her forgiveness then I had it. Which helped me feel a little better, and in fact right after that we had two big weeks of Discussion Hours, one week 10 and one week 13! And one of those weeks we had seven investigators! Not cream-of-the-crop investigators, mind you, just one lonely old man, and three lonely young men, and one fellow who mostly listens to Discussions with his family so he can ask questions about American Indians afterward, but still — seven! But then none of them ended up joining, and no one else has either, and so there's probably something else besides the thing with Lori.

And maybe I know what it is, but I don't want to admit it, because You know how I never like to admit that anything is wrong: it's maybe that I'm still butting heads with Elder Downing. Even though I'm mostly on the line between *Usually* and *Always* for just about all 53 things on the Spirituality checklist, I'm stuck on *Sometimes* or *Rarely* for *Do I make my companion my best friend?* and *Do I love my companion and help him to succeed?* Maybe if The New Program had worked out better, then I could've gotten at least to the line between *Usually* and *Always* on those too, but of course The New Program *couldn't* work as long as I was only on *Sometimes* or *Rarely,* because a companionship cannot baptize unless they have the Holy Ghost, and they cannot have the Holy Ghost if they're butting heads.

It's not like we're butting all the time. In fact mostly we seem to get along fine, like most days he even gives me a chunk of his Cote d'Or bar, which I don't buy any of myself because I've spent too much money on the doctor, and maybe he doesn't love giving me that chunk because each bar has only seven but he does give me one, which is really nice. And almost every week after Companionship Inventory and Evaluation Meeting I write in my journal *We really ironed some things out today!* But then something'll happen like Donny Osmond or the unlawful letter and it'll bring out this really deep-down tension that makes the thing under discussion even bigger than it is. Like at the bus stop that one time, or like when he clenches his teeth and says to me during street-contacting *Don't ever do that again,* if I start talking in English or a little French to anyone on the street who says he doesn't speak Dutch. I mean the reason I do is I'm just trying to get a referral for the missionaries who actually take care of French- or English-speakers, but Elder Downing just gets mad and says *We are called only with Dutch-speaking people to talk,* like I'm breaking another rule, or like while I'm goofing off in English or French a Dutch-speaking guy who probably would've converted just walked past.

Or maybe the really deep-down tension shows up most when he walks 50 yards ahead of me, which is no exaggeration because I've stepped it off. It usually happens a couple nights a week, when it's dark and there aren't many people around and we have a long way to go to reach our bus stop, but anyway we'll be walking along and talking and suddenly he'll just start pulling away, first maybe five or 10 yards, but then 25, and pretty soon 50. And I don't speed up, because I'm too tired.

I always wonder what people watching must think, though of course there aren't many out watching at night in this weather, but if they are, are they wondering why we're so far apart? Or are they maybe thinking, nah, no way could they be together with a gap like that between them — they just happen to be wearing the same sort of outfit and happen to be about the same age and happen to have the same sort of foreign look and happen to be walking along the same otherwise empty street in the same direction.

But mostly I wonder what Elder Downing is thinking. At first I thought maybe he was mad, but then he'd pull away on a pretty good day too. So then I thought maybe he just needed a little exercise for his long legs and was tired of how slow I was. Or maybe it was because I'm pigeon-toed and he's duck-footed, and pigeon-toed people are slow walkers, even if they often run fast, because when they walk they do a lot of waggling that shortens their stride and takes time. But duck-footed people including my dad are often fast walkers even if they're slow runners, because when walking they don't waste any time or motion with waggling. But then I realized that not even pigeon-toedness and duck-footedness could explain 50 whole yards, which brought me back to my original idea that maybe he really is mad or just doesn't like me, and that maybe my mom was right all those years ago about the two missionaries we saw 50 yards apart on their bikes. But I don't like thinking that, especially because 50 yards apart on foot is a lot harder to get than on a bike, so I just keep telling myself that it's no big deal, and even think of cheery things I could yell up ahead to keep things light, like *No big deal, I shall you see at the bus halt! You go ahead and your exercise get!* Or maybe something smart-alecky, like *Okay, you win, you're the fastest, but no big deal!* Or maybe singing the chorus to *You'll Never Walk Alone*, like soccer fans in Liverpool do: that would crack everybody up. But instead I just tell myself it's no big deal. Except then why do I start thinking that short little non-r-rolling Elder Klein would never go out ahead like that, even if he could? And I wouldn't either.

Well of course I had a serious case of eye-beam-itis going on with that last claim, because seeing Elder Downing way up ahead of me like that so many times finally made me realize that I had too gone way ahead of my companion, like 50 Discussion-concepts ahead of Elder Youngblood in the LTM. And thinking that also made me realize a little better what might really be going on in Elder Downing's head when he goes ahead. He's not walking necessarily to be mad or mean or get exercise. He's walking for God, family, and girlfriend (and maybe country too) — he's walking to be the Greatest Missionary in the World. And showing me, his Junior Companion, what it takes to be that too.

Now I can't get inside Elder Downing's head for sure, of course, that's just what I'm guessing from the little tilt he has to his head when he takes off, and how straight he's standing even though he's carrying the heavy briefcase with our slide projector and tape recorder and picture book that he never complains about carrying, and how often he talks about his buddy the Assistant and other top top missionaries and church leaders. And I'm also guessing that the Greatest-Missionary-in-the-World-thing is going on in his head at those moments because that's what was going on in mine when I went so far ahead of Elder Youngblood too: I didn't not like him, in fact I liked him a lot, but I told myself it was okay to go ahead because I was showing him how a GMIW ought to memorize (real fast). Just like Elder Downing is showing me how a GMIW ought to walk (real fast), or how other guys think a GMIW ought to bike (real fast).

Maybe this Greatest-Missionary-in-the-World thing is itself the really deep-down tension lying there between us. We both want to be it. And we can agree on maybe 90 percent of what it takes to be it. But somehow it's like we're afraid that if we don't get that leftover 10 percent that we think matters then maybe we're not going to be it. Or maybe that if the other guy is the GMIW then the first guy can't be too. But maybe it's not even the 10 percent that's the real problem, but the GMIW thing all by itself. Because even though we're telling ourselves that we're doing it for God, family, girlfriend, and maybe even country and companion, well maybe we're really doing it for ourselves, maybe to stand out above everyone else. Maybe that's why Jesus said that whoever wants to be greatest ought to be least and not stand out, because maybe only then will they stop butting heads over who's greatest.

Well whatever it is, the really deep-down tension came up to the surface again after the transfer letter two months ago, because both of us were thinking that since we'd already been together two months we'd for sure be transferred and split up, and probably promoted too, him to District Leader and me to Senior Companion. But then the transfer letter came and neither one of us was going anywhere. Then the same thing happened again after three months, and we just about died, because we were even more sure we were going to be transferred/promoted that time. One guy in Elder Downing's LTM group was even made a District Leader and a couple more in mine were made Senior, and there we were, the all-stars, lagging behind. So maybe it was no coincidence that the week right after the last non-transfer was our worst week yet, with the worst day yet coming that next Sunday, May 23, 1976, when the Zone Leaders came over to our place after church and said they were going to do a training visit with us. But it was pretty clear they were there to get to the bottom of our companion-ship problems, which I'd mentioned once offhand to President Olsen and maybe Elder Downing had too.

So as usual in a training visit like that we split up, me going with Elder Christenson, a plain-looking kid from Idaho who is one of the nicest guys ever, and Elder Downing with Elder Christenson's companion Elder Christensen. I don't know where Elder Downing and Elder Christensen went or what training they did, but I know there was no special training going on between me and Elder Christenson, because we just headed downtown to the Boulevard Anspach and started street-contacting, as usual, but we hardly did any of that either, because pretty soon we were just talking and walking, which was weird, because I'm in the habit of stopping anybody who walks by and I feel guilty if I miss someone. But anyway Elder Christenson started kindly asking how I was doing with Elder Downing, which made me start forgetting about all the people going past, and pretty soon we were talking so much that we actually stopped walking, right on good ol' De Brouckère Square.

175

Next thing I knew I was leaning against a rail and saying more words than I knew I had on the subject of Elder Downing and a lot of other things too, because really I'd never talked about them much or put them all into words because they're hard to explain, since things don't look that bad on the surface between us. But the words just kept coming and coming, then so did the tears for only the second time (in public) my whole mission, and then even more embarrassingly so did the big sobs that make you so you can't talk any more, all right there on the Square, in front of my Zone Leader and all those people staring at me now who usually don't want to look my way at all. And even though I'm always saying that it's no big deal when Elder Downing walks way ahead of me, well guess what I started blubbering about first to Elder Christenson?

But there was more to it than just Elder Downing's fast walking, of course. I was also blubbering about my own shortcomings, because I've been out long enough to know that if I've got a conflict with someone then I'm partly to blame too, maybe even mostly. But I just don't know how to fix this one. And I'm sure it's not easy having your first Junior Companion, because just like my mom always said the first child is sort of the experiment and so the parents will make mistakes and you just have to hope you'll all make up later. But it's also hard to be the Junior Companion, especially as long as I've been one, and in fact that might've been the thing I was really blubbering about most, even though I didn't say so to Elder Christenson because it would sound like I was aspiring. Elder Downing always says that I'm *bucking for Senior,* which I hate him to say, maybe because it's true. I know You told me to stop going grandiose, but I didn't think wanting just to be Senior qualified for that. But maybe it does, because maybe I just want to be Senior as a first step to being something bigger. And even though Jesus said if you want to be greatest you have to be least, maybe sometimes I'm only willing to be least if it's somehow a stepping-stone to being greatest, but so far I'm just least, period. I'm sure that's the wrong attitude, but really it feels like my talents are sort of being wasted. I mean come on, I can understand Elder Larson being a Senior before me, because he's older and was in the army. But Poor Elder Hart? And Metcher? And Whitesides? And

Hudson? And Sister Acey? Okay, maybe her, she's mature, but these others? They probably still can't say the Discussions word-perfect. I'll bet even Elder Furtwangler will be Senior before me. Not to mention all the guys from back home who are Seniors, or Rachelle's brother who's a fetchin' Zone Leader.

Well, Elder Christenson was really nice and even cried a little with me, which maybe isn't that hard for him since his eyes are always watery and his nose is always red anyway, but he made me feel better, and I calmed down and even tried to chuckle at how silly I must've looked there on the Square. He said he'd been in just the same situation once, and told me to just keep trying, and that if things got really bad I should call the Mission President. I don't want to do that, because he'll probably just tell me to stop blaming other people, and he's probably right. So instead of calling him, Lord, I'm calling You, and hoping You might intervene with him about a transfer.

I know I was dying to be Elder Downing's companion once and I got my wish in a big way, like almost four months' worth, so it's my own fault. And again I know it's weak to ask to be transferred instead of just solving the problem. In fact that's probably why I haven't been transferred so far, to give me a chance to solve it. But now I feel like I've solved it as much as I can at this moment, though I'm sure if I had enough faith and worthiness I could solve it all the way. I just can't think of any other solution now. But Your will be done. That's really how I feel after saying all this. I'm too tired to push anymore. If You want me to be a Junior still, I'll be it. But maybe if possible let it be with someone else.

Well that's all I've got. I'm lying here face down on the ground because I can't kneel any more, and don't know how else to get out what I want to say and I'm sorry for bothering You with my many requests but You can go ahead and disregard any others I've made lately because this is the one I really care about. And I promise for real this time that I won't ever go grandiose ever again. Ever. At least I'm feeling a little calmer now than when I first came in the room, so that's good, and in fact maybe that's how I wanted to feel most, because once again somehow that and not the big heroic feeling is what is starting to seem most likely to be from You.

It's my turn to clean up the mess from our curry-spaghetti lunch-dinner, so I've got to go do that so I can get back out to work on time. And You won't mind that I've been praying in English, Lord, because that's one time when it's allowed, as You know, just like You knew in advance everything else I was going to say here too, but I still needed to say it anyway.

Lord have flippin' mercy.

Amen.

fifteen

DELIVERANCE

You have to get the little teeth things through every hole in the top and bottom of the master, then close the little metal cover over both teeth things before you turn the printer on or you'll make another huge mess, warned Elder Randall, the Mission Printer, who was instructing me in the finer points of the legendary AB Dick tabletop, which just as the name promised sat stoutly and greenly on a table.

He was doing the instructing in English because neither one of us knew how to say all the technical terms *(little teeth things, little metal cover)* in Dutch. And he was instructing me at all because despite my God-given inability to understand machinery and an impressive lack of small-motor skills that made me uniquely unqualified for this particular, I was here to take his place.

Missions had printers and therefore Printers because photocopiers were still slow and expensive and uneven, and purple-ink mimeograph was as messy and smelly as ever, but a humming AB Dick tabletop was fast and neat, and messy only in the cleanup. Or if you messed up. That last was what worried me.

Elder Randall had already gone over how to pour in ink and toner, how to get fancy with more than one color, where to whack the machine when pages started smearing, how to tie the belt of your dark green work-coat so it wouldn't get caught in the printer and drag you halfway through, and a lot of other things that were spinning my head. And now he was re-explaining the biggest mystery of all: attaching to the printer's spinning cylindrical drum the special paper — the master — that you typed or drew on to print something. The master had to be attached really tight, because once you pressed the *On* button the drum whirled around faster than a Belgian summer, impressing itself ever so briefly on the top sheet of plain paper in the stack that sat waiting just below the drum, and theoretically spitting out dozens of printed high-quality pages a minute.

Someday I would learn a little about sixteenth-century hand-driven printers, but this newfangled electrified thing was totally confounding me, seeing as how I was possibly the only kid in junior-high history to flunk not only seventh-grade shop but, to prove it wasn't a fluke, eighth-grade shop too. I listened hard and nodded gravely while Elder Randall kept talking, but I had serious doubts about being able to learn everything I needed to before he packed up in a few days and left me helplessly alone.

Okay, try another one, he said glumly, since the first master I'd tried had sure enough been too loose and torn and spun around like crazy, flapping with every revolution and spewing dots of ink onto the wall and my work-coat. How in the world had I been chosen to take his complicated place? Elder Randall surely wondered. The fresh master ran better, but the printed pages still had a few smears, so he turned something here and tightened something there and whacked the machine again, all of which I tried anxiously to follow.

But here was the thing: even with all my fumbling and bumbling, even with all the longstanding enmity between machinery and me, even with a green work-coat covered in old and fresh ink plus a bunch of unidentifiable possibly toxic substances, even with an office that was a windowless bunker deep inside the deepest part of a pretty ordinary four-story building, I was absolutely in bliss. Heaven-level bliss.

I'd been transferred to the Mission Office in Antwerp, right behind the zoo.

The Office was where the Mission President ran things, along with his trusty staff of six: two Assistants, a Personal Secretary, a Financial Secretary, a Recorder (statistics guy), and a Printer. The Printer was last not only on the list but also in the hearts of his countrymen, because everyone knew the Printer was the lowest rung on the Office ladder, and very possibly even a slacker sent to the Office so the President could keep an eye on him. But I didn't care: I was still in bliss.

President Olsen had called me personally just a few days earlier, on Monday, June 7, to tell me the news, five days before the official transfer notice would arrive in the mail, because anyone going to the Office needed special training from the person he'd be replacing, and so he needed to transfer earlier than usual too. I'd left for Antwerp on June 8, the day after the phone call.

I was stunned by the whole thing, partly because I couldn't believe I was finally being transferred, partly because of my checkered history with machines, and mostly because Junior companions never went to the Office. President Olsen even said so on the phone: *I told myself I'd never call someone to the Office who hadn't already been a Senior, but I feel very strongly about this,* he said, which made me feel pretty good. I also felt pretty good when President Olsen also said he wanted to *raise the profile* of the position (no elaboration necessary), which he was hoping I would do, and to help out a little on that front President Olsen was giving the job a fancy new name: ICMR, Internal Communications and Missionary Resources. A clunky title like that was usually hiding something of course, like low status and vague duties, but again I didn't care: everybody fighting in the French Revolution had also said that Italy was a low-status vague-duty battleground until a young Napoleon Bonaparte got there and started raising the profile.

Wait a minute, I thought soon after hearing the news of my move: all that stuff about President Olsen feeling strongly and never calling Juniors — had God actually answered-the-way-I-wanted my lunch-dinner-time prayer last Saturday June 5? Or had President Olsen been planning to transfer me all along? Maybe the second, because after all, this particular transfer wasn't exactly what I'd been pouring my soul out for, which was to be made a clear-cut Senior companion. Everyone at the Office was Co-Senior, which meant I was no longer Junior but I wasn't really Senior either. Plus would God really answer anyone's prayer by making him the Printer or even ICMR? So maybe there'd been nothing divine about it.

Elder Downing confirmed that. After I hung up from talking with President Olsen and repeated the news, Elder Downing was stunned too, maybe because as part of the Office staff even the Printer would theoretically rank a little higher than Senior-Companion Elder Downing (though in practice people thought of the Secretaries and Recorder and Printer as more off to the side of the mission flow-chart than inside it). Whatever the source of his stunning, Elder Downing on hearing the news was only able to muster a *Wow! Is this weird or what? It must be because you sick are!* Pfffft went my excitement. Maybe he was right. Maybe that was the real reason I was moving. Working at the Office wasn't as hard as regular missionary work, because mostly you were inside all day at a desk. Or a printer. Even a sick guy could do that.

At least Elder Downing wrote the customary farewell in my journal, saying that he hoped I would have fun at the Office and that we'd had some good times together and that I was a good missionary. I wondered whether he really meant that last one, especially after the *because you sick are* crack, or whether the protocol of writing in someone's journal just sort of dictated that you had to say that. But it actually felt like he meant it, which made me though glad to be leaving also sad that things hadn't gone better between us.

The reason for my bliss didn't have anything to do with my new responsibilities, which were actually a cause of pretty constant stress.

In addition to printing every single piece of mission communication and even writing some of them (the IC in my title), I was also supposed to man the mission's two noisy 16-millimeter film-projectors and show assorted church films at various film-evenings around the entire mission, plus take care of all orders for books and pamphlets (the MR). I was pretty good at keeping track of books and money, but almost every single print job I ever did featured some sort of smear or fade-out, and I never quite mastered the snake-like film that wound up and around and sideways and down and back up the projector again, and that was especially elusive when a room full of people was waiting for you to fix the clackety-clack broken loop that'd just stopped the projector cold and that you didn't have any clue in the world how to fix, but just started pressing things and hoping. None of that was even in the same country as bliss.

Maybe the bliss came from the new profile-raising assignments I was now getting at the Office, like instead of being hidden away somewhere in the basement when new missionaries arrived, all the Office staff, even the ICMR, were now helping to train them for a day or two, just like the Assistants did. All the Office staff were also now getting up on time instead of thinking that if they never went out and gave Discussions then there was no point getting up early to practice them. And all the Office staff were now going out every night to proselyte like they were supposed to instead of dragging out their Office duties on purpose into evening hours or sitting around at night watching somewhat awful church films we all knew backwards and forwards, especially the really bad lines. But no, not even that little rise in profile was the reason for my happy state.

The real reason for my bliss was this: being at the Office meant that I was mostly inside all day long now, doing office sort of work like a real local businessman, instead of outside all day long in the wet and cold, doing missionary sort of work. I didn't even really care if my particular sort of office work put on daily display my formidable lack of mechanical skills: I was inside. Sure, I still had to go out at night and do ordinary proselyting from 5:30 to 9:30, but that was just about right for me, especially since on a lot of nights it wasn't even as long as that: some nights Office duties really did take you into the night hours even if you weren't trying, and some nights I (and a companion) had to drive around showing somewhat awful films, and it was always at least 9:30 before we got back.

Oh, I felt guilty about my bliss sometimes, especially when I hauled Missionary Resources to meetings and saw the emotional scars on other missionaries, and wondered how in the world they'd ever endure being outside all day long all 22 months in Belgium while I had to be outside only 16. And I knew that my new position had probably put the kibosh on my dream of becoming the Greatest Missionary in the World, because it was unthinkable for a Printer or even ICMR to rise to Assistant (basically the *sine qua non* of being the Greatest Missionary in the World). And being a mostly non-proselyting ICMR even meant giving up my vision of 84 baptisms, and at last lowering it for real now to something realistic like 30. But six months of not having to work outside all day long made up for those losses, I secretly felt. In fact I sensed that those six months might save me as much as Rachelle already was. That was why when my bulldoggedly diligent office companion Elder Higbee suggested that maybe we should turn over film-evenings to other members of the staff, because those evenings were interfering too much with our already-limited real proselyting, I about had a Missionary Resources fit. Sure, I still wanted to get 30 baptisms, but showing those somewhat awful films in person was part of my sacred ICMR duty, I insisted, part of my inalienable responsibility. I about had another fit when Elder Higbee then suggested, okay if you're so indispensable to film nights, then maybe when such a thing was scheduled we could proselyte in the afternoon to make up for any night hours lost. *Impossible!* I responded, *the President has you necessary during the day, and I must Internally Communicate and Missionary Resource!* Plus I loved driving through the Belgian countryside for those film nights. I could easily admire the countryside because it stayed light so late through the summer, and also because we weren't allowed to drive the mission van faster than 50 miles an hour, which it probably couldn't have gone faster than anyway. All that driving helped me love Belgium even more than I already did, plus I was still sort of contributing to missionary work by showing those somewhat awful films, even though sometimes only one or two people showed up to see them.

Even with our fewer traditional proselyting hours, we still had some traditional *Success!,* beyond merely the printing or film-projecting sort. We soon had a not-always-alert investigator named Victor who finally got through every

Discussion and wanted to get baptized! It didn't happen, though, because Victor finally realized during the required pre-baptismal quality-control interview with the Zone Leaders that becoming Mormon meant he would have to pay tithing. But at least we'd gotten close. And guess what, *Zuster* De Smet from Hasselt, the lady who'd also never been convincingly alert during a Discussion and who I'd never given a single Discussion to but who I'd at least visited on a lot of cold nights, was going to get baptized right there in Antwerp! I wasn't going to miss that, and neither were about 11 other missionaries who also had some sort of possibly tenuous connection with her. As we stood watching her go into the water, I realized that just like me these 11 were there to claim a little part of her conversion too. Just like me, they probably all wrote home that week too to tell families and girlfriends the joyous news they'd been waiting to hear: that someone we'd helped teach and/or fellowship had gotten baptized at last! That 1/12 of a baptism seemed to impress my family and Rachelle as much as my news about being promoted to ICMR did, which I tried to make sound as important as I could, like I was some vital new cog or better yet secret weapon in mission strategy. *Wow, the ICMR,* Rachelle'd written back. *I'm sure they've got the right person for the job!* Which she couldn't have known wasn't exactly a compliment.

I was also in bliss at the Office because I'd even lost my ever-lingering mystery illness. Maybe it was the air in Antwerp. Maybe it was the glasses I'd gotten so I didn't have to squint anymore. But maybe it was because I was back to normal relations now with companions, having only the usual petty irritating problems with them instead of unsolvable existential-crisis ones.

And maybe I was also feeling better because a few weeks into my new job I found out the real story behind my transfer.

Elder Downing, as it turned out, was wrong.

One of the Assistants, Elder Bergstrom, one day asked me how I liked being at the Office, and I said very much, thanks, adding that I'd really needed a change.

Well that's really interesting, he said, because President Olsen had had the idea about the ICMR for a few months now and even had in mind all that time the exact missionary he wanted for that new job, starting in June, and that exact missionary was someone besides me. In fact in anticipation of the President's plan, the Assistants had even moved that someone to the new ICMR spot on their big green-felt transfer-board. Then just two days before President Olsen was going to finally call the guy with the news, he suddenly changed his mind, and told the Assistants he was going to call me out of nowhere instead. *It was the strangest thing,* said Elder Bergstrom.

I was speechless. Too speechless to tell Elder Bergstrom that two-days-before-President-Olsen-was-going-to-finally-call had been June 5, the same day I was trying to nudge the heavens. My nudges never got responded to like that, i.e. with a solution I actually asked for. Oh, I'd gotten some unexpected comfort before, like in the dismal upstairs bedroom, and some unexpected joy, like in the snow-covered field near Zichem. But a successful nudge?

Maybe it was coincidence again. Maybe I was doing what believing people always do when they can't find a rational explanation for something really big in their lives: find an irrational one instead. Maybe there was just something to the power of psychic energy across space. But this time maybe the simplest explanation was that God had heard me, and for once I was going to go with simplest.

Over the years I'd wonder about that whole chain of events often, because like the seventeenth-century Catholic bishops and especially Reformed domines I would one day study I'd get really picky about accepting something as genuinely miraculous. In fact sometimes when I'd hear the sorts of miracles my fellow Mormons would claim, I'd start longing for the sorts of review boards with a million witnesses and experts that those old Catholic bishops used to insist on before they'd ever in the world declare *miracle!* And those review boards turned down a lot. Maybe they would've turned my story down too.

Or wait a minute — maybe the whole thing was even more an answer to Elder Downing's prayer than to mine. Because not long after the transfer that I thought vindicated me and that even moved me theoretically above him on the flow-chart, he vaulted back ahead by being promoted to District Leader.

Which was maybe exactly what he'd been praying for, in the room right next to mine, on that same heaven-nudging June 5.

sixteen

VOLO ASSISTANTARI

To reach my dark little windowless Printer's office at the back of the ground floor, I had to walk through the bright gigantic office at the front of said floor, which belonged to my distinguished neighbors, the Assistants to the President, the twin pinnacles of the mission flow-chart.

Usually I just made a wisecrack and went through, since their office bore strong resemblance to a disaster-relief site, and since we all had work to do. But today the Assistants were off in some other town training Zone Leaders, and so I decided to snoop around. I especially wanted a peek at the big green-felt transfer-board on the front wall, with every missionary's picture on it, because transfers were coming up again soon and the Assistants were already busy shifting pictures around, working out possible moves and stays.

I wasn't just interested in who might be going where, of course, but in who was being promoted to what, especially if it was anyone from my own LTM group or near it, like Elder Downing, who'd by the way been promoted again, to Zone Leader. But today I was especially interested in who might be taking the place of Assistant Elder Bergstrom, who was about to go home, partly because whoever took his place would be my new downstairs neighbor, but mostly because I was always curious about just exactly what kind of guy it took to be the thing I'd once aspired to be myself but had promised never to aspire to again. So the first place I looked was at the top of the big green-felt board, where the pictures of the Assistants were always pinned.

Elder Bergstrom's picture was sure enough gone, and smiling out from his most desirable place was none other than my own Flemish-speaking self.

Oh my goodness, I thought. I had to sit down. *It's going to happen after all.* And in the most unexpected way possible: from ICMR to Assistant. Who would've thought?(!) But oh that God, He was tricky sometimes. In fact a lot of times. Just think about some of the things He did, and some of the leaders He chose, like David — who'd have ever known that God had a shepherd boy in mind for King of Israel? And who'd have ever known, after faking me and everyone else out for over a year, that God had me in mind all this time as an Assistant? But there my picture was on the big green-felt transfer-board, glimmering under the fluorescent lights like one of those saint trading-cards I'd seen in Belgian living rooms.

All through that blur of a day, and then the afternoon and evening too, I Internally Communicated and Missionary Resourced in a daze, because despite all my promises to keep him locked away my grandiose self was back, and boy was I glad. I'd have to buy a new suit for sure, I thought. A dark blue one this time, and a little more tailored than what I had now. Maybe new shirts too, even if they didn't have white-on-white over here. Oh, and new shoes. Power shoes.

Every time I walked through the empty office of the Assistants that day — my soon-to-be office — I glanced at the transfer-board, still not believing it, and trying not to stare in case someone walked in and saw me. The other people at the Office were bound to see it soon too, and wouldn't they be surprised! Sure, the other Assistant, Elder Gabberd, had stunned everyone by going straight from Personal Secretary to Assistant, but who would have ever thought that an ICMR ever would? *This* was what the President was thinking of when he said he wanted to raise the profile of the position! This and not sickness was why God had brought me to the Office! I'd barely been out a year, which was pretty rare for an Assistant and was just another sign of the genuine extra-specialness I knew I had all along. And oh wouldn't Rachelle be impressed!

By the time I went to bed that night, the Assistants still weren't back and so the others still hadn't seen the news, since nobody had any reason to venture downstairs. So I just lay there on my lower bunk, full of my private knowledge and unable to think about anything else. I tried to stop thinking about who might be impressed, and tried instead to feel the way I thought I was supposed to feel, which was that this was not a huge honor but a huge burden. Yes, I told myself soberly, now I knew how Moses felt being summoned up to Sinai, or Jonah being sent to Nineveh, or maybe even Jesus himself taking up His cross. Yes, I would manfully take on my new charge too.

But actually I was being a lot more like medieval bishops than like these guys. Oh, on the surface medieval bishops seemed humble enough when they were nominated for their new jobs. Because when asked if they wanted to accept their nomination, every single one of them said *No*. Twice. *Nolo episcopari,* they'd say, *I do not want to be bishop.* But that was just a warmup for the third time they were asked. Because on the third time almost every single one of them said *I sure do!* or words to that effect. The only bishops who really meant *Nolo episcopari* were the ones who said it the third time too and then ran away before they could be consecrated, or had to be dragged to the episcopal throne by soldiers and forcibly held in it. And there weren't many guys like that.

Including me. Oh sure, just like the old bishops, I always said *nolo assistantari* if the topic of wanting to be an Assistant ever came up. But now that I actually was about to be asked, I was practically running to my new office and shouting *volo assistantari! I want to be Assistant!* I probably wasn't alone, because from what I could tell, plenty of missionaries felt the same. Maybe most churchmen in most churches did too, about high office. Oh, the burdens of office were real, but not enough to make most people stop wanting office, especially when someone with as much credibility as Paul was shouting from the biblical sidelines that it was okay: *If a man desire the office of a Bishop, he desireth a good work.* Of course you couldn't ever tell for sure what mix of ambition or humility was going on inside someone, but you couldn't always say either that ambition was completely missing in someone's ecclesiastical DNA. Mormon scripture even said as much, warning that almost *anyone* who got a little authority was bound to start throwing it around a little more than he probably should. And even though Mormon church leaders were typically laypeople and so didn't get all their status in life from their church position, the spiritual sort of approval and awe they *did* get from church people or their mother-in-law for reaching such salvation-guaranteeing heights was pretty hard to resist. Including for missionaries. We heard often enough, after all, that whatever heights we rose to on our mission would pretty much determine the heights we'd rise to in the church after we went home. There were even rumors that the files of Returned Missionaries at church headquarters were color-coded, something like red for District Leader, blue for Zone Leader, and white for Assistant, to give top leaders a quick glimpse of likely candidates for future church office.

Boy was I glad, I lay there thinking, that I'd gotten over my irritation with Elder Trimbo, and had parted with Elder Downing on decent terms, or this never could've happened.

And good thing I'd been nicer lately to Elder Hurst, the sometimes annoying Recorder, who when the staff was too busy for a morning devotional would go into the next room and have his own private devotional by punishingly singing at the top of his lungs that pedantic old hymn *Who's on the Lord's Side? Who?* As if the rest of us weren't. Or who'd take advantage of those rare devotionals we did have, now that he had everyone together, to instruct us on such highly religious subjects as the one true way to shift gears in the mission cars.

Oh, and really good thing that I'd even become friends with my old nemesis Elder Furtwangler, because you couldn't have the sorts of feelings I'd once had for him and hope to become Assistant. I'd managed to avoid him for over a year because of our opposite locations in the mission, but then Math-Genius he was moved to the Office as Financial Secretary and I couldn't avoid him anymore. I soon gotten tired again of his bragging, and talent, and now wouldn't you know it he was actually speaking perfect Dutch, despite all the things people said about mouth muscles not being able to change after age seven. He even seemed to be speaking French now, too. But then I had to proselyte with him a few times, and it was astounding how at one Discussion when I'd just given up he completely turned people around with his charm and language. And also the two of us drove to a few film-evenings together and I found out that in private he was actually a really interesting and thoughtful guy. And so even though one of the hardest things in the world is to give up what you regard as a legitimate grudge against someone, it wasn't long before I wasn't jealous any more of Elder Furtwangler's perfect Dutch, but was admiring it along with everyone else, including when he got a standing ovation during some activity at church, because Flemish people were thrilled speechless if you even tried to talk their language but if you spoke it perfectly for even just a few minutes, well, then you got a standing ovation. I was actually glad for him as he stood there slow-blinking and for once not knowing what to say. And I laughed now when he and I would ride our bikes home after an occasional night of proselyting together, and out on some quiet road he'd sit up straight and ride with no hands and burst out singing the Will Tura favorite, *I am so lonely without you,* in perfect Dutch and pitch.

So good thing I'd had that change of heart, because now I was going to have to get along with everyone, including Zone-Leading Elder Downing, who I would now actually be training, but I was trying really hard not to gloat too much about that. In fact I'd already decided I was going to be nice to him and not hold grudges or act like I outranked him even though I did.

And what a great thing, I kept thinking, that Elder Gabberd had handpicked me as his new companion! I'd gotten to know him thanks partly to our adjoining offices but mostly because we liked to joke around on the same sort of what must've been leaderly wavelength, I realized now. So maybe this elevation from ICMR to Assistant wasn't as outlandish as it looked. Oh, he was a bigger personality than I was, no doubt about it, but he was bigger than everyone — a guy who didn't so much fill a room when he entered as take it over, with a charisma that would someday make him the national sales director of a big company. EG's dad had summed it up best by giving Elder Gabberd the nickname *Big,* which was about as imaginative as giving the nickname *Lefty* to a lefty, but it was still perfect for him. As far as I could tell, his only missionary weakness besides singing off key (and maybe getting on the nerves of quieter missionaries with his spilling-over personality) was how messy he was. In fact no one would share a bedroom with him, which was a violation of mission rules, but at the Mission Office there were spare bedrooms and everyone was happy to let him have his own in order to quarantine his mess. But his gigantic office gave him an even bigger canvas to work on than his bedroom did, and it soon featured his stained ties lying across sheets of messy papers on his desk, or a dirty hand-kerchief he'd scotch-taped over a hole in one of the wall-tiles and called the repair good. But how important was messiness anyway, especially since there was still no doubt that no one was as good at real missionary things as Elder Gabberd was? And wouldn't I be glad to work alongside him all the time, because the times that I had worked alongside him, mission work was actually fun.

He must've been impressed by me too, was all I could figure, and not just by my skill at joking around either, but like by the time just a couple of weeks before at church when two of the assigned three speakers had failed to show up for Sacrament Meeting and I volunteered to the person in charge that I was willing and able to speak right there on the spot in their place, because I knew I could just recite a couple of long concepts from the I Dis-cussion and none of the members would recognize them and maybe most missionaries wouldn't either. And I recited those concepts as flawlessly as ever, and though I didn't get any standing ovation like Elder Furtwangler did, the locals complimented me on my Dutch, and more importantly Elder Gabberd was just about bursting with pride that a non-Assistant member of the Office staff — and the ICMR at that — had stood up and saved Sac-rament Meeting, and what an example that was to the whole mission. For days afterward he'd gone on about that to everyone, and soon after that the mission even started another push for missionaries to re-master the Dis-cussions word-perfectly (*re*-mastering implying that they'd mastered them in the first place, I thought dubiously). All because of me. Maybe *this* was why I'd been blessed to memorize all the Discussions so fast and perfectly: to help draw the attention of people who chose Assistants.

So it'd been nice to be the ICMR, I thought as I started to doze off now.

Nice to have done my bit to raise the profile of the position. Nice to have done so many different sorts of things too, like not just Internally Communicate and Missionary Resource, but also to help with publicity when the BYU Folk Dancers came through town. And who could forget my signature piece of printing, the bright and awkwardly stapled yellow program I'd composed and printed for the regional conference in Amsterdam when a lot of big church leaders from Salt Lake were in town? Even though I ran out of stencils for the capital *R* on the program and had to improvise by hand-drawing a shaky little leg onto a *P*, you almost couldn't tell it was fake. Or what about the time President Olsen assigned me to drive Sister Redding down to Brussels, all by ourselves, because she was going to be the drummer for the cultural evening at that very same regional conference and there was only enough room in the car for her and the drum equipment and a driver, and since Sisters weren't allowed to drive cars, that meant an Elder (me) had to drive her? That was the talk of the Office, and it changed my whole view of Sisters. Maybe she changed President Olsen's view too, because he unprecedentedly created an entire Zone of Sisters Only, with Sister Redding as one of the Zone Leaders, until some high authority passing through essentially said if Sisters couldn't even drive then they sure as heck couldn't do something as important as Zone Lead.

But now it was time for me to move on to bigger things, I thought, soberly. To be a man at last, just like 1 Corinthians 13 said. Just like Elder Downing had so often told me to be. I fell asleep, dreaming.

When I woke up the next morning at 6:30, sun rays were streaming in but I hardly noticed because I had a job to do. Actually two: get ready for my new job and get things ready for my replacement.

After Discussion practice, and scripture study, and breakfast, and prayers, I went to my office to get started, which meant of course walking through the Assistants' office. And there they were, finally back from their overnight trip. I hadn't seen them since I'd first laid eyes on the big green-felt transfer-board, which was what they were working away on that very moment, with my picture up at the top next to Elder Gabberd's. I was dying of embarrassment and anticipation at the same time, and kept walking back and forth through their office during the next half-hour waiting for one of them to say something about my imminent promotion, but they just made their usual wisecracks to me, and I avoided looking at the board like it was Medusa herself.

A few minutes later, with me again in the room, annoying little Recording Elder Hurst came in to ask the Assistants something. Of course he snuck a look at the transfer-board, and upon seeing my picture up at the top he burst out laughing. *Yeah right!* He said. I pretended like I hadn't noticed, and looked at the board now too as if surprised, while thinking to myself, *What's an annoying little Recorder know?* I sort of hoped that the Assistants would say something in my defense, but instead they looked at what the annoying little Recorder was laughing at, like they'd forgotten what they'd done there at the top.

Now Elder Gabberd started laughing too, like he'd just remembered what they'd done, and said, *Hey Elder Harline, what'd you think of my joke?* in a voice that assumed I knew it obviously was one. Crushed, I had no choice but to laugh now too. I knew from deep deep context that Elder Gabberd wasn't trying to be mean by doing something like that: our friendship rested almost solely on teasing, and in fact I made a lot of jokes at his expense too, and he usually laughed harder than anyone at them. So he'd probably just been trying to keep up, maybe throwing my picture there on the way out the door, like *Hey here's a thought, but not a serious one. He'll know it's a joke because we're always joking around, and we'll get serious and choose someone for real when we get back.*

I did my best to gather myself, then walked on through to my office, and workbench, and put on my gross, stained, dark-green, possibly toxic workcoat, resigned to being ICMR again and solemnly promising yet again never to go grandiose ever again, while Elder Gabberd and Elder Bergstrom kept chattering away and moving pictures around on the green-felt transfer-board, including unceremoniously moving me back to my proper place among the Office staff, off to the side. The last picture in the row.

Many years later, when one of my books got some attention, Elder Gabberd noticed, and even though he hadn't talked to me in 15 years he looked up my number and called me. I wasn't home, so he told my son that he was a producer for the *Today Show* and was interested in interviewing me. It wasn't quite as preposterous as Elder Gabberd supposed, because I'd already done a radio interview in New York for the book, and a few years later actually would do an interview on the *Today Show.* But he thought it hilarious. When I got home, my son excitedly told me the news, and I excitedly called the number back. EG tried again to pretend he was a producer, but pretty soon he started laughing and I recognized that laugh right away, even after all those years. *Hey Elder Harline, what'd you think of my joke?* he asked. *Not as funny as you think,* I said this time, instead of feebly laughing along. But then I started laughing too, for real, because you couldn't help it with Elder Gabberd, even if he'd once put your picture up at the top of the big green-felt transfer-board and almost made your grandiose illusions come true.

seventeen

A Three-Meal Kind of Guy

The **bold-type** idea I'd been hoping for to prove just what a bold missionary I really was hit me on the train ride down to Halle.

It was bolder than telling the atheist couple there was a God no matter what they said and then getting thrown out for it.

Bolder than planting myself in front of actual local businessmen on the streets of Brussels and getting looked at like I was from Mars.

Bolder than standing up in front of classrooms full of slouching teenagers or clubrooms full of cigar-smoking men daring me to prove I was more than a zoo-exhibit with an accent.

Bolder than going where no missionary had supposedly gone before with the Discussions.

Bolder than buying my white-on-white shirts.

Even bolder than writing an unlawful letter.

The real and true bold thing was this: we missionaries in Halle, where I was now headed, would from this day forward eat three meals a day instead of just two.

Just thinking about that level of boldness was enough to churn my stomach. Those other bolds had all taken some *nerve* and determination, sure, but they weren't what you could call seriously *bold,* because while doing every single one of them I'd been able at least to assume that most of my fellow missionaries and most people back home — the people whose opinions I cared about most — would've unanimously and back-slappingly approved. I hadn't always assumed rightly, of course, but when you could at least *assume* that people-whose-opinions-you-cared-about-most would unanimously and back-slappingly support you, well, that wasn't being seriously bold. It was more like going beaver-eagerly along. But changing from two meals a day to three? A fetchin' revolution, that was. Because I didn't think any of the current people whose opinions I cared about most (like mission leaders) were going to like my plan at all.

Okay, so maybe the three-meal plan wasn't even in the same solar system of bold as Rosa Parks not budging from her seat on the bus, or as Galileo daring to say we earthlings actually live in a solar system rather than an earth system. Or to bring in another metaphor here, on a comparative or even absolute scale of bold, switching to three meals a day barely weighed anything, because after all *three* was the official number of meals officially suggested in the official white book itself. But the undisputed not-even-needing-discussion and therefore-really-powerful custom of the Antwerp mission, a custom meant to show just how dedicated you were as a missionary, was to eat just two meals a day: breakfast from 9:00 to 9:15, and lunch-dinner from 2:00 to 3:30. Anyone thinking like me (or the white book) of having lunch (from 12:00 to 1:00) and dinner (from 5:00 to 6:00) separately, and thus reducing the work day from 10½ to 10 hours, wasn't just upsetting the system but was on the exceedingly broad road to slackerhood, and many there be who find it.

So it was a little bit bold. Even if at least part of the reason for this sudden burst of boldness was, let's just say it right here, my being terrified of having to go back outside all day long again to proselyte.

I was in the powerful position of boldly decreeing things like meal-frequency because I'd just been named the new District Leader in Halle, a town southwest of Brussels with a famous statue of the Virgin.

My last month at the Office had been a smashing printing *Success!,* coinciding as it had with *Miracle Month,* so-called because to celebrate Christmas the mission had set the unheard of goal of 41 conversions for December, way past the usual monthly 8 or so. But as the almost flawless bulletin I produced to announce the occasion familiarly said, if everyone had enough faith it could happen: Moses parted the sea, David slayed Goliath, and the ancient apostles raised the dead because they'd believed. If the mission couldn't get its 41 conversions, it would obviously be because we didn't (believe).

For this my crowning bulletin the long-awaited day dawned at last, not of lion finally lying down with lamb or of crooked ways finally being made straight, but of ink and toner mixing perfectly together, of master sheet staying whole, and of smears disappearing from the land altogether. It was a great printing triumph, capped by the nearly square box I drew around the big *41* on the center of the front cover. In the end, we didn't quite get 41, more like 24, but that was miracle enough for most.

With nothing left for me to achieve on the AB Dick, I was sent back out to proselyte full-time, just in time for winter.

I put on a brave face about it, especially since my new companion Elder Roy had just arrived in Belgium and was already constantly looking at me for guidance, including right here on the train, but I worried for days about how I would cope with being outside all day again. Still, I just kept smiling at Elder Roy to let him know everything was going to be fine.

Luckily for me a lot of things were working in my favor in Halle, starting with the place itself, located just above the invisible language-line that ran horizontally across the country and divided it in Flemish- and French-speaking two. Like the way the town's small-but-not-too-small size was so much more manageable than Brussels or Antwerp, yet its location near Brussels made it a lot less provincial than Hasselt. Or the way the rolling hills in the landscape and cityscape were just so calming to my nerves. Or the way the wide canal to Charleroi ran so picturesquely through town. Or the way the railroad tracks that divided the town geographically didn't divide it socially, because the single rail crossing was more a gathering place than a barrier, as people piled up there 20 times a day on foot and moped and car and bicycle, nodding greetings and chattering until the train passed by. Or the way the basilique, which didn't look like any other church I'd ever seen, stood out so enchantingly in the skyline.

There was also the favorable thing of being able as District Leader to at last do things pretty much the way I wanted.

There was also the other favorable thing of me now having only about eight months to go before going home, which just didn't seem as impossible as say 15 months to go seemed when you were walking 50 yards behind your companion.

And most of all there was also the unusually high concentration of fantastic people in Halle. Not that I hadn't met fantastic Belgians before, but I'd never before noticed so many in one place. Like *Mevrouw* Marcelis, who ran the stationery store where local businessmen bought special pens and notebooks and paper, but who would sometimes just give us things because she was so friendly, maybe because she had boys our age and couldn't imagine them so far from home. Or like the Timmermans family with college-age kids too, who would end up listening politely to three Discussions before saying *Enough,* but who would keep insisting that we keep coming back to visit and eat and then would drive us on P-Day in their big 1950s-style Peugeot to Waterloo and then to some ancient Christian sites in the town of Nivelle, both of which would really fire my imagination as much as the old tower-ruin in Zichem had. Or like Josephine de Waele, who at first glance was just your ordinary precious old lady, but who on second glance would turn out to have been 40 years before a chef in some of the finest kitchens of Brussels, and who every Thursday would make the missionaries of Halle a four-course meal the likes of which they'd never experienced before, including her revelation-quality chocolate mousse, and all of which she would insist on making for free but we would always sneak a whole 40 francs ($1.25) under our plates anyway for that fantastic (unknown to us) 800-franc meal. Or like the family who would tell us they didn't want to hear one more Discussion, but who would insist that before leaving we all sit arm-in-arm on the couch and sing along with their new New Seekers album. Or even like the local packs of teenage boys, who would yell their usual *CIA** at us but who would also prove to be friendlier than most such packs, moseying on over to chat with Elder Roy and me and even offering us a smoke instead of just running away and laughing.

Or like maybe most of all Angelique Martel, the only Mormon in all of Halle, who would do more than anyone to make us feel at home, because she knew how lonely lonely could feel, since her husband had left her alone with two kids a long time ago, and after the kids had grown up and left home she'd finally realized just exactly how lonely she actually was, and for years she'd been *deep in the pit,* as the Flemish say, and she'd gotten out of it by going every day after work in Brussels to the narrow little Gothic Chapel of the Madeleine near Brussels Central Station, where for months she sat for hours and hoped for hope, and one afternoon sitting there she remembered she had a copy at home of some Book of Mormon she'd gotten somewhere, which she decided to read, and that made her interested enough to call the number inside, and though the missionaries who answered were stunned at being called up by someone, they gladly taught her the Discussions and baptized her just months before I arrived, and she'd been a big help to the missionaries and the branch in Brussels ever since, even though she had to travel an hour and a half each way to church every Sunday.

There was also Elder Roy himself, so eager to get along that he'd do things like wash dishes when it wasn't his turn, or make my bed in the morning while I was in the bathroom getting ready, and who would be as all-around pleasant a companion as you could have, even though he'd never ridden a bike before and had a really steep learning curve in that regard and kept crashing, causing me to keeping turning and see him waving from the tangled mess on the ground that he was okay, and even though the crash would inevitably send my special little visual-aid book (which I'd trusted him to carry and that was guaranteed to convert dozens) into a puddle, well, you couldn't get upset for long with a guy like Elder Roy, who even though

---

* Especially after all of us, to fight off winter winds, bought some black full-length fake-leather coats at the local thrift store.

he was from Canada would never complain about me saying at the door, *Hi, we are Americans.* He was the kind of guy like Elder Trimbo who you were glad to have around on hard days, which happened even in Halle.

There would also be in Halle even better letters from Rachelle, so maybe she wasn't as unimpressed as I'd feared that I was a measly District Leader, because soon she'd be telling me that I was the only person she ever wrote to besides her brother, and she'd also add some really daring P.S.es, like *I never get bored with your letters, they are really quite exciting!* or *You really write good letters,* or best of all, *There had better be a result from this activity!* a line she stole from something I'd said so authoritatively about missionary activity.

There were also my new Zone Leaders in the Brussels Zone, maybe not so much Elder Downing, whose Zone-Leading presence made me slightly nervous, but more Elder Downing's companion, my old friend Elder Gabberd, who decided that after being an Assistant he wanted to try being a Zone Leader before he went home. Of course he got along as well with Elder Downing as he did with me, but pretty presumably because of my mixed history with Elder Downing, Elder Gabberd himself would always do the District-Leader training visits with me. Which visits all ended up being a lot of fun, maybe because they all ended in disaster, like the time he tried to train me in how to take local members along to contribute to Discussions, in this case a rare F Discussion about Repentance, which went fine until it was time for the local member to explain how repentance had benefited him, and he explained how he'd once had a problem being attracted to little boys but now thank goodness he mostly wasn't, which caused Elder Gabberd and me to die on the spot and the investigator not to invite any of us back ever again. The best part of the training visits, though, was watching how impossible it was for anyone to resist Elder Gabberd; people even seemed to feel rude if they didn't stop and talk to this big, messy, sloppy-walking fellow with the huge smile and voice who took up most of any sidewalk.

But even with all those things about to go on for me in Halle, I was pretty sure that the three-meal plan would do as much as anything to help me survive all-day-outside missionary life again, and even to start finding a little contentment that had nothing to do with food.

I might not have been brave enough to try the plan in any other town, but because Halle sat there at the extreme bottom of the mission maybe I thought no one would notice.

The train ride down from Antwerp was my last desperate moment to come up with something that might make the long days bearable, so maybe that's why the plan hit me then. After arriving I nervously presented it to the three others, taking care to show them chapter and verse in the white book, which astonished them, and to my surprise they were all for it. I was still a little nervous, though, about what might happen when some Zone Leader came around for a training visit and discovered that the missionaries of Halle were heretically splitting lunch-dinner into two separate meals, but for now I felt a huge sense of relief. And daring.

Oh sure, in the dismal upstairs bedroom in Hasselt I'd learned the theory of daring to be myself. But it was safe to say that in Brussels the theory had been flat-out forgotten, and in Antwerp I'd spent most of my time just trying to recover from Brussels. Mostly it was safe to say that I was still highly interested in doing and being what people whose opinions I cared about most wanted me to do and be, especially people like the Zone Leaders.

I wasn't the only guy like that, of course. Even Saint Augustine got mad at himself for stealing some pears with his friends, mad not so much for the stealing itself as for stealing because his friends wanted him to. If you were always doing and being what people whose opinions you cared about most wanted you to do and be (even supposedly good things), then you'd not only never figure out what you yourself wanted to do and be but would almost certainly end up doing and being a lot of actually dumb things. Like stealing pears. Or aspiring to positions. Or maybe even the worst sort of dumb thing, treating people badly because people whose opinions you cared about most said it was okay to treat them badly. Like atheists. Or slackers. Or people like unto it.

I knew all about that sort of going along firsthand, precisely because it was the worst sort you could do. In a weird sort of way the horrible awful memories of that were actually the main reference point, the inspiration, the thing I thought of most, when I started thinking about the possibility of *not* going along with something just because the people whose opinions I cared about most wanted me to. Like if I could just remember how awful I felt about going along with those really dumb people-treating moments, then maybe I would have enough nerve to do what I thought was best when other going-along moments presented themselves, even little teeny tiny ones, like meal plans.

It was hard enough to think about the dumb people-treating moment I'd gone along with in seventh grade. A lot of kids called Curtis Nash Peg Leg because one of his legs was just a stump attached to a thick piece of rubber and wood with a point on the end that squeaked really loud as he limped along. Also he could barely see except out of one tiny corner of his eye, so sometimes guys would run in circles around him just out of his eyesight and make noises and laugh while he limpingly whirled around trying to see who it was. Then one time he whirled too fast and his fake leg fell off and he fell down and people started really laughing, which made him yell and cry and grab his heavy fake leg and try whirling around on his good leg so he could hit people with the fake leg — that's how tired this really gentle and usually smiling guy was of being laughed at. I didn't laugh but I didn't do a single thing to help either, and so I might as well have gone along, mostly because like everyone else watching I was afraid of the opinions of the people who were laughing.

But even harder to think about than Curtis Nash, in fact the dumbest people-treating moment I'd ever gone along with, was the cringe-worthy treatment of Danny Clevenger. This time I wasn't just a passive guilty bystander but an active champion inflicter of pain, just because I cared so much about what certain other people thought.

I and Danny and three other guys had all been friends through seventh grade, but then one day early in eighth grade the leader of us five came running out of the locker room after basketball practice laughing so hard he could hardly talk, but when he caught his breath he declared to the world the news that Danny was a *fag,* because just a few minutes ago when a bunch of them were still in the shower the leader had seen for himself that Danny *had a boner.* I wasn't entirely sure what it all meant, but I laughed with everyone else and then ran away with them too from the locker room as fast as possible, because our leader had spoken, and it didn't need saying that if you wanted to stay in the now four-man group and keep your reputation intact, then from that day until the end of the world you would never have anything to do with Danny again, except at practice or a game when you had to pass to him. The leader's claim didn't require anything like actual empirical proof, didn't require any second witness, didn't require any discussion of the fact that unlike most of us barely pubescent fellows Danny was already fully mature, didn't require any answering of the question as to whether any of us were actually entirely sure of how things should look in the nether regions of an entirely mature male. Nope, none of that, because our leader's opinion was all we needed, and so all through eighth and ninth and even part of tenth grade we all kept up this boycott of Danny Clevenger, who quickly became a pretty lonely fellow thanks to us, because the leader of course told the story to everyone else at school too.

Still, treating Danny this way felt funny enough that something inside was actually almost screaming to me *not this, not this.* But I didn't listen. I even heard words at church and home about treating other people kindly, but surely that didn't apply to someone who the people whose opinions you cared about most said didn't have to be treated kindly, like the sort of person Danny supposedly was. Even my Mormon friends could agree with that. Maybe my Mormon friends would disagree with my pack of friends at school about smoking, and drinking, and drugs, and sex, but they could all agree on the categorical imperative to never be friends with a guy like Danny, or even be friendly to one. That's why I couldn't just, say, decide to be kind to Danny knowing that I could fall back on my Mormon friends once the School-pack disowned me, because what mattered most in defining yourself as a Mormon kid was never smoking, never drinking, never doing drugs, never having wrongful sex, and if you were a girl never showing certain parts of your skin. All those mattered way more than the great and fluffy commandment about treating other people the way you wanted to be treated yourself. Oh, sure, it was fine to be nice and everything, but it was more like a bonus point than something at the top of the salvation-giving list, and it had its limits, and Danny was pretty obviously it.

But going through all that here is just a way of delaying my awful horrible moment, when I wasn't just a bystander any more to the boycott but right at the front of the picket-line. It started the day I walked into the school library and saw Danny sitting at a table reading the sports page of the *San Francisco Chronicle,* the way all of us had once done together, and in fact what I'd come into the library that day myself to do. And so I grabbed the other copy of the *Chronicle,* and feeling a little guilty about the whole Danny thing actually went and sat down across from him, kind of like saying I personally didn't really think Danny was such a bad guy but you know how it is with friends, which really surprised Danny when he looked up, and he and I even exchanged a few friendly words. But then within minutes wouldn't you know it the other three members of the pack came wandering into the library too, which I knew not because I saw them (because I had my back to the door), but because I heard them, as all of a sudden there was a giant commotion as they all took one look at my proximity to Danny and broke into library-violating laughter, then started pointing at me and practically knocked down the door trying to get back outside.

Here was my big chance to be bold, and here was when I understood what real boldness really involved: I could be the kid who was actually listening to the voice inside and keep sitting there with Danny and become his friend again, could be the kid who stories would be told about for years afterward because he'd been kind to someone even when the people whose opinions he cared about most hadn't; or I could just do what I did, which was to jump up from the table as fast as I could and leave Danny and the *Chronicle* in the asbestos-laden dust, then go running after the people whose opinions I still cared about most, yelling all the way out the door so that even Danny could hear, *I didn't see him there!* And then when I finally caught up with them outside, I lied again that Danny had been the one to sit down across from me and not me from Danny, basically just saying with Peter, *I do not know the man.* They made it pretty clear that they didn't buy my stories, and that I was on pretty serious probation with all of them, but I promised it wouldn't happen again.

I wasn't sure how Danny put up with this all that time, just going on day after day playing basketball and being one of the best players actually, and doing his school work with practically no one at school being brave enough to talk to him. At least until maybe tenth grade when the whole thing sort of fizzled out, and people started talking to him again like nothing had ever happened, or that he hadn't suffered or anything like that.

What happened to Danny was still hanging heavy on me here in Belgium — sure, mostly because I still thought that the real tragedy had been that Danny had turned out not even to be gay rather than because anyone should've been treated that way period, but it was still hanging heavy — and that horrible awful memory of going along with something I knew was wrong just because important others wanted me to suddenly helped me realize that maybe I should start doing what I felt was right even if important others thought it wrong. Maybe that could somehow start making up just a little for what I'd done to Danny. Maybe it was even a tiny clue of what it meant to *be yourself.*

Maybe most 13-year-old kids in 1969 or any year wouldn't have been bold enough to follow up on a feeling that they should be kind to someone who'd been universally condemned, or that maybe they should walk up to help a kid who was clumsily whirling around with his fake leg. Maybe having that kind of nerve would've taken a Rosa Parks of junior high. But at least as a 20-year old I could muster up enough nerve to come up with a really-small-potatoes three-meal plan that went against hallowed custom but that I still thought was right. That the plan was so microscopically small, and the amount of genuine raw boldness necessary to carry it out so minuscule, said a lot about how little scope I imagined there was in the missionary world, or even religious world, for true boldness. But it was something: it was a tiny step down the road toward being able to ignore pear-stealing, Danny-Clevenger-avoiding, two-meal insisting others, and listening to my insides.

In fact the three-meal plan turned out to be spectacularly right. The breaking up of the day into three made everything easier to bear. But just *doing* the plan was what helped me most to start feeling a little contented at last.

eighteen

JUST ONE MORE LAST CIGARETTE

After my mission I'd sometimes dream about Lieve de Clercq, but it was never a bad dream.

It usually happened around February 4, Lieve de Clercq day. The day I observed silently to myself every year. The day (well, half-day) that Lieve was Mormon.

Elder Roy and I met Lieve soon after we got to Halle, where the missionaries we'd replaced had left a cassette tape full of information about the few people they'd been working with and Lieve was the undisputed star. We wasted no time going to see her.

She was in her mid-30s and tall and striking and married with three kids between 8 and 12, but the most striking thing of all about her was that she kept saying she wanted to be baptized.

No one ever said that.

A few said they'd think about it, then didn't (think). A very few said they'd be baptized, but then acted like they weren't home the next time we came by. And one couple told me they wanted to be baptized, but it was impossible because the wife had the ground-transportation-sickness trifecta* and so couldn't go to church, while the husband was a big cigar-band collector whose biggest meetings were always on Sundays and if it

---

* Car, tram, bus.

came down to cigar-bands or church, well you knew what was going to win that battle. But in my experience that was about as close as anyone usually got to saying *I want to be baptized.*

But Lieve was serious. During my first visit to her home, she said in her strong and slightly slurred voice (that came from all the medications she'd had to take for the dozen or so operations on her back) that she'd had a vision about it. I just sat there open-mouthed, because again no one said that, even if they were on drugs. Maybe this was the conversion that would make all the hurt and pain disappear and start me down the road to baptizing regularly. Sure, back at the Office I'd ratcheted down my vision of 84 conversions to a more realistic 30, and just the month before I'd ratcheted down again to an even more realistic 20, which was a measly convert per week for the rest of my mission, which even though I still hadn't baptized a single person yet, still sounded like nothing. But even 20 would be extra-special.

The only trouble-spot emerging in my mind about Lieve was whether she'd count as a full baptism for me, because the missionaries we'd replaced had found her and taught her most of the Discussions and so probably deserved most of the credit. Those guys had even said as much on the cassette tape. I thought they were just being selfish though, because hadn't Paul said not to worry about who got credit for converts? But I was thinking that mostly of course because I wanted the credit myself.

How much credit I got, I decided, would depend on how much I ended up working with Lieve. If she got baptized within say a week or two, then it would be pretty hard to claim much. Sure, I'd be able to write home and finally say *I baptized someone this week,* but if I were really honest I should add *even though I didn't have much to do with the process.* In that scenario, I'd maybe get only a quarter baptism, and adding that to the 1/12 baptism I already had with *Zuster* De Smet, plus the two 1/64 baptisms I could go out on a limb and claim for shaking hands with two people who eventually got baptized, well, all that still wouldn't add up to even one. Luckily for me though, Lieve still had a long ways to go, not because she was slow-minded (in fact she was unusually bright) but because her medications made it hard for her to concentrate. So if it took long enough then I could make a legitimate claim to at least a majority share of credit, especially since Elder Roy was still learning Dutch and I'd end up doing all the talking. All that might nudge me up to a very solid 1 or even 1+. Twenty baptisms would be just around the corner from that.

We ended up visiting Lieve two or three times a week for a month and a half, finishing and then reviewing the Discussions and clearing up any questions she had, which I thought was plenty for me to lay claim as chief converter. I was even able at long last to give those I and J Discussions I'd gotten extra divine help with at the LTM 16 months before, the ones that'd made me sure someone in Belgium was just waiting to hear them. But even after we finished I and J, and even after I was pretty sure that all that work with Lieve would give me (and secondarily Elder Roy) the credit I deserved, something was still nagging me. Nothing big, I told myself. Just that maybe Lieve didn't have a clue of what she was actually getting into.

She kept smoking like a local diesel bus, for instance, even though she knew that Mormons weren't supposed to smoke. Not only that, but Halle was part of the Brussels branch, 35 kilometers away, and like a lot of Belgians Lieve didn't have a car, which meant an hour and a half walk-and-train-and-tram-and-walk each way every Sunday. I seriously doubted she could do that, especially since she'd never managed to attend church even once so far just to see what a Mormon service was like. And what about her husband Ludo and their kids? Ludo was a postman but what he really liked to do was cook, including assorted fantastic meals for local businessmen (who knew that eel could be fantastic?), but he wasn't the least bit interested in the product we were selling. The kids always wandered in and out of Discussions with Lieve like they were torn between their mom and dad, or maybe they were just curious about the foreigners.

But then Lieve finally went in person to the church in Brussels to see a baptism, which gave me new hope. She had to take a cab, which I doubted she'd be able to afford every week, but the baptism was so beautiful to her that she couldn't even sleep that night, thinking about how she wanted to do that too. And she promised that Ludo'd said he was fine with her getting baptized, if that's what she wanted to do. And so I just kept moving ahead.

Lieve was far enough along that I decided to schedule a pre-baptismal quality-control interview with the Zone Leaders on Tuesday February 1 at her home, and the baptism itself on Friday February 4 at the church in Brussels. But when Ludo found out that he'd be asked during Lieve's interview to sign a form saying she had his permission to be baptized, just so there'd be no hard feelings, well his feelings turned hard fast. In fact when the Zone Leaders drove down Tuesday night at 7:00 to do the interview, Ludo was already in bed, on purpose, so he couldn't sign. Which meant no interview. And no baptism. I took the form from the Zone Leaders and said I'd go by and ask Ludo the next day whether he wanted to sign, and if Ludo did then the Zone Leaders could come back and do the interview on Thursday, still in time for the scheduled Friday baptism.

In fact Ludo signed the next day (Wednesday), but he wasn't happy about it. Especially not when his 10-year-old son Jonas, who was watching, then asked whether he could be baptized too, which just made Ludo bark *No!* and slam the door on his way out of the room. He was still worked up on Thursday, because when we all showed up in the afternoon to do the interview, Lieve opened the door and the first words out of her mouth were that Ludo'd changed his mind. She suggested that maybe they do the interview on a sort of provisional basis, and then if she managed by the next day to talk Ludo into it again everything could go ahead as planned. But then a big question mark started forming in Lieve's mind about why she had to get any formal permission at all from Ludo, especially when she found out that if things had been the other way around spousally then the church wouldn't have asked her for her permission. Finally she calmed down enough to go ahead with the interview, and she passed, which made me breathe out a sigh of relief, but the whole situation was now loaded with more tension than I thought everybody involved might be able to handle.

I also thought that maybe it'd be a good idea for Elder Roy and me to go back over that same Thursday night to try talking to Ludo again, and soften any hard feelings, so the baptism could still happen the next day. But Ludo said he couldn't understand why Lieve needed to be baptized when she was so obviously sick, because even if it turned out that the Mormon baptism was the real and true baptism, he just didn't see how God would require that of her, in her condition. With nothing really settled, we went back to our apartment that night and prayed that Ludo would soften up.

By the next morning, the morning of the scheduled baptism, he still hadn't. When we went by, Ludo was already out delivering mail, and Lieve said he hadn't changed his mind — and so she just couldn't feel good about going through with it. I didn't know what to think. I didn't want her to have any trouble with Ludo, but I was also sure that if she really wanted to convert then Ludo's heart really would soften, because Conversion Motif 3J or so said that was how it always went. So I told her that. And Lieve said okay, then she'd go through with it. To steel herself a little, she shakily pulled another non-steel cigarette from her purse, assuring horrified me that it would be the last one.

All excited again and sure that with God's help Lieve would be able to all of a sudden stop smoking, Elder Roy and I went to shop for some things to eat for the post-baptismal celebration at her home that night. But while we were riding home loaded down with groceries, here came Jonas running toward us, saying that his mom had changed her mind again. She just couldn't do it, even though the post-baptismal goodies were already bought and paid for and unreturnable.

I was in full crisis mode now, so I rode home and climbed up into the attic to be alone. Oh, I was still aiming for 20 baptisms, but deep deep down I wondered whether I'd ever get even one, or whether I'd ever be this close again. Didn't I have to get at least one full-fledged put-them-in-the-water-myself baptism before going home? If the whole point of being a missionary was to baptize people? I couldn't stand that thought of having only one, but then one thought saved me: Conversion Motif 5C, the Unexpected Exponential Qualities of the Number One. This said that okay, so maybe a missionary might baptize only one, but that one might go on to convert someone else, and those someone elses still more someone elses, until maybe the whole bunch was up to, say, 20, or even maybe 84. That little unexpected exponential kick from one, which just completely ignored the number's usually non-exponential powers, actually made your single baptism even more crucial than baptism number 37 or something, because the one that you'd gone to all the trouble of getting was the linchpin, the one that if you wouldn't have gone to all the trouble of getting would've caused those that followed never to happen. That was a story you could be proud of telling people. Including girl people. Because I was sure that the third thing a Mormon girl with top top standards in a prospective husband would want to know about me was *How many people did you baptize?* The most sophisticated, like Rachelle seemed to be, might cut you a little slack for going to Europe, but they'd still expect you to have *something* to speak of. And if you could tell about an exponential kick, well, all the better.

I just kept lying there on the attic floor thinking about all this, not looking out the little window in the slanted roof across all the houses in the rolling cityscape feeling like I was responsible for the salvation of them all, the way I usually did. No, I just lay there the way I usually did when I was in crisis mode: eyes down, head on my hands, wrestling with myself.

After about an hour of that, I started feeling a little like maybe I was making this whole thing a little too much about myself, instead of about Lieve, even though I kept telling myself that yes it really was Lieve's salvation that was at stake here. I also kept telling myself that I also really cared about the local branch, and the brave people who kept hanging on, and wouldn't it be nice for them to have some more new people? But did they really need another totally uninvolved member, like the other 90 percent on their rolls, a lot of whom had been baptized because missionaries had just been so fetchin' determined to baptize them so they could feel good about their missions, and most of whom had by now pretty much been forgotten by those same missionaries who'd gone back home in a big blaze of glory? All that back and forth made me a little woozy by the end of my lie-down, but believe it or not I felt just a little like I could actually let Lieve go, and stop worrying so much about how many I baptized. Sure I'd feel bad, and maybe a little humiliated, about going home with zero baptisms, or even 19/192 of a baptism ($1/12 + 1/64$), but I'd get over it.

Of course that little bit of letting-go disappeared real fast when an out-of-breath Jonas came knocking again at our door about ten minutes later, saying *My mother is of opinion changed! She wants baptized to be!* Full of new hope, we rode right over to her house again to hear the news for ourselves, which Lieve confirmed as she lay there on the couch in pain, smoking another cigarette. *The last one,* she promised again, without me even needing to say anything. She wanted to go through with the baptism, and if Ludo gave her any grief, she said, then I should just give her a little push and make her go through with it anyway. I didn't like the thought of that, but if Lieve wanted me to push then maybe I would, a little. She told us to come back at 5:00 and we'd all ride to the church in a taxi.

On the way back to the apartment, I stopped at a phone booth since we had no phone of our own, because I needed to call the Mission President, technically to follow mission rules about clearing all possibly almost certainly problematic baptisms in advance but really mostly hoping that a real authority figure would tell me it was okay to baptize someone who was still smoking like a local diesel bus, and who probably would have a really hard time making it to church every week, and whose husband didn't really want her to get baptized even though he'd signed the official form. Because if the Mission President said okay, then I wouldn't have to take responsibility and could even feel good about it. But I didn't feel good, not only because of her smoking, but because the church was supposedly about families, yet here I was feeling like I was causing a lot of trouble for one. The Mission President sighed, because he saw all the danger signs too, but said that if she wanted to be baptized so badly and seemed like she was willing to do what she said she would do (stop smoking), then I shouldn't stop her, because technically she could toss away her last cigarette even while she was wading into the baptismal font. (He didn't actually say that.)

So it was okay. The Mission President said so. My hands were clean.

We got back to Lieve's place as promised at 5:00, worried that maybe she'd change her mind again, especially since Ludo was sure to be home by now. But there she was, all smiles and ready to go. Her oldest and most protective child, Valérie, was ready to go too. Ludo acted friendly, but when the four of us went out the door to the taxi he went into the other room and didn't say goodbye. We all crowded into the back seat of the big blue Mercedes, as the driver didn't want anyone up front. When we pulled away, I breathed out and allowed myself to think for the first time: *it's really going to happen, I'm really going to baptize someone.*

Or maybe not. Five minutes later Lieve pulled out a cigarette and lit up.

I didn't always mind cigarettes, believe it or not. When I smelled cigarette smoke in a super-diluted form outside, for instance, it actually reminded me of some happy things, like baseball, where any memory I had of some epic catch or big hit or great pitch always played out against a haze of bleacher-filling parents lighting up and blowing out. No, I only minded cigarettes when they were indoors, or maybe most of all when they were in a taxi on the way to what might be my only baptism ever.

With the calmest voice I could muster without coughing, I reminded Lieve again that once she was baptized she'd have to give those things up, and as usual she said it was the last one and this time handed me the pack. I'd never held a pack of cigarettes before, and not knowing what to do with them I just stuck them inside the coat pocket of the hand-me-down brown stainless-steel suit I'd recently inherited from a going-home missionary. The rest of the ride I just looked out the window and sweated.

When we finally got to the church at the north end of Brussels and walked inside, the famously grumpy janitor walked up to me and asked, *Well? Goes it through?* He'd seen plenty of cancelled baptisms in his day and he wasn't going to fill the baptismal font all the way up with precious water until it was a sure thing.

Hoping that the janitor wasn't noticing the bulge in my coat pocket or the cigarette smell rising up from every stainless-steel fiber, I just said, *I think it.*

Think?

I mean, yes, it goes through, keep filling please.

I wasn't sure though, and went down the hall to be alone again while Lieve with the help of Valérie and a couple of ladies went down another hall to change into her big white baptismal dress. There in the little bare classroom I felt like I was on an even bigger roller coaster than I'd been up in the attic in Halle just a few hours before. In the attic I'd been ready to give up the baptism, but then after Jonas came knocking and especially when we climbed into the taxi my hopes had gone soaring again and I just had to have that baptism. But then when Lieve pulled out her cigarette, I had to think really hard that maybe I should just give up baptizing her after all, that maybe it wasn't the best thing for anyone, except maybe for me.

I didn't want to be one of those missionaries who was so desperate to baptize someone that he'd baptize anyone. Rumors about missionaries doing just that were already floating out of Latin America, where missionaries were baptizing plenty but they were under serious pressure to baptize even more, and so maybe they'd do things like the missionary in Brazil my friend saw, who in his desperation to reach a goal late one night finally grabbed a drunk man at a bar and took him outside and dunked him in a barrel of water and called it a baptism. Or like some missionaries in Mexico who just wrote on baptismal forms some names they got from tombstones in the local cemetery. And those were just two examples, without even mentioning the missionary-sponsored ping-pong tournaments where players couldn't move onto the next table until they'd listened to another Discussion. Oh, those Latin American missionaries.

But I didn't even have to look at Latin America, because there'd been the famous baseball baptisms in England and France a decade or two before, where kids were told they couldn't play this really cool new church-funded game unless by the way they were baptized first. Oh, those English and French missionaries.

But I didn't even have to look to England, either, or France, because guess what, right there in Belgium, right in Hasselt where I'd first worked, it was very possible that the 20 or 25 people who'd quit being Mormon almost the instant they'd been baptized had pretty possibly had some dubious methods used on them as well, by the legendary Elder Fisher, the one who'd proved you really could baptize in Belgium, because when my companion and I had gone looking those people up to learn their stories, well almost all of them said they hadn't really known what they were doing or even what the baptism was about when they'd done it, and they were still pretty obviously angry about it too. Oh, that Elder Fisher.

But maybe I and a lot of others were a lot more like Elder Fisher and these other sneaky missionaries than we thought, because didn't we all put some serious pressure on people too, maybe just without the same level of skill as Elder Fisher and Company? Like a certain breed of car salesman, maybe I too believed that just about no one was capable of making a serious decision, like buying a car or saving a soul, all by herself, but needed a little pushing and pulling and nudging to get there, for her own good. I tried pushing people into committing to this or that behavior too, and even told Lieve de Clercq that if she had faith and went through with her baptism then her husband's heart would be softened. Maybe it was more about making myself and all the people back home feel good than about making locals feel good, because you could bet that all those really skilled missionaries had written home some mighty strong and grateful letters about how they'd been blessed with baptisms, and that their parents probably wept because that's what they'd been waiting to hear, and that their bishops probably read the exploits right from the pulpit during church, and that no one was ever going to hear any retraction. No bishop was going to stand up and say, *I have a little correction to the fantastic baptizing* Success! *we heard about from Elder _____ , namely, that as well-meaning as he was, quite a few of his baptisms might have been a little hasty, before people really knew what they were doing. So please make a note that just about all 20 or so of the baptisms that made us so happy when we heard about them, that made us feel like if people were getting baptized in a foreign place like that, it just proved our church was irresistible, were mostly about Elder _____ feeling good about himself and us about ourselves.* Nope, no such retraction in the history of Mormondom. And if there had been or ever would be, well I didn't want it being said about me.

But kneeling there in the classroom I had to admit that part of me wanted to make my parents weep just like Elder Fisher's parents no doubt had, part of me wanted to make my bishop proud, and a lot of me wanted to make Rachelle swoon. And I even started thinking that I deserved a baptism, what with all the hours I'd put in, and all the wind and rain I'd ridden through, and all the sweat and emotion and bicycle spills I'd endured, and all the will-breaking times I'd forced myself to talk to people in public places, just for starters.

But then just like in the dismal upstairs bedroom in Hasselt long before, and sort of like in the attic just a few hours ago, came that calm that I now recognized as the closest thing to sure I ever felt about God. And that feeling said, without any words, that I didn't have to baptize Lieve or even 83 other people to feel good about what I was doing. The whole mission business, it hit me for at least a nano-moment, was more about suffering a little with people and feeling connected to them than it was about baptizing them. It was about being a friend, however trite that sounded, however much breaking-up boyfriends and girlfriends debased the term by saying they *just wanted to be friends* without even really meaning it, however much leader types were always saying to missionaries *you're not here to make friends,* like that was some bad thing. Jesus had a pretty strong view about friends, as in laying your life down for them, which went way beyond the casual sort of relationship most people meant by that term. That's what the whole mission business was about, it now seemed to me. Maybe even the whole religion business. Maybe even the whole life business.

I felt a huge sense of relief. I was even almost ready (but not quite) to give up my vision of 84, or 20, or even 1+. But after all that, I also improbably felt like the right thing to do at that particular moment was actually to go ahead and baptize Lieve, and not for my sake but because of the big beautiful dream she'd had.

Still, it should be Windex-clear by now that any noble feelings I had inside were not always the most stable things in the world. In fact they pretty regularly traded places with all the ignoble feelings lurking inside me too. In even more fact the two sorts of feelings were so familiar with each other by now that they casually waved at each other in passing all the flippin' time. Because after I got up from my prayer in the sterile little classroom and went and changed into my own baptismal whites, some of those less noble feelings somehow snuck back in right during the baptism itself.

All 15 or so people there that night, including the skeptical janitor, were watching from the baptism room, while Lieve walked down the steps on one side of the font and I down the steps on the other. I then held her wrist with my left hand and raised my right arm to a square and said the short baptismal prayer, then put her under the water, back first. For the rest of my life, I'd remember the exact weight of Lieve in that heavy gown as I eased her into the water with my right hand on her back and my left on her wrist and then lifted her out again with a loud WHOOSH. She was beaming, and so was Valérie, and so was I. But the thing was, the main reason I was beaming was that despite the noble feeling I'd had moments before in the classroom, the primary thought taking over my head when I put Lieve into the water was that now I could say I'd at least baptized someone.

I didn't want to admit that that was the thought that won out in the end, but it was true. That's what I felt most. I didn't even know how it'd snuck in there, and not just snuck in but actually forged its way to the front. And yet there it was, dominating all those other feelings also running through me.

That's why I wasn't so much different from all those really slick Elders. Just less skilled. Or maybe wasn't even so much different from a going-home Senior Companion in my friend's mission who dressed up in white and punched out the just-arrived Junior Companion a converting woman had asked to baptize her, so desperate was the puncher to get a baptism before he went home. I probably wouldn't have punched out Elder Roy, but if Lieve had asked him to baptize her I would've understood a little how that other guy felt.

After the baptism, the really good-hearted Branch President of Brussels went 20 miles out of his way to drive Lieve, Valérie, me, and Elder Roy back to Halle, so we wouldn't have to take another expensive taxi, and we all ate a few goodies at the post-baptismal get-together. Ludo was nowhere to be seen, despite his food-preparation skills. The really good-hearted Branch President promised to visit her every month, but I wondered whether he really could, since he lived clear across Brussels from her and already had so many other people to visit and ten times too much responsibility as it was. (Within a few years he would quit the church, exhausted.)

In fact, trouble with Lieve started that very night, because just after we all left she fell down the stairs on her way up to bed and hurt her back again. Elder Roy and I heard about it when we went by the next morning to say hello. Ludo answered the door and told us the news, saying we could go upstairs and see her if we wanted, but she was on more medication to deal with the pain. Ludo said it like he was blaming me for everything.

I smelled the cigarette smoke as soon as I hit the stairs, breaking my heart. She couldn't stop being Mormon already, I thought. Not like those people in Hasselt! Not like all those bad baptisms in France and England and Brazil! I thought the situation so serious that I told Elder Roy to stay downstairs and talk to Ludo while I went and had a serious talk with Lieve in her bedroom, which was against all sorts of mission rules but that's how serious I thought it was.

Lieve was barely lucid, but she did manage a *Hello Elder.*

I smiled tightly and asked, *How feel you, Lieve?* But then instead of waiting to hear or instead of consoling her, I just said, *Remember that you promised have never more to smoke?*

I know Elder, said Lieve groggily, *I forgot because of the pain.*

She handed me my second pack of cigarettes in two days, and I tried to convince myself she really meant it instead of even entertaining the idea that maybe she'd never be a practicing Mormon. Now I tried consoling her a little, and wished her a good recovery, but I left feeling uncertain about everything.

That happened on a Saturday, which meant the next day was Sunday, which was supposed to be Lieve's first day at church, but of course she never made it to church. Not that Sunday, and not any other. We went by her house later that day, to see how she was feeling, but this time she wasn't even friendly. Maybe she was blaming us for her fall too, like Ludo, that somehow it'd been a bad omen of her baptism. Even the kids seemed mad at me. In fact when we went by again on Monday, even friendly Jonas wouldn't let us in, except to let us stick our heads in the door and say hi to Lieve lying on the couch, her pack of cigarettes lying right next to her. Where did she get them all? I thought, dejectedly, as we left.

I stayed in Halle another month or so, but whenever we tried to visit Lieve no one answered. Once I saw the curtains move, the universal sign in Belgium that people didn't want to answer the door.

At least I got to see Lieve and her family a few months later, just before I went home to California. They even invited me over for a farewell dinner, maybe because it was pretty clear to Ludo by now that he wasn't going to lose Lieve after all. I even gave my old purple bike to Jonas so he wouldn't have to run everywhere any more. And when I started going back to Belgium as a historian, Lieve and Ludo were always glad to see me. Lieve never mentioned her dream again, or getting baptized, but her health got a little better. She even gave up smoking, which made me laugh. And Ludo made even more great meals for me. One year, though, when Ludo was out delivering the mail, someone hit him on his motor scooter, which damaged the part of his brain that let him taste. But Ludo kept cooking anyway because he loved it so much.

Then another year I called and Lieve said *Ludo is dead.* Some complication from his accident. Lieve and her dozen operations had outlived almost-always laughing Ludo, who'd practically single-handedly kept the family together during Lieve's bad times. Lieve took me out to visit Ludo's grave. I'd really liked Ludo, and always felt bad about the worry I'd caused him.

And then finally one other year, I called and Lieve's number was disconnected, which made me fear the worst, and sure enough when I finally found Lieve's daughter Valérie at the restaurant she now ran (she was Ludo's daughter too), she confirmed it. Lieve was dead, barely 60 years old.

I'd hardly seen Lieve during those 25 years since my mission, and her baptism hadn't exactly been Gibraltar-like in Mormon or world history. But when I heard she'd died, I felt a hole inside, and thought about her, and lamented any unkindness I might have shown her. And just like when I dreamed about her, I smelled the cigarette smell curling up from the lapels of my old stainless-steel suit.

nineteen

IN NO TIME

In Belgianland, in forests and fields, there are places where time has never been.

These places aren't easy to find, mind you. And don't even think about going to look for them, because they'll close right up if you do. If you're lucky enough to find such a place, it's because it's decided to let you stumble in accidentally, like Alice stumbling into her rabbit hole to Wonderland. Except in Belgianland you don't actually fall, you just suddenly realize you're in another world.

These timeless places shouldn't be confused with places where people are trying to stop time, like at a game where vein-popping coaches yell *Time Out!* or in a house full of kids where a fun-loving mother also yells *Time Out!* when things get out of hand again.

They shouldn't be confused either with places in Belgianland where time actually *has* stopped, like at a medieval ruin, or a 1920s Art-Deco building, or a still-working eighteenth-century farmhouse where steam is still rising up from piles of eighteenth-century-looking manure in the courtyard.

And they certainly shouldn't be confused with places where time is said to go on forever and ever Amen, like the classic versions of heaven and hell drawn up at church.

In fact the timeless places of Belgianland shouldn't even be confused with places where melancholy hangs so heavy that it practically squeezes past into present, like in Brussels at De Brouckère Square, although that sort of melancholy is getting really close to what actual timeless places feel like.

Nope, a bona fide timeless place just floats around in another dimension altogether. Time doesn't stop there, because it never got started. It doesn't go on forever and ever Amen there, because it was never present to begin with. And past time isn't squeezed into present time there, to be brooded upon, because there simply isn't any past. Everything just exists at once. There's no becoming, and no still-dormant potential, but only being. There's no remembering, and no prognosticating, but only awareness. There's no bawling, and no wild joy or heroic feeling, but only contentment. There's no hoping for the future, and no worrying about the past, but only present. Because there is no time.

Oh, it feels crazy when you start sensing all this. Crazy crazy. Loopy crazy. On drugs crazy. And it sounds even crazier when you start trying to explain it, to myself or especially to someone else — explaining that when you're inside a timeless place you feel like you've never been anywhere else, but then when you're back in the world of time you're not sure how long you were gone, or even whether you really were gone, or oh yeah even whether you're sane. So you can imagine the relief when you learn a lot of years later (because you've kept these crazy feelings to yourself for so long) that you're not the only one who's felt this way.

It turns out that finding timelessness has been the sort of nondenominational holy grail of all the great yogis and mystics over the centuries. Oh sure, a lot of early Christians thought of eternity as something classically linear and never-ending instead of as all-things-always-present-at-once, but Augustine set them straight when he said that *in the Eternal nothing passeth, but the whole is present,* and that *in Eternity all things stand still,* while *in time one thing comes, another succeeds.* Then there's Jesus's *Take no thought for the morrow,* which after an encounter with a timeless place gets a whole new meaning. And then you see that not only Jesus and Augustine and the yogis and mystics and Alice are with you, but some big names in science too, like Einstein, with his famous *the distinction between past, present, and future is only a stubbornly persistent illusion.* Sure, he and his physicist friends came to that conclusion through a whole lot of math, and the yogis and mystics reached theirs through a whole lot of meditation, while you got yours through just a few chance encounters with rabbit holes in the forests and fields of Belgianland, but what they're all talking about sounds enough like what you're feeling to make you feel relieved anyway.

My first place without time opened up early on, near the village of God-sheide outside Hasselt, where I never got in a single door for a Discussion but I did find at least one rabbit hole. My companion and I saw a small woods in the distance, then through the autumn-bare branches a small house inside the woods, so we started walking toward it, and the next thing I knew we were in some other world, like I and every person, thing, and place I'd ever known, done, or been were all there too, at once. Maybe it was the fairy-like effect of Belgianland's late-afternoon winter-light, or maybe it was how new everything still was to me there, or maybe it was just late-onset jetlag, or maybe it was that since no earthlings were talking to us I started hearing some otherworldly voices instead. But whatever it was, everything was there together — like *déjà vu,* already seen, except a hundred times more intense. Like *toujours vu,* always seen.

A second timeless place opened up in the snowy field near Zichem at Christmas, even if I didn't recognize it that way at first.

Then a third and fourth place popped up near Halle, the third when my bicycle tire went flat miles from home and I had to walk most of the way through a woods where a timeless place just snuck up again, and then the fourth when I was riding through the hills that led to the village of Pepingen, which happened to be at the edge of what was so magically called the Pajottenland (Pa-yoat-un-lont), and by the way, a bike wasn't the best place in the world to feel another dimension, with what it did to balance and all.

And finally after those four timeless places I found bunches more of them, near the end of mission time, all of them now in the hilly fields and forests of the Pajottenland, which spread out like a fan from the western side of Brussels all the way to the countryside. In fact as far as I could tell there were more timeless places in the Pajottenland than anywhere.

Okay, maybe not in the parts right *next* to the old western wall of Brussels, because those were all urbanized and disenchanted by now. But you could find a few rural and enchanted patches in the next ripple of villages heading west, like Dilbeek where Mormon missionaries lived, or Itterbeek where Pieter Bruegel used to paint. And you could especially find enchanted places in the most western and rural stretch of villages — from just above Halle in the south all the way up to Affligem in the north, like in the enchantingly named Lennik, Gooik, Schepdaal, St. Ulriks Kapelle, Ternat, Wambeek, and dozens of others in between.

Maybe I found more timeless places in the Pajottenland just because that was where I worked longest as a missionary, 12 whole months to be exact. But it was probably more than dumb time, because after all during most of those 12 months I didn't even know that's what the name of the place was. No, it was the place itself, and the people who lived there, that did it to me.

Twelve months in the Pajottenland like this: four in Dilbeek with Elder Downing, three in Halle with Elder Roy, and finally, to end my mission, back to Dilbeek for five more months. And mostly during those last five did I realize where I was and what was going on.

When I got word that I was headed back to Dilbeek, I couldn't believe it, because just the year before I'd been ecstatic to leave that awful old apartment behind forever, where I wasn't allowed to shower except on weekends, where the male half of the old landlordly couple was friendly but the female half made me tremble because she did things like diagnose sickness by reaching uninvited inside my pajama-shirt and sticking under my armpit a thermometer that probably belonged to Anders Celsius himself (d. 1744), and where the couple's only child, 35-year-old Alphonse, yelled just as furiously at big-time wrestling on TV as he did at his parents.

But it didn't take long to see that things would be better this time in Dilbeek. And not just because the end of mission time was looming, because I still couldn't believe that. And not even because I was now a big-shot Zone Leader, which except for being an Assistant was the highest honor you could hope to have.* In fact all the tracking of time and *Success!* I had to do as a Zone Leader, in the form of all the statistical reports I had to write, had zero to do with timelessness. Oh, I did other things too, like interview the very occasional person for baptism, and attend Zone Leader seminars at the Mission Home in Antwerp, and train the District Leaders and regular missionaries of my 20-member zone, and sometimes I even felt like my training helped in non-time-bound ways, like with Elder Wood, a really sensitive fellow in third-stage post-traumatic-shock after three months of riding busses and trams around Brussels, or with Elder Beaumont, a 28-year-old mailman from New Jersey who did even more wondrous things to Dutch than most missionaries did. But the overarching purpose of all that training was to give a NASA-like boost to everyone's *Success!* Their time-bound time-laden *Success!*

Nothing except local business could have been more time-bound or further removed from a rabbit hole than a proselyting report divided into 27 categories that could be turned into flow-charts, fancy colored graphs, and three-dimensional conical shapes. And probably nothing could have been further removed either from one of Aquinas's five proofs for the existence of God, Who after seeing such a report was maybe shaking His head and saying *not this, not this.* At first I'd just assumed that the thing bugging me was the sort of report I'd been given to work with, and so I'd used some of my newfound being-myself boldness to invent a new report, which nar-

---

* Was it just coincidence that Rachelle in the same letter both congratulated me on my elevation to Zone Leader and invited me to come visit her when I got home? No way, I thought.

rowed *Success!* down to just a few crucial categories, but the real genius of the system lay in the sheer frequency of reporting, as in twice a day every single missionary being required to call me up to tell me their precious statistics. And my being-myself boldness paid off, because the chronically underperforming Brussels Zone jaw-droppingly witnessed 100 percent improvement in its famously low statistics, and neither I nor anyone else ever stopped to consider that maybe the improvement was just very possibly due to nerve-racked missionaries getting a whole lot better at reporting rather than necessarily at proselyting. I never dug around to find out whether that was maybe the case, but why should I have, when I was getting so much praise for my wonder-working system? So much that I was invited to present it to the other 10 Zone Leaders, which should've been a really proud moment for me, because I was the lead author of the system, and because Elder Downing was in the audience (probably not taking notes). But even before my button-popping presentation was done, even while I was still yapping away about the myriad virtues of high-frequency-reporting, even while I was assuring all the other Zone Leaders that they too could have *Success!* like this if they really wanted to, inside I was already hearing, *not this, not this,* and actually listening now. Because the way I felt talking about this report was just the opposite of how I felt in no time.

No wonder that after the presentation was over, I kept up my wonder-working system for only a week or so longer and then quit it. I even stopped charting my own personal statistics on graph paper, the way I'd done for so many months. Because all that charting, even though so clarifyingly color-coded, just didn't mean anything anymore. And so even though I as a big-shot leader had to keep up my statistics somewhat, I mostly tried to ignore them now. And here came that calm again.

And feeling like that, not being a big-shot Zone Leader, was what made my second time around in Dilbeek so much better.

To ride your bike into the western-most, rural-most, and rabbit-hole-most part of the Pajottenland you had to first brave the hard-charging time-bound cars on the Ninoofsesteenweg that ran just outside your front door.

Most roads in Belgianland had pretty generous bike lanes on each side, and even where there were no lanes local drivers were pretty good lookouts, because this was the land of blesséd Eddy Merckx after all, not of cars. But it was also the land of whatever-cars-there-were-tended-to-drive-really-fast, especially on the barely four-lane Ninoofsesteenweg that was so tight it had no bike lanes at all. Even the most careful drivers had nowhere to go to try to get around anyone dense enough to ride a bike here, so if you were going to be one of those dense anyones then you had to ride in a sort of rolling tip-toeing style along the big white stripe running along the outside of the road, which gave you about six inches of room to work with, and which meant that sometimes in fall, winter, and spring your billowing overcoat was going to be brushed by a whooshing car, and in summer your already suffering wristwatch might be grazed by the gigantic side mirror of a roaring bus.

If you were headed to the village of Schepdaal that lay exactly due west from Dilbeek, then you just rode the Ninoofsesteenweg straight for six nerve-racking kilometers and hoped you'd arrive alive. You always did (arrive alive), so when you reached the village you turned left off the *steenweg,* up past the usual picture-perfect parish church, and headed into the village's hills and fields, and there after the last house, out amid the grain waving in the breeze, you had a pretty good chance of leaving time.

If you were headed northwest from Dilbeek to St. Ulriks Kapelle or to Ternat and Wambeek beyond, then you had to stay on the Ninoofsesteen-weg for only a daredevil kilometer or so before veering right, up a side road, cresting a hill, then making a long lung-restoring descent past scattered houses and shops until you suddenly found yourself on a quiet and mostly flat country road bordered by lumpy pastures with rickety fences and fields mostly green and gold. After a few calming kilometers like that, you'd come to another village, where the brick houses and shops would begin again, including the shop owned by the fellow who sometimes worked on your fragile purple bike for free, but then just like that you were past the village and in between fields again, and it was the fields you noticed most. Like the triangle-shaped field just before the church of St. Martens Bodegem, where the only Seventh-day Adventist in all the Pajottenland was always working and always waved at you, a fellow suspect person. Or like the field with a giant sweaty old horse pulling mightily some creaky old farm machine. Or like the field with a single bent old man or woman whacking away at the ground with a hoe, making you wonder how in the world whatever they were doing in that little tiny spot could possibly make any sort of difference in that big old field. Or especially like the quiet fields where on hot and thus humid days all you could hear were the bugs buzzing around your suitcoat, stuck like glue to your sweaty white-on-white shirt, because it was in the quiet fields in the heat of summer that you were most likely to leave time.

If you headed southwest from Dilbeek you would see a lot of the same scenery. You'd turn left this time off the Ninoofsesteenweg and ride past the tiny church of St. Anna Pede that Pieter Bruegel liked to include in his paintings, even if you had to go a little out of your way, because what a lovely tiny church it was. Then you kept going through the mostly French-speaking suburban neighborhood until you got to sacred countryside, then you rode under a mammoth concrete railroad bridge that was completely out of place in the Pajottenland, and that your still chronologically undisciplined mind let you think was some Roman aqueduct instead of just a twentieth-century bridge for trains. Then you'd pass farms with wobbly signs inviting you in to buy their ice cream, but you'd already spent the last of your snack money on a waffle at Cave Man's, which was one of the few reasons you still went downtown now. So instead of stopping you'd just keep riding all the way to the edge of the Pajottenland, all the way to the castle of Gaasbeek, which didn't itself have any rabbit holes, but the forest all around was full of them, as you discovered when a missionary and then just about every year since, during the countless timeless walks you take through that forest, feeling every time like you've never left and that nothing's ever changed and that there's never been time.

And last of all if you were headed northeast from Dilbeek then you didn't have to ride on the Ninoofsesteenweg at all but just cross it, except there were almost no timeless places going that way, because riding that way you were just riding back toward Brussels, but even that road had a few magical fields alongside.

Of course the point of all this riding wasn't just to see a bunch of scenery, or just to look for magical places, or just to dull the pain of rejection by killing time with long cycling tours. It was to go talk to people, yes way out in the countryside now instead of on the streets of downtown Brussels.

What an ingenious idea it'd been to start going into the villages around Brussels, where Flemish-speaking people actually were, instead of downtown where they mostly weren't. Flemish-speaking missionaries in Brussels had mostly avoided the Flemish-speaking villages because they mostly wanted to conquer the exciting city itself, and also because going out to Flemish-speaking villages wasn't easy on busses and so would mean long bike rides that got even longer in the rain. So sure, your odds of getting rejected downtown were even better than in the countryside, but downtown at least you were getting rejected on warm busses and trams instead of on a wet bike. But Zone-Leading Elder Gabberd had been bold enough to change all that, and by the time I arrived back in Dilbeek to take his place, the missionaries had been riding way out to the villages in the countryside for several months.

Of course plenty of Flemish-speaking villagers were as suspicious as all villagers were famous for being, but plenty of them were also famously hospitable. And after only a couple of months, I'd already met a lot of both sorts, knocking as I had on just about every door in all the villages within a 12-or-so-kilometer half-circle away from Dilbeek and ATAP-ing everyone I met on the occasional street. But I wasn't knocking or ATAP-ing as usual anymore, in fact wasn't doing anything else as usual anymore either, but instead using my newfound boldness to just list with the wind, in a good and even somewhat graceful way now instead of an unaware tossed-around-like-a-sock-puppet way, just striking up and maintaining the most casual sort of conversations with people, the sort of conversations I'd been told missionaries didn't have the time or the vocation to strike up, much less to maintain. And a casual conversation, mind you, was no easy thing to strike up or maintain for a CIA-looking guy with an accent, but there I was just trying to get to know people, just trying of all things and completely against protocol to make friends, even going back to visit people who'd told either me or my predecessors that they didn't want to hear any more Discussions but who were genuinely interested in being friends, which somehow felt right now.

And what a lot of friendly people there were to meet in the Pajottenland, more than anywhere I'd ever been. Like Marilu and Bernard Huys in Schepdaal, who I myself never taught a single Discussion to but who always welcomed me and always invited me to Bernard's organ recitals at the village church, and who in letters and conversations until the near-present liked to fondly recollect the old talks they had with missionary me about *philosophy, art, and music* in their Eden-like backyard, which recollections might have embarrassed me because they included no mention of any talk about Mormonism, but it doesn't embarrass me because I was so glad I knew them.

Or like Louis and Charlotte De Ridder in St. Ulriks Kapelle, who the closest they ever got to a Discussion was when they drove me and my companion and their four kids to a Mormon choir festival in a city far away, but they have always kept the welcome mat out for me, even to the very present.

Or like *Meneer* and *Mevrouw* Peeters in Ternat who were so regal that I didn't ever learn their first names, and who lived in a now-palatial remodeled barn and insisted on serving us every Monday head-spinningly elegant dinners that began with a phone call(!) to the mysterious room next door, and who kept writing to me for years.

Or like *Meneer* and *Mevrouw* Strubbe, who lived on the street behind us in Dilbeek and were heart-warmingly friendly even though they had an old encyclopedia that said Mormons sacrificed young girls on the upper floor of the Salt Lake Temple and threw them into the Great Salt Lake, to which I could only flabbergastedly say that whoever was doing the throwing must've had a heck of an arm, because the lake was about five miles away, which made them laugh.

Or maybe especially like Raymond and Yvonne Aerts, who lived at the edge of Brussels instead of in the countryside but who might have been the most magical people of all. I'd met them the year before with Elder Downing actually and had already enjoyed a memorable meal with them and had already felt their unusual level of goodness, but Elder Downing and I had felt guilty about continuing to visit a couple who weren't interested in hearing any more Discussions. But one of the first things I did when I came back to Dilbeek was to look them up, because interest in hearing Discussions wasn't my big criterion for talking to people anymore.

Yvonne and Raymond had grown up near each other in villages to the west but came to Brussels for the now-retired Raymond's job as a local banker. Their house was classic Belgianland narrow, full of traditional but at least not brown furniture. But Raymond's real joy was his manicured backyard garden or more accurately mini-farm, right here in Brussels, full of potatoes and vegetables just like the fields back home, because stick-thin Raymond loved most of all to eat, even more than most people, owing to his barely surviving four years in a German POW camp, where he dropped to 40 kilos (about 88 pounds). Those four long years must've shortened him too, because he was only about 5′4″ now. Ever since the war, it was like Raymond was trying to make up for lost meal-time, because he cultivated his garden and attacked every meal with an intensity surprising in a guy his size and temperament. You never heard a peep from Raymond during a meal, and he always finished first, which was saying a lot at a table that included at least one fast-eating bad-mannered local businessman. Raymond never did catch up to all those meals lost during the war, because even though he ate like a Belgian plow horse he stayed as thin as a backyard goat. Luckily for him, Yvonne was a heaven-sent cook, even in a land full of heaven-sent cooks. But here's the thing: eating and gardening and local banking weren't even Raymond's best features, and cooking wasn't even Yvonne's, and that was saying a lot for the both of them. Because even better than Raymond's little farm, even better than Yvonne's salads and *friets* and tomatoes with tiny shrimp and homemade tarts soaked in something that made your throat burn but still tasted good, was how ineffably *good* they

233

both were, Yvonne's food just being the main vehicle for expressing that goodness, evident for instance in the fact that in spite of her 2' wide girth on her 4'11" frame and her obvious love for food, she almost never ate as long as guests were there to be served and talked to, she just got so carried away talking and listening.

Oh sure, we could've justified visits to Raymond and Yvonne's and to every last one of the Friendly People of the Pajottenland in classic mission-ary PR style: they were all well-respected pillars of the community and so even if they weren't actually taking Discussions you could bet they were saying good things about missionary us to other well-respected pillars in the community, so we were therefore still at least indirectly proselyting when we visited them. Or maybe their kids would convert when they got older! But I had to admit that I didn't really have classic missionary pur-poses in mind when I went to visit them. I even had to sheepishly admit that I was probably learning more about religion and life from them than they ever would from me. Oh, I didn't think they were perfect or even over-estimate them the way I was wont to do with people I liked: among other things they held some pretty alarming views of immigrants, especially those from North Africa, and also held some deep old sentiments against Walloons (French-speaking Belgianlanders) for reasons I couldn't quite grasp. And every last one of them liked to eat and drink too much at spe-cial occasions, according to old Burgundian tradition. But those were all historically conditioned and thus time-bound things, not things that rose above time, and it was the latter I learned most from them and that made me feel like I'd always known them — and that surprised me as much as falling down a rabbit hole would.

I'd never have guessed that as much goodness as could possibly exist in the universe could be packed into a 4'11" tall 2' wide 65-year-old very ordinary- and even stereotypical-looking Belgianland woman named Yvonne. Or into her 5'4" equally ordinary- and even stereotypical-looking husband Raymond. In fact my understanding of what goodness was didn't any longer come from studying any list of 113 or however many rules my particular culture said really and truly constituted goodness, or even from the really important guidelines laid down by my parents and teachers and leaders, but instead from just seeing it personified in two ordinary- and even stereotypical-looking Belgianlanders named Yvonne and Raymond.

I'd never have guessed when I was a boy dreaming of a mission and of fame and love that I'd find my greatest contentment ever not through playing baseball or through a (picture of a) beautiful girl or through baptizing 84 but instead through moving for a while in the same orbit as a 4′11″ tall 2′ wide 65-year-old Belgianland woman (who as far as I could tell rarely shaved her legs and almost certainly never her armpits) and her food-loving Belgianland husband. Despite their foibles, the goodness inside them was whole and indivisible, like a holograph, or like the host of the Catholic Eucharist: no matter how many times you divided it, it was still as whole as before. Or like the wholeness of the physicists, who say that a tiny cubic inch of what looks like plain old space actually holds as much energy as the entire universe. Well, that was Yvonne's amount of goodness too: it couldn't get any bigger.

It was a total shock to me, realizing that — a shock on the level of Peter's when God told him that Gentiles weren't unclean after all, or of people when they saw Jesus touching beggars and unwanted children and sinners and lepers. I not only was shocked to feel goodness that big, but I especially was shocked to feel it in a place so far away among a bunch of strangers speaking a strange language and almost all belonging to the great and abominable church of the devil. I'd have bet-my-life supposed instead that I was there enlightening and saving them, but now it looked like they were enlightening and saving me, and maybe even causing me to go a little native.

But maybe going native wasn't so bad. Even the champions of the local-business look at the Mission Home understood that you had to go at least a little native to understand people. Hadn't Jesus himself gone native, by being born human so he could understand humans? So was it so bad to go a little native, a little local, so you could understand locals, beyond even the businessmen? Or to end up actually learning more from them than they did from you?

Whether it was bad or not it was still shocking, especially when it hit me that maybe the Friendly People of the Pajottenland were the way they were not in spite of their great and abominable Catholicism but to a big extent because of it. Maybe even local Mormons were too, because it was pretty hard to separate local Belgianism out completely from local Catholicism, even for those who'd officially become something else. Most of the time the sort of Catholicism on display in Belgianland wasn't the sort that would march in the streets to defend transubstantiation or the infallibility of the pope, or that would send Mormon missionaries packing: you wouldn't find Yvonne or Raymond doing any of that. In fact if any of those subjects ever came up, you were more likely to find Yvonne saying something skeptical about infallibility and flicking her wrist backwards at you and tossing her head sideways, like *oh come on,* the way she always did when she disapproved of something, and to find Raymond glued to the Tour de France and inviting Mormon-missionary me to sit down right next to him and watch wide-eyed like he was instead of talking about theology. But there was no doubt that Yvonne and Raymond had learned their thoroughly inculcated senses of duty and obligation and modesty and politeness and hospitality from their thoroughgoing Belgianism, which included a lot of Catholicism, and that Catholicism had a lot to do with the sort of timeless uncontainable goodness oozing out from them.

People like Raymond and Yvonne were the reason I stumbled into more rabbit holes in the Pajottenland than anywhere else, not because rabbit holes were just arbitrarily popping up there as purely objective geographical phenomena. Because the whole point (or just result) of reaching the timeless state mystics and yogis and scientists are always trying to reach, and that I was beginning to experience, was to heighten the sense of connection to everyone and everything around me, more connection than I ever felt just languishing in plain old ordinary time.

It's another one of those crazy-sounding things, and not only because I'd never expected to get a thing like that from my mission but because I'd never expected a thing like that to be what I'd get *most,* instead of, say, a lot of grateful converts uttering my name in reverential tones to their equally grateful descendants. But once again a few physicists would weigh in to help me here. Like Neil DeGrasse Tyson saying that the greatest discovery of science was that all things were made of the same stuff: *We are part of this universe, we are in this universe, but perhaps more important than both of those facts, is that the universe is in us.* The stars in the heavens were made of the same stuff as earthlings, and American landers and Mormons of the same stuff as Belgianlanders and Catholics. So people don't just *want* to feel connected to others or to nature, or even just feel mystically connected, but literally are, so that maybe Jesus's urging people to be one and Paul's talk about nobody being strangers anymore weren't so much instructions as reminders. Which makes you realize how it was possible for places and people so far away and foreign to feel like they'd always been home.

Oh, I looked hopelessly like a stranger in Belgianland, I did, and not just because of my suits. But I felt at home there anyway, and not coincidentally started feeling as well a sense of who I really was. I still wasn't entirely sure what that meant, because *myself* could be a long and confusing business,* but I knew it first emerged noticeably not just among but because of the Friendly People of the Pajottenland. Because what I came to realize was that when I felt most connected to other people was also when I also felt most timeless and most myself — like these people were seeing me for who I was, not who I was supposed to be. And I was doing the same for them. Maybe just to mutually feel that was what I'd really come to Belgianland for.

I wanted to keep feeling those connections even after I went home, even though none of the Friendly People of the Pajottenland or their kids ever became Mormon. So I wrote letters and Christmas cards, slowing down a little over the years but still visiting whenever I was nearby, which was pretty often. Yvonne insisted on every visit that I come over for one more Gargantuan-level dinner where she'd wave away my ecstasy over her food like it was the silliest thing she'd ever heard and where I'd eat gratefully

---

* Maybe that wasn't terribly surprising, because according to theologians Jesus Himself had two natures, so why wouldn't humans possibly have even more or get confused about their own? Or say like Walt Whitman, *I am legion?*

alongside a silent and even more grateful Raymond, and sometimes along-side my wife and kids and even parents too, because Yvonne insisted on fitting my whole clan inside her narrow house if they were in town, and even though she didn't speak a word of English she acted like my parents were her best friends, and then at the end she'd secretly stuff 1000-franc bills inside my coat for the kids. And when she and Raymond celebrated their 50th wedding anniversary, and my family and I just happened to be in town again, we were all invited to the special Mass and dinner, which is a big deal if you know how much a Belgianland special dinner costs per head, and as usual the dining festivities went from six to midnight with one course per hour and increasingly noisy talk and dancing, all of which my now-adult kids still talk about. And then when Raymond had to go into a care center and silently wolf down the inferior-but-still-not-bad institu-tional food (this was Belgianland after all), I'd go with Yvonne to visit him, and she'd apologize for not being able to make meals for me anymore, but boy was I glad that I could finally do something for her for once, and treat her to a meal every declining year at the restaurant she liked, out near the cemetery where Raymond was finally buried, out along the road where I used to ride my missionary bike toward her house, and I always had to tell the waiter in advance not to take Yvonne's money because I was absolutely paying, even though Yvonne always tried to sneak the waiter something. And then finally Yvonne died as well.

And then the others started dying too, including saintly Marilu, and charismatic Louis, who went quiet in his last years because of dementia, but luckily his 45-year-old Down's syndrome son Karel was around to watch him like a hawk, and to keep Louis out of the street just like Louis had kept Karel out all those years.

I have only pictures of some of them now, with myself posed alongside in my local-businessman suit, pictures that look for all the world like the classic pose of a Mormon missionary with some of his converts, but in fact they're all pictures of Belgianlanders with one of theirs. Sometimes I miss them and lose contact, but mostly I've felt over the years like they're all still inside me, like they shaped my views without even ever trying to, more than

I ever shaped theirs while actually trying. And when they're with me inside like that, I don't have any melancholy or time-boundedness at all.

Oh sure, just like a lot of other things I learned on my mission, I didn't learn that sort of contentment overnight. And oh sure, I later learned that I was actually connected to everybody, not just to the Friendly People of the Pajottenland. I went on to feel connections in Sweden (where I didn't even look like a stranger) and France and even of all things near my American-land home. But you first learn feelings like that in a particular place among particular people, and where they'd come first and fastest and easiest for me was among people in places I'd never even known existed when I was a boy dreaming of converting people.

In the Pajottenland.

In Belgianland.

twenty

OUT WITH A THUD

Have to hurry myself, still much to do, I thought in Dutch as I almost ran from the Delhaize grocery store to our Volkswagen Polo that was parked along the edge of the busy street, right in front of the fruits and vegetables.

It was my day to drive, so Elder Vogel got in the passenger's seat and I jumped behind the wheel and started the Polo and checked my rearview mirror before backing up. But I didn't turn my head to check my blind spot because I was in a hurry and it'd been clear just a second before when I'd walked through it, and for fetch sake I only had to back up a little, so I started backing up and *then* turned my head to look, just in time to hear the thud against the right rear bumper that always signaled you'd just hit a little old man.

It couldn't be. Not now. Not the last week of my mission.

The little old man must've started walking behind the Polo in order to wave down a bus, because at this stop like so many others in Brussels the bus couldn't pull all the way over to the curb, because the curb was lined with parked cars, so a waved-down bus just pulled up next to the parked cars and stopped in the middle of the street. Any little old man waving at it had to wade in between the parked cars to climb aboard. I'd seen the bus coming in my left mirror but not the little old man in my rearview mirror (no right mirror), because he had entered the blind spot at the very instant I'd started backing up without checking.

241

I slammed on the brakes, jumped out, ran around the car, and saw the little old man lying on the ground, surrounded already by several fiercely protective people. At least he wasn't dead or even seriously hurt, but the fiercely protective people were already yelling at me. Especially when they caught an eyeful of the suit and an earful of the accent that on a young foreign-looking and -sounding guy my age gave me away as a possible CIA-agent or even religious fanatic.

I immediately saw the headlines sure to plaster the covers of especially less respectable Belgian papers the next day: *Mormon Cult Missionary Scheduled to Go Back Home This Week Is Detained in Belgium Indefinitely for Hitting Little Old Man in Front of the Fruits and Vegetables at Delhaize.*

It was Monday August 8, and I was supposed to fly away this coming Saturday August 13. But there was now some serious doubt about that.

Too bad I didn't yet know the seventeenth-century rhyming Dutch proverb, *haastig spoed is zelden goed,* which in unrhymed English means *hurrying up is almost never any good.*

Several of the fiercely protective helpers shot assorted dirty looks my way, but then to everyone's astonishment the frail little old man, who was at least 80, got on his feet, determined to catch the bus that had since pulled up and was still waiting for him in the street. Everyone on the bus was now looking out the windows and watching too. I stood there apologizing with arms out, offering to help, but the fiercely protective helpers wouldn't let me any closer. The little old man climbed gingerly up the stairs, moaning and groaning for everyone to hear, which made the bus driver glare at me, and then keep on glaring while he shut the door and pulled away, the little old man bent over in the front seat, no doubt still moaning.

I felt completely helpless as the crowd started dispersing. What was I supposed to do? Was someone going to call the police? Was I supposed to stay there until they showed up? And would the police detain me for weeks or months and ruin my going-home? Especially if the little old man's injuries turned out to be more serious than they seemed? I could always just report the accident myself to our landlords' son Alphonse (who unfortunately for the citizens of Brussels was a cop) when Elder Vogel and I got back to the apartment, but you never knew with Alphonse: he might wave it off and say not to worry and go back to watching big-time wrestling, or he might handcuff me on the spot and drive me down to headquarters personally. With uncertainty swirling all around, Elder Vogel and I finally climbed back in the car and drove off, with me having visions of the police dragging me from the plane just before it was supposed to take off and carry me to my home.

During these last weeks in Belgium I badly wanted to tell people just how sad I was that my mission was about to end, like other missionaries did all the time.

But I couldn't. Because even though I loved the Pajottenland and certain friendly people there, my relief at almost being done overwhelmed everything else. I never thought once about *extending* for a month or two, that magical word that got everyone back home speaking in reverential tones about just how *dedicated* you obviously were. I didn't even want my parents coming to pick me up so we could travel around Europe for a couple of weeks, the way some missionaries did. No, I just wanted to go home, and worried that the Mission President would call and say I *had* to extend.

But finally the last week arrived and I almost started believing I really was going home. Then I hit the little old man.

That wasn't the only thing threatening my home-going. There was also the (usually) even worse driving of my very last companion, the tall and gangly Elder Vogel. He actually turned out to be one of my favorites, to my great surprise, because we seemed to have very little in common at first. But he did have one great and unforgivable flaw: he didn't know how to drive a car with a manual transmission, and it was my job to teach him.

We had a car because all Zone Leaders had cars. Sure, there were such severe restrictions on them (Zone business only) that we still ended up riding our bikes most of the rainy time anyway. But when you did drive them, you were supposed to take turns — one guy one day, one guy the next — and it would have been a most assured loss of authority for one member of the Zone Leaderly team not to take his turn at the wheel.

I wasn't sure which was harder: teaching Elder Roy to ride a bike or Elder Vogel to use a clutch, but I knew for dang sure that teaching Elder Vogel was more dangerous, because it involved exponentially higher speeds and because his hand-eye coordination was about the same as a tree's. For weeks we'd devoted half an hour a day to his driving, mostly on country roads where cars were rare, but as always when a car appeared in Belgium it appeared really fast, which appearance would make Elder Vogel forget what he'd learned not only about driving a clutch but about driving period. As soon as a car loomed on the horizon, he'd exclaim *Oh no!* in his nasal voice (that miraculously didn't bother me) and start jerking and lurching until he'd finally stall, then cry out in total panic, *Elder Harline what happened? I did everything right!* And I would try to explain through clenched teeth what part of everything he hadn't done right, while he just kept insisting that the nefarious clutch had betrayed him again.

I'd put off his maiden drive into the busy streets of Brussels as long as I could, in fact until the very last week of my mission, but I finally ran out of excuses the day after hitting the little old man, because really would Elder Vogel do any worse? So the next day when it was his day to drive, and we had to go into town to cash my last check, he nervously took the wheel and I even more nervously the passenger's seat. Maybe his maiden drive into Brussels would be my last, I feared, and maybe my mission instead of ending on August 13 might end today, August 9, along with my entire life, in a fiery crash with Elder Vogel yelling, even as flames were licking at the both of us, *But I did everything right!*

And so I buckled in tight and we drove into town, lurching along just fine most of the way, until we got to the last big intersection near our destination at Rogier Square, where Elder Vogel sure enough killed the engine and panicked and almost killed us while I clenched my teeth giving instructions to save us.

That non-leisurely drive and little scene in the intersection weren't the only things that day threatening my return. On Rogier Square stood a little trailer run by a money-exchanger the historically-and-culturally-clueless missionaries had always affectionately if still cluelessly called The Jew. This 60-year-old fellow had from his trailer with the mysterious plastic circle on top been cashing missionaries' checks for 30 years, when few other places would, and cashing them with a lot of humor too. I cashed one that day for $50 at 34.4 Belgian francs per dollar, and in-between the usual banter asked whether he would please pose for a picture, since I was going home in a few days and wanted to remember him. He dramatically obliged, jumping through the swinging door in the counter and fanning out a big pile of bills in front of his smiling face while I clicked away. I even told him I'd miss him, after the 15 or so checks he'd cashed for me and all his hilarious missionary observations.

Then Elder Vogel and I drove off, me at the wheel this time even though it was still technically his day to drive. We had a couple of referrals to look up downtown, and I was thrilled to plunge into the giant five-to-ten-lane roundabout on Montgomery Square, full of speeding, honking cars, just like in a European movie. When none of the referrals were home, we started back to our apartment, but as we got near Rogier Square we heard a screaming-loud siren and saw the mysterious plastic circle on top of The Jew's trailer flashing like crazy. Everyone was slowing and looking, and horrifying word quickly reached us that he'd been robbed and shot to death, about a half-hour after we'd left.

What a disturbing last week this was turning out to be.

And there was more. Even church on my last Sunday had been disturbing — all three, in fact.

For one of the only times in my life, I'd not only attended the usual Mormon services that Sunday but those of other churches too. And what was disturbing was just how comfortable they were. The first was a Mass in the parish church of Wambeek, where we'd gotten to know the friendly pastor a little, not to fulfill the favorite missionary fantasy of converting a rival clergyman, but just so maybe he wouldn't preach against us like some pastors had. He'd invited us into the rectory to chat, and told us about how he'd been in a concentration camp during the war and how that had helped him as a priest, because until that'd happened he'd always told people who were suffering that trials were good for them, so cheer up. But after being locked up himself he'd realized just how empty his words must have sounded, and how debilitating and lonely suffering could be, as his time in the camp just about broke him. It made him empathize with people now instead of trivialize their troubles. He also invited us to Mass on my last Sunday, and we thought why not, but then his sermon was just as unsettlingly insightful as our chat with him had been. Despite my new openness to others including Catholics, I had to admit that I'd still been expecting something great and abominable at a Catholic Mass.

The second disturbing service was at a tiny Protestant church, where we'd been invited by an investigator who'd said he would attend a Mormon service if we would attend his. I'd agreed to go with the same attitude I'd had the time I traded invitations to church with a friend a few years before: *Sure I'll come to your church, but I'm inviting you to the true church, while yours is just a play church. And I'm a little worried about being brainwashed at your church, whereas at mine you'll just get obvious truth.* But the sermon at this church was also inspiring.

It always bugged the heck out of me when people would say to us, *Oh, religions are all the same,* because the whole point of me and every other missionary being there in Belgium was to show that no they weren't. But then when I went inside these two other churches to check them out for myself, I had to at least admit that by focusing so much on all the differences I sure had missed all the sameness.

The third service of the day, the Mormon one, might actually have been the most disturbing of all, mostly because it was so bad, thanks in no small part to me, one of the featured speakers. Since I was to give my goodbye talk, our landlord Bernard asked if he could come listen. I tried to deliver an inspiring message, but maybe I didn't believe it enough, because it had all come across as give-me-cancer-now depressing, with all those empty pews and that big old tall slanted wood ceiling and that sad late-afternoon light coming through the windows, even though it was the only genuine Mormon church-building in the whole mission. I looked out over the audience while I spoke and realized that most of them, 19 to be exact, were fellow missionaries, not locals, despite all our efforts. And I didn't fool anyone, including Bernard, with my attempted enthusiasm, because when I optimistically asked afterwards how he'd liked the meeting, he looked me in the eye and said only one word: *triestig.* Dreary. Sad. Unlike the Catholic or Protestant services that day.

And finally the last disturbing thing that week was the let's-just-call-it unthinkable incident with the white shirt. Elder Vogel and I had a 30-something investigator way out in the Pajottenland who'd eagerly let us in for a couple of Discussions but who then kept fidgeting and fussing the whole time instead of doing any Discussing, until near the end of the second Discussion he suddenly went radically off-topic and blurted out with a part-hopeful and part-sheepish smile, *I know not how I this must say, but I like not women,* punctuated by a half-giggle twist at the end. We sat there stunned, not feeling timeless at all, even though we were in the middle of the Pajottenland. Oh, I still felt bad about Danny Clevenger, but of course he'd turned out not to actually be a non-woman-liking guy, like this guy was, who was an absolute puzzle. Determined to be polite, and also to get in a full Discussion-hour, I said *Well okay* and just kept going. When it ended, the guy wanted us to come back again but I for once resisted the chance to pile up some easy Discussion-hours and made the excuse that I was going home in a few days and wouldn't have time, sorry. At which point the guy said well in that case he'd like to give me a small goodbye present, and I said sure. He said he'd noticed we always wore white shirts, and he had one for me, if I could just wait a second. So he went into the back room while Elder Vogel and I sat awkwardly waiting for more like five or ten minutes. Maybe he's ironing it or something, I thought. Finally he walked back out with a folded white shirt, and set it behind me on top of the couch. I thanked him, and made some more awkward small talk while the household cat jumped up and laid right on top of the shirt, acting really protective about it.

Finally we got up to leave, but the cat wouldn't budge. At last the guy shooed it away, and I picked up the shirt, which obviously wasn't new. Plus it was plain white. Plus I wasn't sure it would fit. Plus probably the last thing I wanted in the Belgian world was another white shirt, especially a used one from a guy I didn't really know. I'd just throw it out when we got back to the apartment, I thought. But wait: at second glance the shirt had one of those nice stiff European collars you couldn't really get in the US yet. I'd admired those ever since my own limp collars had been boiled one too many times by local launderers. And I'd still need at least one or two white shirts at home anyway: with a collar like that, this one might last for years. So maybe I would try it on. I thanked the guy and we left.

Reaching my bike, I started folding the shirt even smaller to fit it into my bike bag, but when I did I felt something slimy and sticky inside.

Gross, I said, in spontaneous English.

What is it? asked Elder Vogel.

Know not, I said. Then I knew: *Darn cat.*

Still, I took the shirt back to my apartment, washed it out in the sink, and that night when it was dry tried it on. A perfect fit! And what a collar! It really did last for years, and became my go-to shirt for special occasions, like my college graduation picture. So maybe one good thing came out of that meeting after all.

Or not. Again, one of the advantages of being a little naïve about matters sexual or of not knowing exactly what it was some of your friends and non-friends were up to was that you weren't tormented all the time by detailed sexual thoughts. But one of the disadvantages was that it could make you absolutely clueless about what might be lurking inside a white shirt. Maybe missing Maturation Day in sixth grade, plus a couple of crucial days in tenth-grade biology, hadn't really paid off for me.

I figured out the real story of the shirt only a couple of years after college, after I was married and had finally figured out all the actual and not merely theoretical details of male plumbing. One day, after not thinking about the incident for years, there rushed up out of the deep subconscious a panicky thought of what might've actually been inside the shirt, and that it had nothing to do with cats. Hoping I was wrong, I screeched to the nearest library to research whether cats ever excreted any substances the likes of which I'd seen and touched. Alas.

By the time of my screech-accompanied research, I no longer thought that the tragedy of the story was the guy's crack about not liking women, but instead his epically disastrous methods for expressing interest in someone. Still, I wasn't exactly hoping to remember the event, and I never told it to anyone: it was too embarrassing, and even made me feel guilty like it was my fault or something, or shouldn't be told in company mixed or otherwise, maybe especially given the very real possibility that the story maybe didn't show me (not to mention the guy) at my (or his) absolute best, okay maybe not quite along the lines of poor old Noah or Lot or even Boaz in their not-absolute-best moments, but still trending in that unenviable direction.

But then it turned out that I'd have no choice in future years but to remember the incident on a pretty regular basis, yea even weekly, because once my parents and I were living in the same town again and I started visiting them every Sunday, I had to walk through the front hallway, where on the wall next to other proud moments in family history hangs my college-graduation picture, right where no one can miss it.

Still, after all those mostly immediately and partly retrospectively disturbing events, my last week suddenly looked like it would go out with a bang.

For one thing, I got my third final letter from Rachelle, and what an encouraging P.S. it contained, even more encouraging than such recent P.S.'s as *Be sure to come on down* [actually up] *when you get home!* and *Man, I'm getting excited to see you!* and *Just give me a call when you get home, you'd better 'cause I'll be waiting by the phone! Just kidding.* Just kidding? She probably wasn't but was just saying that, and it all terrified me, because just like Cyrano I knew I was better in writing than in person.

But the biggest thing of all, guaranteed to impress Rachelle as well, was that someone wanted actually to get baptized right away, as in now. And not just any old someone, but someone able and willing to make it to church every week. Her name was Coralie, and we'd run/tracted into her weeks before while she just happened to be preparing a school report on Mormons. She wanted to learn more, but strictly on an informational basis, and we agreed to meet with her a couple of afternoons a week, using the Discussions as our basis of discussion but leaving out all the usual leading questions and commitments and the baptismal invitation/challenge. And whadda ya know, that really laid-back approach worked, because Coralie found herself actually believing the information she was hearing, and pretty soon she was asking to come to church on more than an informational basis, and pretty soon was friends with people like Angelique Martel, and pretty soon without having even been invited/challenged by us was asking the really good-hearted Branch President of Brussels whether she could get baptized. On August 11, the night before I headed to the Mission Home to go home.

It was too good to be true. What a perfect ending! I'd get a really good baptism after all! *Yes, children (and grandchildren), I didn't have any real baptisms until the very last day of my mission, but all that waiting was worth it, because look what it's turned into now!* I saw my elderly sweatered self saying to future generations. There was only one classic glitch: Coralie's parents were going nuts. Absolutely bonkers.

Coralie had just turned 18 and the age of majority in Belgium was 21. Plus she still lived at home, which meant that her parents' authoritative and opposing thumbs were doubly strong. Once again, I and my family-loving religion were helping to upset a local Belgian family.

Like Lieve de Clercq months before, Coralie insisted she wanted to go ahead with the pre-baptismal interview anyway, because she was sure her parents would come around in time for the big day. Oh, how I hoped that would happen, because despite all the warm timeless feelings I'd gotten in the Pajottenland I still felt like maybe only a really good baptism would be enough to wipe away for good all the pain. And not only that, but with someone as bright and devout as Coralie I had a real chance at the exponential kick: she'd bring in all sorts of new members! And so two days after getting confused by uplifting Catholic and Protestant church services, a day after hitting the little old man with our VW Polo, and on the day I got Rachelle's third final letter, and almost died in a car crash with Elder Vogel behind the wheel, and The Jew was killed, and just a few days after getting my new white shirt, we set up an interview for Coralie, that very night. Tuesday August 9.

None of us loved going ahead with the interview without her parents' permission, but we justified it by saying that it would take place in her home, and that she really was emotionally and mentally capable of making a decision like this. Besides, it was pretty clear by now that any baptisms that did occur in Belgium, or in fact almost Any Time Any Place in Christian history, usually provoked some sort of family fight, so if we waited until everyone in the family was for it, well, there would never be any baptisms.

But the glorious ending I'd envisioned, that I was sure was going to be a final reward for all my hard work, the fulfillment at last of the long-awaited promise of The Missionary Story, lasted about an hour. Coralie's father learned about the interview and came knocking late that afternoon on our door, to say that no one would be home at the scheduled time and so don't bother. Then he stormed away. We tried walking after him, to smooth things, but he turned around and told us to go away, he wanted nothing to do with us.

We went by Coralie's house that same Tuesday night, not to try to talk the father into anything, but to make amends. It didn't work, as it ended with the father saying sarcastically to me, *Good trip!,* as in get out of here! One last thud. That wasn't how I'd hoped my mission would end.

It ended like this instead. Thursday morning Elder Vogel and I drove to Halle one last time, for a brief training visit, but mostly so I could say goodbye to Lieve and Ludo de Clercq, and to Angelique Martel, and to my other friends there. I wondered whether I would ever see them again, which was the same thing I'd wondered when I'd said goodbye to Yvonne and Raymond, and Louis and Charlotte, and Bernard and Marilu, and other non-converts the last couple of days, which goodbyes had despite my eagerness to go home made me really sentimental.

Then late Thursday afternoon we went to Coralie's house, because Coralie and her mom wanted to have us over one last time to actually make amends this time. Her father even apologized for being rude, maybe because it was now clear we'd given up trying to baptize his daughter, and this time he genuinely wished me a good trip home. Of course I kept clinging to the hope that Coralie would someday convert anyway when she left home. (She didn't.)

Then finally Thursday night Elder Vogel and I made one last training visit, Elder Vogel training the District Leader this time and I matching up with the District Leader's brand-new companion, who'd arrived just a few weeks before from South Africa.

He was obviously in a lot of trouble. We did a few usual missionary things, even down near De Brouckère Square, but mostly we just talked. *It's just not at all like I pictured it,* Elder Jacobs said in his South African accent, without quite weeping. He didn't have the usual language problems, because he spoke Afrikaans and that was just a dialect of Dutch. No, the problem for him was what he'd said: the reality wasn't matching the image. I listened with full empathy, and told about my own experience in the dismal upstairs bedroom in Hasselt, which I'd never told anybody, and understood how badly you wanted to do what you'd heard others had done, and how discouraged you could get when you didn't, and how you could even think you were really bad for not doing it. Oh, I sounded like a wise old man, I did, full of calmness and assurance and back-patting, and I meant what I said too, but deep deep down I knew that the real foundation of my calmness and assurance was that I was going home the next day. It was a lot easier to talk for 10 minutes about something like this than actually to go through it, especially when you were leaving. If I'd had as long to go as Elder Jacobs now had, well I just might be as sullen as he was. But I couldn't say that.

Finally, the last thing we did was to actually get in a door and teach one last Discussion — a C of course, just like the first one I'd given in Belgium. I could give it backwards or forwards now — and in fact for a lot of years after I went home.

When the sun rose on August 12, my twenty-first birthday, I got ready to go to the train station for my final ride to the Mission Home and my final interview and my final dinner before flying home the next day.

While I loaded my bags into the Polo, landlord Bernard came out to say goodbye. He'd known me at least as long as he'd known any other missionary. He just stood there for several minutes staring at me, alternately bursting into his loud cigarette-throated laugh and then getting all quiet again. But finally he shook my hand goodbye, and to my surprise he was crying as he said *You're always welcome here back to come.* It almost made me cry too. I'd been looking my whole mission for converts, but maybe I should've just been looking instead for people like the guy standing right in front of me, as well as like my other non-convert friends around the Pajottenland. And I really wasn't sure I'd ever come back, because in those days flying overseas was still just so out of the ordinary.

The final interview with the Mission President went fine. He even reassuringly said that he was sure the Lord was pleased with me. I'd been hoping to hear that, hoping it'd transform my very unsure feelings on that score into some real concrete sense of accomplishment. But it didn't. I felt as flawed as ever.

Still disbelieving I was going home, and still fearing until we were in the air that Belgian Special Forces might storm the plane and drag me off for hitting the little old man with the Polo, I flew the next morning to London with four other missionaries, without incident. From there I went on alone to California. And only when I was alone on the big TWA 747 did I finally actually believe I was really going home. My anxieties about having to Any-Time-Any-Place anyone within conversation-distance started shedding a little, like I was losing a layer of skin. Unlike my plane ride over to Belgium I had the skills to talk to strangers now, but was too tired. For the first time in eons while riding public transportation I didn't Any-Time-Any-Place Any One, but just closed my eyes and laid my head back, and rested.

THE CHAPEL OF THE MADELEINE

I arrived home in California that same night just fine, which I can't say for my giant green mostly-cardboard suitcase: right there on the conveyer belt it fell apart at last, exhausted.

I gave my homecoming talk the next Sunday, but somehow it wasn't as magical as the ones I'd heard as a kid. Maybe it was because I realized while standing up there just how much the talk had been written for me, by the whole expectant audience. I said the usual *hardest thing I've ever done,* which was absolute truth, and the even more usual *best two years,* which was basically true too because it beat any other two-year grouping I'd known (except maybe years 5 and 6), but I left out almost all the details that might've added some nuance and even meaning to those clichés. And even though I didn't have any real conversion-stories of my own to tell, I told some other people's anyway, because a homecoming talk wasn't a homecoming talk without real conversion-stories. The most original thing I did was to talk at excessive possibly even record-setting length in my new exotic language, one last desperate attempt to offer a semi-conventional proof of what a bold missionary I'd been.

I adjusted back to ordinary life just fine, which of course made me feel guilty, because in The Missionary Story really dedicated Returned Missionaries always struggled with *adjusting.* But there I was, calling up Rachelle just hours after I got home, and days later making a trip (up) to visit her. Or maybe I wasn't adjusting as well as I thought, because even though our first in-person conversation was promising, she lost interest in record-breaking time (many records were being set here). I tried again a couple of weeks later when we both got to school in Utah, but she was completely disillusioned by then, and our last conversation ended with a non-eye-contact goodbye, my conduit to God gone just like that. I saw her once more a few months later, at the bookstore, where she was working as a cashier, and even from a distance I could see a big engagement ring on her finger. At least things had gone right for her with someone.

Not long after that, though, I met my actual future wife, and not long after her own mission to France we got married and started having our three kids.

Not long after the wedding, the Belgium Antwerp Mission closed (1982), also in record-setting time: too many rabbit holes and not enough converts, I liked to think was the official word. It merged back with the Netherlands Mission, the way things had been before we'd all started arriving in 1975. In fact all the European missions have been merging ever since, while the Latin American missions just keep on dividing. There aren't 150 missionaries any more in Flanders, like in the glory days, but only 20 or 30, like just in case.

Shortly before the wedding, I started having the bad dream about going on another mission. It came in all sorts of variations over the years. Sometimes I'd be headed out the door of my first mission only to be stage-hooked by someone saying *Two more years for you!* Sometimes I'd be back in college and single and couldn't believe I was already climbing on the big ol' jet airliner again. Sometimes I'd be married with kids and would have to leave everyone behind, and other times they'd all go with me. And sometimes I'd be headed back to Belgium, but other times I'd be going to a town just down the road, which was so much worse that I wanted to faint, though that turned out to be really hard to do in a dream.

No matter the plotline, I always felt guilty and confused. You weren't supposed to have bad dreams about your best two years. Surely no traditional **bold-type** missionary ever had. I could even hear the **bold-types** saying that they'd fetchin' had the exact same challenges of missionary life that I had but had met them with a firm handshake and steady gaze and manly smile, not some weak dream, *so get over it! And if you can't then at least don't talk about it because who would admit something like that?(!)* And I could see them looking down on me the same way strong soldiers looked down on weak soldiers who had *soldier's heart* in the Civil War and *shell shock* in World War I and *combat fatigue* in World War II and *post-traumatic stress disorder* now, and hear them blaming my *missionary heart* on not enough faith or worthiness or obedience or something. Not enough something.

But then I finally got bold enough to start asking other former missionaries about the dream, including at the charmingly dreary annual Antwerp mission reunions I never miss, and realized I wasn't even close to alone. Oh sure, guys like Charlie Gabberd, who'd actually already and happily gone on another mission thanks to his *surplus income* from his sparkling career in sales, doubled over laughing when I asked him about it. And sure, guys like my easy-going son dreamed they were going again but were happy about it. But a lot of people I asked knew exactly the dream I meant, even saying *Wow, you blew my mind mentioning that, because I thought I was the only one.* All the unscientific non-random sampling I did over the years made me think that whether someone had the bad dream or not wasn't so much a matter of where they'd been on a mission, or of how much faith they'd had,* but of how well they'd managed to fit into mission-culture-as-currently-constituted. The born salesmen and born leaders and born followers, who fit easily, rarely had the dream: they were like Mozart finding music or Arnold the Pig mud. Laid-back types, who didn't really care whether they fit, didn't usually have it either. The ones most likely to have it were the born introverts and born introspectives and born sensitives who engaged in all

---

* It emerged that missionaries to Latin America, for instance, were just as capable of having the dream as missionaries to Europe were.

sorts of personality-bending and will-breaking and metaphorical Chinese-foot-binding *trying* to fit, but who in the end were still more like Mother Teresa as general or Francis of Assisi as CEO. If there'd been some other sort of mission culture, or if mission culture'd bent itself a little more to fit them in too, maybe they'd have avoided the dream altogether, instead of just having to get over it later on.

Oh, I still would've gone on a mission despite the bad dream, because I couldn't have imagined not going, and because I wouldn't have met the Friendly People of the Pajottenland or learned Dutch and a lot of other life-altering things. And it's always good to stretch yourself and reach beyond your grasp and do all those other metaphors somewhere out of your comfort zone. But knowing stuff like the theory of personality-fit, and the anthropology of butt-kicking, and the deeper meaning of *perfect,* and the fact that our supposedly measly 100 converts per year was actually way ahead of the typical 40-percent-per-decade average-growth-rate of new churches,* would've made a lot of things easier to bear and help you feel a little less bad.

So would've being able to do other sorts of missionarying, like humanitarian or educational or generally serving sorts, and I don't mean the measly four or so service hours a week of recent Mormon missionaries but more like 40, and not just as a sneaky backdoor way of proselyting either but as a no-strings-attached way of helping just to help, just like the Book of Mormon missionary hero Ammon was ready to do a sheepherding sort of mission forever.

And so would've just hearing in advance another missionary story or two, or a hundred, instead of just the culturally approved One True Missionary Story, because when your own highly idiosyncratic story isn't even coming close to matching the One True Story, well then you're in a real fix,

---

* In 1975 there were around 1,000 Mormons in Flemish Belgium; our supposedly measly 100 converts per year would've put the mission at around 2,000 by 1985, which was a 100 percent growth rate. Not counting those who like Lieve de Clerq never made it to church might've dropped things closer to 40 percent, but that was still average, not horrific, growth.

sure as you are that the problem can't possibly lie with the One True Story you've never heard anything but, and instead must absolutely lie with you, you, and you. And so to get out of the fix you try mightily to fix yourself, and though such trying is a mighty fine thing to try, it entirely predictably falls short, which can get you depressed really fast, and the only thing that saves you is practically out of desperation realizing that your highly idiosyncratic story itself may actually be the *actual* true story, despite its screamingly blatant non-One-True-Story elements.

It's not easy to accept that sort of realization, mind you, touching as it does again on that thing about being content to *be yourself,* but just like that afternoon in the dismal upstairs bedroom *that* thing is always the one that hangs on longest and feels most right. And it feels even more right over the years as you finally start sharing highly idiosyncratic stories with a few others, not in public of course, out of deference to the One True Story everyone is so eager to protect, but in quiet little tête-à-têtes off in some unsanctioned corner somewhere, because even this low-level undergroundish sort of telling helps you see not only that hmm, other people have highly idiosyncratic stories too, but even bigger hmmm, maybe *everyone* does. Maybe *no one* ever lives up to *any* One True Story, maybe not even the people who seem like the flippin' incarnation of it. Like when an interviewer practically gushed-over asking Cary Grant what it was like to be Cary Grant, and old Cary floored the poor interviewer by famously saying, *Everyone wants to be Cary Grant. Even I want to be Cary Grant.* Maybe multitude-baptizing Wilford Woodruff would've said something like that too, if he'd been asked such a thing, maybe after one of his two divorces, for instance. Which makes you think that maybe the point of a One True Story isn't so much to be an ending point as a starting point, not so much to be something to measure yourself against as something to inspire you to reach inside and to make your own highly idiosyncratic true story. All of which is why you also think that maybe if you could've heard a few of the latter such stories early on, and if they'd maybe been accorded the same sort of respect as any One True Story, well then maybe you would've dodged a bad dream or two, or a hundred. Or at least thought them funny sooner.

And finally, way before I finally got over the bad dream, I became a fun-loving historian. Especially of European religion, meaning especially Catholicism and Protestantism. That meant I actually started going back for real to Europe, especially to Belgium, almost annually, instead of just in my dreams almost weekly. In real life, just like in the dream, I sometimes went alone and sometimes with the whole family. But mostly I always went out of my way to (1) avoid De Brouckère Square and (2) drive into the Pajottenland, trying to get lost on its tiny beautiful roads but never succeeding, because everything was still there at once for me, and when you feel like that there's no getting lost.

I also soon started making it a point to wander into every Gothic space I saw, and not because my young son loved testing the echo with his big new voice but because I soon realized that even though Gothic was a manmade style and was invented in a particular earthly time and place and was despised by a whole lot of Renaissance architects who said that Gothic decidedly was *not* eternal, it managed to feel timeless and otherworldly anyway.

In fact after my silly little drama on busy De Brouckère Square during my May 23, 2011, lunch break, I calm down not by heading to some big noisy café but to a small quiet Gothic space near Central Station.

I've got one more thing to think about today, and even though any Gothic space is good for thinking and feeling, what I've got in mind and heart needs to be thought about and felt in this particular space: the Chapel of the Madeleine. Angelique Martel's chapel.

It's 800 Google meters away from De Brouckère Square, just below Central Station and the archive where I'm working. Even though none of the tourist books give it any stars, even though the Masses are depressing, and even though its modernist stained-glass windows clash abominably with its medieval bones, it's still a Gothic space in its vaults and shapes and air and stone, and thus still good for thinking. Especially about Angelique.

She died several years ago, but I just found that out this week, and that depresses me. Going to the chapel where she used to go to feel God might help, I think. And so I sit down on one of the straight-backed straw-bottomed chairs and soon feel coming over me all the meals she made for us and all the rainy cold nights she always gave us something warm to drink, and how cheerful she mostly was despite all her years in the pit, and how happy she was when former missionaries came through and visited over the years, including me. But then people stopped writing and visiting her so much, including me, as in not responding to her last four or five New Year's cards because I was too busy, or in not visiting because down there in Halle she was after all out of the way. And I wonder how alone she was at the end. She was alone from Mormons for sure, which I knew because she'd stopped going to church when the trip to Brussels got to be too hard for her as well as for those driving her, and also because her two sons, who were married with kids and who cared for her and who'd always been friendly to me and other missionaries, in the end made it a point not to invite any Mormons to her Catholic funeral. Was that her idea, I wonder? If so, then she obviously felt ultimately alienated from people she'd given so much to for at least two decades. If it wasn't her idea, then her sons must've felt she'd eventually been hurt for sure. I want to tell her how sorry I am, and that I'll come here to the chapel often, every year, to try to make up for it a little, however too-little that may be. I also want to light a candle here for her, especially if she wanted to die Catholic. But I'm not positive she did, so I decide instead just to whisper some Catholic words that were made for a Gothic space like this but that no Mormon could possibly object to: *Requiem aeternam dona ei, domine.* Give her eternal rest, Lord.

I don't feel just Angelique here, but a lot of others too, because of course everything is connected in a timeless place like this, including other local Mormons, dead and living. Like the old Mormon television producer *Broeder* Pimentel in Brussels. Or *Zuster* De Zitter, who was recruited into the Mormon Missionary Choir because it didn't have enough sopranos and whose voice I can still hear soaring over everyone else's on the cassette tape

I still have from 1975. Or *Broeder* and *Zuster* Rogiers in Antwerp, who persisted with such dignity despite the real troubles caused by their conversion. Or the Lambrechts and Goosens and Puymbroeks who didn't persist but grew weary. Or poor suffering *Zuster* Jaspers, who I saw on her deathbed and didn't bring any comfort to. And of course the very briefly Mormon Lieve de Clerq, who I kept pestering so much about her cigarettes, even when she was sick. I want to tell all of them how much I admire them for even daring, and how sorry I am for so quickly forgetting most of them after I went home, and how insensitive we missionaries could be about what locals had to go through to be Mormon, and how sorry I am for so often making my mission more about me than about them, and for imagining that God cared so little about locals that He made their salvation entirely dependent on whether young mostly North-American missionaries got out the door on time or wrote letters on the right day or thought about girls too much. And I'd say by way of explanation (but not justification) that being conditioned to be almost obsessed with examining your own worthiness so that you could be blessed with *Success!* probably made it pretty predictable that you'd end up thinking the whole mission business was not just mostly *up* to you but also mostly *about* you.

Requiem aeternam dona eis, domine. Give eternal rest to them, as well.

I also feel here the people we tried to convert, and not only Yvonne and Raymond or Bernard and Marilu or Charlotte and Louis or landlord Bernard who finally just became my friends, but also the Blind Man who turned us away at the door, or the little butt-kicking vintage old man who sent me flying, or Coralie's father who sent me packing, or even the man who pulled a gun and sent me running, and hundreds and thousands more. I want to tell them that we weren't much different from any of them, even though we seemed like it, and that we at least didn't mean any harm even though we caused some and should've thought a little more about that. And that I'd want to try to make up for it a little by letting them know that good chunks of whatever good we have inside us came from the unusually big-hearted people of Belgium. Even the guy who gave me the white shirt probably wasn't so different from me, or even from Saint Augustine, because just like me and the Saint this guy too just wanted to love and be loved: he just didn't know a good let alone non-epically-disastrous way how to show that.

Give rest to them too, Lord.

And of course I feel all the other missionaries, but especially those who don't bother to attend our charmingly dreary reunions, not because they live too far away or because they've seen what's on offer but because maybe they feel like they failed on their missions or at life or have quit the church or think they have some flaw or characteristic the rest of us there won't accept, like Elder Arthur, who is gay and supposes others won't want to know that, or hilarious Elder Gunnerson, who after his second divorce stopped attending, or Elder Koepnick, who almost never got letters and was always so sad and maybe never wanted to think about his mission ever again, or gentle Elder Wood, who became a sullen and beaten person from all the rejection, or Elder Bergstrom, who rumor says doesn't go to church any more even though he wrote in my journal *Make our dream here in Belgium come true.*

I'd bet we'd all accept whatever they think their unacceptable flaw is, because we finally know we all have one or two or twenty more that need accepting too.

I also feel here Elder Trimbo, who's a band teacher and can play brassy music to his heart's content now, and Sebastian St. Croix, who I want to tell about the big Station of the Cross with the flaming gold actual cross on top hanging from my living room wall at home, and Elder Nelson, who fell from a ladder just this year and died, and Sister Redding and Sister Acey, who were so inspiringly sane, and Elder Youngblood, who never would've gone ahead of his companion like I did, or Elder Furtwangler, who I've lost track of, or Elder Huddleston, who died in his thirties from cancer and had a saintly aura about him and who really liked Elder Downing, and yes Elder Downing himself. I want to tell all of them how glad I am to have known them, and their good hearts. Their missionary hearts. Their Belgian missionary hearts. Which are maybe just empathetic hearts.

They all got some of that, I'm sure, even the strong ones, because when you expose yourself to ridicule and failure and the elements and God and suffer for it, you're bound to learn a little empathy, at least if you're paying any kind of attention. You don't have to go on a Mormon mission to Belgium to get that sort of heart of course, but I'll bet most of us got a pretty good dose of ours there. And I hope no one's suffering from it anymore.

Give rest to them all, Lord.

I take in one last Gothic breath, then stand up and walk to the exit, where a tattered man holding a tattered paper cup opens the door. I recognize him and nod and drop in the coins I've got, then step on through, back into time.

Thanksgiving

I wanted to write this book in the first place because I couldn't understand why I was having a dream that not only made no sense to me but that I was actually ashamed to have, and figured there must be some rough stuff in there somewhere, and that I'd better sort it out if I ever wanted to get any serious REM-type sleep.

Then I wanted to write it in the second place because once I started nervously chatting up other Still-Believing Former Mormon Missionaries in below-the-surface sorts of ways, I realized that I as usual wasn't as special as I thought, in this case in needing to talk out the rough stuff, and so I supposed that maybe some others would be glad to see some of that talking done in public, since it was at least potentially partially akin to their own particular experiences. And when I saw that a few of those other Still-Believing Former Mormon Missionaries were also starting to write honestly and publicly about their particular dose of rough stuff, as opposed to the relentlessly heroic sort of mission book on the one hand, or the astonishingly scandalous sort on the other (the two basic sorts that had long dominated the Mormon-missionary-memoir genre), well, then I realized that what I was feeling was putting me right in the middle of a flippin' zeitgeist and that yes maybe this sort of talking out most definitely needed to occur, blended right in with all the good stuff we talk about too, part and parcel of the whole, as it were.

And finally I wanted to write in the third place because once I started chatting up other-believers about their particular sets of faith-experiences, the more I saw yet again how un-special I was, because what I (and they) had once imagined to be our own particular and highly sectarian experiences actually ended up looking a lot like each other, in fact made me (and them) see that we were all pretty consistently tooting a lot of the same spiritual horns, so to speak. And so it struck me that sharing warts-and-all intrafaith experience was doing a lot more to promote interfaith understanding and empathy than talking/arguing about theology had ever done for me — in fact was doing a lot more than sharing only-the-best-and-carefully-screened-bits of intrafaith experience had ever done too. Because only the warts-and-all sort of sharing and admitting was somehow able to stun you into seeing yourself in people you'd always been positive were total strangers.

All that chatting-up over the years means I have a lot of people to thank for helping to bring this book about, even if they didn't know that that's what they were doing. I'll start with those many fellow former missionaries who endured my often tiresome questioning, including Kendall Brown, Chris Hodson, Mike Lenhart, Laura Lenhart, Ed Harris, Shawn Miller, Eric Dursteler, Paula Kelly Harline, Steve Smith, Amy Harris, Kevin Kenner, and more whose contributions I have no doubt forgotten.

I thank as well those many fellow other-believers (because who isn't one?) who were willing to talk so frankly and honestly about their own faith-experiences, such as Carlos Schwantes, Carlos Eire, Jim Fisher, Eddy Put, Brad Gregory, Ralph and Doris Heritage, Bill and Char Larson, Luke Larson, Diarmaid MacCulloch, Emily Michelson, Louis Perraud, Jan Roegiers, and the authors of too many inspiring spiritual memoirs to mention.

Many thanks as well to the embarrassingly many people who agreed after usually only mild coercion to read at least parts of the punishingly long original manuscript, including some of the people above, plus Gary Bergera, Charles Callis, Sam Cardon, Karen Carter, Randy Christiansen, Victoria Christman, Wilfried Decoo, Carine Decoo-Vanwelkenhuysen, Paul Halladay, Kate Harline, Rachael Givens Johnson, Carole Kelly, Sara Madsen, Heather Nibley, Stephen Nibley, Jana Reiss, Kathryn Richey, Troy Richey (actually the whole Richey family), Peter Wright, and Tim Wright. A huge thanks to Jane Barnes for heroically editing the whole of the original, and for accepting so whole-heartedly my favorable comparison of her to the immortal Eleanor Lavish. Whether offering detailed or one-sentence or in some cases even one-word responses and encouragement, the opinions of all helped.

Thanks further to David Bratt at Eerdmans for being willing to consider the book, then embracing it so enthusiastically and putting the final touches on so expertly, along with all the other talented and helpful Eerdfolks. Without them, my big hope of reaching other-believers probably wouldn't even have a chance of happening.

Thanks to my parents for supporting me in so many ways over the years, including on my mission, and to so many family and friends for enduring so many times so many undoubtedly disturbing stories, especially my mission-going wife Paula (Paris, France), and our children Andrew (Chinese-speaking Australia), Jonny (Spanish-speaking New York), and Kate (Toulouse, France). Thanks as well to fellow and sister missionaries of the short-lived Antwerp Mission, *buitengewoon zendelingen allemaal,* especially those who had to be my companion. And of course deep thanks to so many extraordinary people in the extraordinary land of Belgium.